# PARIS INSIDE OUT

**An Insider's Guide for Residents, Students & Visitors on Living in the French Capital**

EDITOR

DAVID APPLEFIELD

CORY MCCLOUD, LAYOUT & DESIGN
LAURA HAUGHEY, COPY EDITING

PUBLISHED BY AUP OFFICE OF STUDENT AFFAIRS
&
FRANK BOOKS, S.A.R.L.

**PARIS INSIDE OUT**
THE AMERICAN UNIVERSITY OF PARIS
31, avenue Bosquet
75007 PARIS
FRANCE

ISBN: 2-908171-01-5

SPECIAL THANKS TO JOHN NISSEN, RENÉE KETEL,
KAREN WAGSTAFF, ITALIA JAN, JOHN STRAND & STEPHEN PLUMMER
COVER: TIMBRES "SÉRIE LIBERTÉ," "PANARAMA DE PARIS, 1989,"
PH. © MUSÉE DE LA POSTE, PARIS.

ACHEVÉ D'IMPRIMER EN JUILLET 1990
SUR LES PRESSES DE L'IMPRIMERIE FRICOTEL
ÉPINAL - PARIS  —  TÉL. (1) 40 23 00 17
DÉPÔT LÉGAL N° 2504, JUILLET 1990

# BIENVENUE À PARIS !

THERE ARE SCORES OF TOURIST GUIDES ON PARIS, PERHAPS TOO MANY. YET VIRTUALLY ALL existing guidebooks fail to educate students, new residents, and long-term visitors about the essential requirements of day-to-day life in Paris: housing options, legal status, employment possibilities, student life, social customs, and, perhaps most importantly, the cultural traditions often subtly lodged in the habits and gestures of Parisians. What sets *Paris Inside Out* apart is its attention to the practical needs of individuals coming to *live* in, not just pass through, Paris.

When I arrived in Paris in the late Seventies, my first days were riddled with confusion, lost time, and minor trauma. Having come to Paris to work in a culinary school, I found myself on Day One being ordered by an overweight chef to fetch ten fat pigeons for his afternoon cooking demonstration. As I dashed out of the door with my apron strings dangling, the only place I thought to look was the nearby park. Finally, I asked for pigeons at a local butcher shop, where the meat-stained men burst into laughter. How could I have known that pigeons are easily found at the neighborhood *marchand de volaille* (poultry dealer)? There was that first telephone call, too, when I confused *Ne quittez pas* (Don't hang up) with *Il n'est pas là.* (He's not here). Inadvertantly, I had hung up on a potential employer when in fact I had been instructed to hang-on. (I didn't get the job, of course, but I soon learned how not to use the phone.) Several days later, I learned in a Latin Quarter*café*. never to pull the flush chain too soon in a Turkish toilet—unless you want wet feet!

Inevitably, there will always be a degree of awkwardness in those first days of acclimation to a new country. There will be strange little moments when you crave blueberry pancakes or the Sunday edition of your city's newspaper, and then others when you simply desire the sound of your own language or don't want to have to struggle to be understood. That is all normal. But there is no need for the process to drag on longer than necessary! *Paris Inside Out* will help minimize that struggle, saving many precious hours and lots of francs. It has been conceived to provide practical information, answer a wide variety of questions pertinent to student and residential life, and is presented in a simple format that allows you to find the essential facts and details necessary for daily academic, social, and administrative requirements. Although the guide tends to be more American than British in its perspective and cultural references, every attempt has been made to resist ethnocentricity and provincialism.

Of course, you can't expect to wholly understand French manners, traditions, and institutions—what is commonly called, "*la mentalité*"—from a book. Experience is the key. Learning how a new country and culture functions is a gradual and evolutionary process. It takes time and patience, and a willingness to experience both the exciting and lonely sensation of being isolated and anonymous in a far-off place. But with that sense of isolation can also come a sense of excitement.

One of the extraordinary joys of Paris is that the myths about the city not only endure but are true. Paris, as a celestial city of beauty, grace, and bohemian self-discovery, continues to thrive in the imaginations of those who choose to spend time here. Even in the rapidly changing Nineties, the most exhausted clichés miraculously still apply.

Great experiences await you.

*David Applefield*

# TABLE OF CONTENTS

# SOME BASIC FACTS

Living in a foreign country requires at least a basic knowledge of a few key facts. Here are some facts, statistics and background data that will help you situate yourself in France.

**Capital**: Paris
**Official Language**: French
**Regional Languages**: Basque, Breton, Catalan, Corsican, Provençal
**Surface Area**: 551,965 square km

---

**POPULATION** (WITHIN CITY LIMITS) 1990 CENSUS

| | | |
|---|---|---|
| France: 58,452,500 | Toulouse: 359,000 | Nantes: 247,227 |
| Paris: 2,147,000 | Nice: 348,000 | Lille: 174,039 |
| Marseille: 803,000 | Strasbourg: 252,000 | Grenoble: 159,503 |
| Lyon: 414,000 | Bordeaux: 210,000 | Dijon: 145,569 |

---

**DISTANCES FROM PARIS TO:**

Amsterdam: 504 km
Athens: 2918 km
Berlin: 1054 km
Boston: 5531 km
Brussels: 308 km
Budapest: 1257 km
Cairo: 3210 km
Chicago: 6664 km
Dublin: 854 km
Edinburgh: 867 km
Florence: 878 km
Frankfurt: 465 km
Geneva: 402 km
Helsinki: 1894 km
Hong Kong: 9982 km
Istanbul: 2243 km
Kuwait: 4403 km
Lisbon: 1817 km
London: 414 km
Los Angeles: 9107 km
Lyon: 460 km
Madrid: 1316 km
Marseille: 776 km
Mexico City: 9194 km
Miami: 7361 km
Milan: 826 km
Montreal: 5525 km

Moscow: 2851 km
Munich: 832 km
New York: 5837 km
Oslo: 1337 km
Prague: 1035 km
Rio de Janeiro: 9166 km
Rome: 1388 km
San Francisco: 8971 km
Stockholm: 1549 km
Tel Aviv: 3289 km
Tokyo: 9998 km
Toronto: 6015 km
Venice: 838 km
Vienna: 1227 km
Warsaw: 1044 km
Washington, D.C.: 6164 km

**RELIGIONS**

Catholic: 90%; 1 out of 5 French claims to be "practicing"
Muslim: 1.7 million
Protestant: 1 million
Jewish: .7 million

**ETHNIC MIX** (Population in 1982 Census)

Algerian 8,050,000
Portuguese 7,570,000
Moroccan 4,410,000
Italian 3,400,000
Spanish 3,270,000
Tunisian 1,900,000
Turkish 1,220,000
Polish 640,000
Yugoslavian 620,000

Belgian 530,000
German 440,000
Cambodian 380,000
British 340,000
Vietnamese 340,000
Senegalese 320,000
Malian 240,000
American (USA) 190,000
Cameroonian 150,000

## CONVERSIONS

### Weights
1 *kilo* = 2.2 pounds
A *demi-kilo* = 1 *livre* = 1.1 pounds

### Lengths
1 centimeter = .394 inches
1 meter = 3.28 feet
1000 meter = 1 kilometer = 0.62 mile
(to calculate miles multiply kilometers by .6)

### Measurements
1 litre = 0.265 US gallon
1 gram = .033 ounce

### Temperatures
Converting Celsius to Fahrenheit:
Multiply Celsius temperature by two and add 32 for approximate conversion.

| Fahrenheit | | Celsius |
|---|---|---|
| 0 | | -17.8 |
| 32 | (freezing) | 0 |
| 50 | | 10 |
| 68 | (room temperature) | 20 |
| 77 | | 25 |
| 86 | | 30 |
| 98.6 | (normal body temp.) | 37 |
| 100.4 | | 38 |
| 104 | | 40 |

**CLOTHING SIZES**

**Women's dresses**:

| France | 36 | 38 | 40 | 42 | 44 | 46 | 48 |
|--------|----|----|----|----|----|----|----|
| US | 06 | 08 | 10 | 12 | 14 | 16 | 18 |

**Men's pants**:

| France | 42 | 44 | 46 | 48 | 50 | | |
|--------|----|----|----|----|----|----|----|
| US | 32 | 34 | 36 | 38 | 40 | | |

**Shoes**:

| France | 37 | 38 | 39 | 40 | 41 | 42 | 43 |
|--------|----|----|----|----|----|----|----|
| US | 6 | 7 | 7.5 | 8 | 9 | 10 | 10.5 |

**Men's shirts**:

| France | 37 | 38 | 39 | 40 | 41 | 42 | 43 |
|--------|------|----|------|-------|----|------|----|
| US | 14.5 | 15 | 15.5 | 15.75 | 16 | 16.5 | 17 |

# BASIC SURVIVAL TIPS

**Dates**: In France, 1/3/65 is not January 3, 1965, but March 1, 1965.
**Time of Day**: Generally expressed by the 24-hour clock. Thus,
8 am = 8h or 8h00, and 8 pm = 20h or 20h00.
Midnight = 24h, 24h00, or *minuit,* Noon =12h, 12h00, or *midi.*
12:30 am = 0h30; 5 pm = 17h or 17h00.

**Electric Current**: France's sytem is 220 volt, 50 cycles. To use standard American 110 volt, 60 cycle appliances you will need a plug adapter and a transformer that is appropriate for the wattage of the appliance. Some 220 volt appliances have a combination 50/60 cycle motor that allows them to operate in France without any problems. Lamps from the U.S. will work without a transformer with 220 volt bulbs. Clock radios work but the clock part is not always reliable. Plug adaptors and transformers can be found in the basement of the BHV (Bazaar de l'Hotel de Ville) on the rue de Rivoli, which has a special section for adapting foreign telephones, answering machines, fax/computer equipment and other appliances.

**Floor Numbers**: The floor in which you enter a building is not the first floor, but the *rez-de-chaussée* (RC). In France the street level is not officially an *étage* (floor). Thus, the *premier étage* (first floor) is actually the second level of the building, one floor up from the *rez-de-chaussée*.

# RED LETTER DATES IN FRENCH HISTORY

**30,000-15,000 B.C.:** Cro-Magnon man, whose cave paintings still exist in the southwest, roamed France during the last Ice Age.

**600 B.C.:** Greek traders found Massilia, later to be called Marseille.

**59-50 B.C.:** Julius Caesar conquers France.

**AD 987:** Hugh Capet, first of the Capetian monarchs, elected king of France.

**1207-29:** King Philip Augustus brutally suppresses the Cathar (Albigensian) heresy.

**1226-70:** Louis IX (St Louis), greatest of the the Capetian kings, founds Sorbonne (1253) and wages 7th and 8th Crusades.

**1309-77:** The papacy establishes itself in Avignon.

**1337-1453:** The Hundred Years' War (against England)

**1515-47:** Reign of François I; Renaissance flourishes in Europe.

**1562-98:** The Wars of Religion between Catholics and Protestants (Huguenots), ending with the Edict of Nantes under which Protestantism is officially recognized.

**1643-1715:** Reign of Louis XIV, whose revocation of the Edict of Nantes (1685) leads to mass Huguenot exodus.

**1715-74:** Reign of Louis XV (who was heavily influenced by his mistress, Madame de Pompadour).

**1789:** The attack on the Bastille starts the French Revolution, leading to the execution of Louis XVI (1793) and then of the revolutionary leaders themselves, notably Robespierre (1794).

**1799:** Napoleon Bonaparte appointed first consul and then crowned emperor (1804).

**1812:** Napoleon's empire reaches its zenith with the capture of Moscow, but he is then forced into a humiliating retreat from Russia.

**1814-15:** Napoleon is forced to abdicate and is exiled to the island of Elba. He escapes, raises a new army, but is defeated at Waterloo. He dies in exile on St Helena (1821).

**1814-30:** Bourbon monarchy restored, under Louis XVIII, then Charles X.

**1830:** Revolution in Paris: Charles X replaced by Louis-Philippe.

**1830-48:** Conquest of Algeria.

**1848:** Another Paris revolution. Napoleon's nephew Louis-Napoleon elected president, then becomes emperor (Second Empire, 1852-70).

**1870-71:** The Franco-Prussian War: France is defeated at Sedan, then cedes Alsace and Lorraine to the victors.

**1871:** In Paris, the revolutionary government of the "commune" is bloodily suppressed.

**1875-87:** French vineyards ravaged by phylloxera epidemic.

**1894-99:** The Dreyfus affair: Jewish officer falsely convicted of treason.

**1909:** Louis Bleriot is first to fly a non-balloon aircraft across the Channel.

**1914-18:** World War I, leading to Treaty of Versailles (1919) and the return of Alsace and Lorraine to France.

**1936:** "Popular Front" left-wing government under socialist Leon Blum. The railways, some factories and the Banque de France nationalized.

**1939:** Outbreak of World War II, leading to German invasion and fall of Paris (1940): a collaborationist government is set up at Vichy, in the unoccupied zone, under Marshal Pétain.

**1944:** Allies liberate France and de Gaulle forms a provisional government. Sweeping nationalizations begin.

**1946:** Fourth Republic formed.

**1954:** Fall of Dien Bien Phu leads to French exodus from Indo-China.

**1957:** Treaty of Rome is signed, setting up European Community.

**1958:** De Gaulle returns to power: Fifth Republic is created.

**1962:** France grants independence to Algeria, after an eight-year war.

**1968:** Student uprising and general strike. De Gaulle resigns (1969).

**1974-81:** Presidency of Valéry Giscard d'Estaing.

**1981-86:** Socialist-led government, with François Mitterrand as President. Continued nationalizations.

**1986:** Chirac government elected and a period of "cohabitation" begins.

**1988:** Socialists regain power and Mitterrand names Michel Rocard as *premier ministre*.

**1989:** Celebration of Bicentennial of the French Revolution.

(source: *The Economist Guide to Paris*)

# POLITICAL GEOGRAPHY

*Départements:* The division of France into *départements* is a result of the Revolution and was accomplished in 1790. The three following principles were decisive in its formation: the size of each *département* was to be approximately 6,100 kilometers; the *département* seat was to be located strategically so that it could be reached in the period of one day on horseback from any point in the *département;* and the name of each was to refer to its provincial history and character. There are 96 *départements*.

France is also divided into regions, which are less important for administrative purposes and should not be confused with the *département* names. The present organization of the regions dates from only 1960 and is the result of economical considerations. There are 22 régions.

**Principle cities and** *départements:* The numbers found after the name represent the postal codes for the *département*. These codes are used in the postal codes, on license plates, and other standardized nationwide forms. People tend to refer to certain *départements* by their numbers:

Paris 75

    Seine et Marne 77

    Essonne 91    (Ile de France)

    Yvelines 78

    Haut de Seine 92

    Seine St. Denis 93

Bordeaux (Gironde) 33

Toulouse (Haute-Garonne) 31

Grenoble (Isère) 38

Montpellier (Hérault) 34

Lille (Nord) 59

Strasbourg (Bas-Rhin) 67

Dijon (Côte d'Or) 21

Lyon (Rhône) 69

Aix-en-Provence

    (Bouches-du-Rhône) 13

Nice (Alpes-Maritimes) 6

# GETTING TO PARIS

Traveling to and from Paris is relatively easy from all corners of Europe and the rest of the world. If you are coming from the United States or Canada, there are a number of reduced-rate travel possibilities available to students. Reduced rates are also possible for those under 26. The Council on International Educational Exchange (C.I.E.E.) issues international student and youth cards which allow substantial discounts on flights. Otherwise, you should consult your travel agent for the most recent rates on scheduled airlines serving Paris.

**Council on International Educational Exchange**
205 E. 42nd Street
New York, NY 10017
(212) 661-1450

**Council on International Educational Exchange**
Centre Franco-Américain Odéon
1, Pl. de l'Odéon
75006 PARIS
tel: 43.59.23.69 or 46.34.16.10
Director: Mme Andrea MASON

Other locations across the United States:

**CALIFORNIA**
*Berkeley*
2511 Channing Way
Berkeley, CA
(415) 848-8604
*La Jolla*
UCSD Price Center
Q-076
La Jolla, CA
(619) 452-0632
*Long Beach*
1818 Palo Verde Avenue
Suite E
Long Beach, CA 90815
(213) 598-3338 (714) 527-7950
*Los Angeles*
1093 Broxton Ave
Los Angeles, CA 90024
(213) 208-3551
*San Diego*
4429 Cass Street
San Diego, CA 92109
(619) 270-6401
*San Francisco*
312 Sutter Street
Suite 407
San Francisco, CA 94108

(415) 421-3473
919 Irving Street
Suite 102
San Francisco, CA 94122
(415) 566-6222
*Sherman Oaks*
14515 Ventura Blvd.
Suite 250
Sherman Oaks, CA 91403
(818) 905-5777
**CONNECTICUT**
Yale Co-op E., 77 Broadway
New Haven, CT 06520
(203) 562-5335
**DISTRICT OF COLUMBIA**
1210 Potomac Street NW
Washington, D.C. 20007
(202) 337-6464
**GEORGIA**
12 Park Place South
Atlanta, GA 30303
(404) 577-1678
**ILLINOIS**
*Chicago*
29 East Delaware Place
Chicago, IL 60611
(312) 951-0585

*Evanston*
831 Foster Street
Evanston, IL 60201
(312) 475-5070
**LOUISIANA**
*New Orleans*
8141 Maple Street
New Orleans, LA 70118
(504) 866-1767
**MASSACHUSETTS**
*Amherst*
79 South Pleasant Street
(2nd floor rear)
Amherst, MA 01002
(413) 256-1261
*Boston*
729 Boylston Street
Suite 201
Boston, MA 02116
(617) 266-1926
*Cambridge*
1384 Massachusetts Ave
Suite 206
Cambridge, MA 02138
(617) 497-1497
Stratton Student Center
M.I.T., W20-024
84 Massachusetts Ave
Cambridge, MA 02139
(617) 225-2555
**MINNESOTA**
1501 University Ave, SE
Room 300
Minneapolis, MN 55414
(612) 379-2323
**NEW YORK**
356 West 34th Street

New York, NY 10001
(212) 661-1450
35 West 8th Street
New York, NY 10011
(212) 254-2525
**OREGON**
715 S.W. Morrison
Suite 600
Portland, OR 97205
(503) 228-1900
**RHODE ISLAND**
171 Angell Street
Suite 212
Providence RI 02906
(402) 331-5810
**TEXAS**
*Austin*
1904 Guadalupe Street
Suite 6
Austin, TX 78705
(512) 472-4931
*Dallas*
Exec. Tower Office Ctr.
3300 W. Mockingbird
Suite 101
Dallas, TX 75235
(214) 350-6166
**WASHINGTON**
1314 NE 43rd St
Suite 210
Seattle, WA 98105
(206) 632-2448
**WISCONSIN**
2615 N. Hackett Ave
Milwaukee, WI 53211
(414) 332-4740

If you are a student, a number of university programs are accustomed to making special travel arrangements for their in-coming students from New York City and other cities in the United States at special group rates. Inquire with the program that concerns you. (See University and Exchange Programs in Paris).

If you are coming from other parts of the world, you should consult local airline schedules for information on youth and student reductions. Many national airlines offer reduced rates. Students may be required to show a certificate of student status completed by the registrar of their university: make inquiries well in advance of your departure date. University registrar's offices will usually certify the student status of any new student on the form provided by the airline, but it is your responsibility to send the form to the university in a timely fashion. Student airfare certificates are not transferable to other persons.

The national student associations of most European countries participate in an international network of student flights under the aegis of the Student Air Travel Association. Connections between Paris and cities in Europe, Africa, the Far East and Australia do currently exist. The fares on SATA flights are normally 40% below commercial fares. More information is available from the national student association of your country of residence. These same offices can supply information on special student train and ship fares. For example, the *Deutsche Bundesbahn* offers a reduction to students traveling from Germany to Paris. The reduction applies only to the portion of the trip made in Germany. Applications, which must be certified by the University Registrar, are available in any German train station.

If you live in Europe and intend to return home by train several times during the year, you should be aware of two reduced-fare plans offered by the French National Railways (SNCF). The first is a 50% reduction card *(une carte demi-tarif)* which, when purchased at a flat rate for a given distance and period of validity, entitles the bearer to a 50% reduction on each trip made between his or her home and Paris. For international travel, this reduction applies only to the part of the trip made in France. A second reduction-plan possibility is a subscription card *(abonnement ordinaire)* which allows you to take an unlimited number of free trips and is purchased for a fixed period of time. Whether the *carte demi-tarif* or the subscription plan is more economical will depend on the number of trips taken in a given period. Information on these reductions is contained in a brochure, *cartes demi-tarif et cartes d'abonnement ordinaire*, available from any major French train station. Similar reductions are offered by other national railways in Europe.

# ARRIVING

## The Airport

Most likely you'll be getting to Paris by plane. The two main international airports are Charles-de-Gaulle (also known as Roissy because it's located in the northern suburb of that name) and Orly, the older of the two, located twenty kilometers south of Paris. Both are very well served by taxis, public buses, and commuter subway lines called the RER (see Transport-ation). Those first moments in a foreign airport are always filled with a rush of impressions—you'll immediately notice the racial and ethnic mix indigenous to France. The culture's sense of style and aesthetics are present in the design and advertising. The cars and signs are new.

If you're flying into Paris from North America on a regular sched-uled flight, you'll most likely be arriving in the early morning. The sounds of Roissy announcements and the strong wafts of express coffee are details that you will pleasantly recognize upon each return. After passing through immigration, nabbing one of the numerous and free baggage carts, and claiming your baggage, you are faced with the choice of whether or not to make a customs declaration. The two exits are side by side. Most likely, as a student, you will have nothing to declare and will be able to pass freely without stopping through the exit marked in green *RIEN A DECLAR-ER*. Americans are rarely bothered, but should you be carrying many large packages or computers or electronics in their original carton, you could be asked to open them

and be assessed a duty (see Customs Regulations).

If you need to change money right away, proceed to the Société Générale, one of France's largest and most popular banks (for detailed discussion of currency exchange and French banking practices, see Banking).

If you're not overloaded and are trying to keep down the expenses, the best options for getting into Paris are the public buses which take you to Porte Maillot (Bus 350) in the 16th *arrondissement* (see map) or Nation (Bus 351) in the 12th *arrondissement*, or the well-equipped and comfortable Air France buses which take you to the *aerogare* at Les Invalides, the Gare Montparnasse or the Porte Maillot. These can be picked up at the curb outside all terminals and are well-marked.

Additionally, there is the RER (*Direction St. Rémy-les-Chevreuse*), which can be easily accessed by a free airport shuttle bus. This train makes stops in Paris at the Gare de Nord in the 10th *arrondissement*, Châtelet (the transportation hub for the RER and Métro lines in central Paris), St. Michel (Notre Dame-Latin Quarter-Left Bank), Luxem-bourg Gardens, Port-Royal, Den-fert-Rochereau, and *Cité Uni-versitaire* (international student residences). The price of a one way ticket to any of these Paris stations is 27 FF and includes the shuttle bus from your terminal to the RER station at the airport. The buses from Orly take you to Denfert-Rochereau or the Air France terminal at Les Invalides and cost 17 FF. The RER line from Orly serves the Gare d'Austerlitz, St. Michel, Invalides/Orsay, Pont de l'Alma (get off here for The American University of Paris), or the Champ de Mars (Eiffel Tower). The price for any of these Paris stations is 22 FF. Save your ticket; you'll need it to get out at your desired station (see map for all these options).

If you are loaded down with luggage, you'll probably want to take a taxi into Paris. First, you must wait your turn in the clearly marked Taxi Stand line. This is a strict rule and taxi drivers will almost never break it. A normal drive into central Paris without heavy traffic should cost between 130-160 FF from Charles-de-Gaulle and 80-130 FF from Orly. If traffic is very heavy, count on an additional 30%. Baggage, pets, skis, bicycles each cost 3 FF extra. You may tip a bit, but don't overdo it. A ten franc tip from the airport is fine. In the city, a few francs is all that is really expected. No need to calculate 15%. Taxis in Paris always operate with set meters.

## Customs Regulations

No vaccinations are required to enter France from any country. As for customs, if you are 17 years or older, you have the right to bring in 300 cigarettes or 75 cigars if arriving from an EEC country, or 200 cigarettes or 50 cigars from any other country. As for spirits, from EEC countries you can bring in one and one-half liters of over 44 proof alcohol, or three liters of sparkling wine, and five liters of non-sparkling wine. From other countries, the limit is one liter of alcohol over 44 proof, two liters

each of sparkling and non-sparkling wine. A few no-nos: no more than two kilograms of fish, 250 grams of caviar, and no meat products from Africa. New goods or provisions originating outside the EEC for personal use are limited to 300 FF per person. Goods originating in EEC countries can value up to 2400 FF per person.

## Train Stations

If you're arriving by train the sensation is very different. If you've never been to Europe before, pulling in under the metal hooded roof of the Gare du Nord can be exciting. The smell, the pigeons, the cold echo all ruminate with a Europe that hasn't changed in a half a century. There are few baggage carts along the long *quais* (platforms), so luggage hauling can be painful. Some porters with large carts can sometimes be hired at the general rate of 5 FF a bag. All Paris train stations have currency exchange points and information stands. Additionally, all stations are served by at least two subway lines (see Métro Map). For a list of Paris train stations and the general directions they serve, along with reservation and ticket information, see Transportation.

Upon arriving, again you have the choice of RER, Métro, or taxi. Note that taxi lines at Gare du Nord around rush hour (6 pm, or 18h)—French rush hour is about one hour later than its North American equivalent—can be very long and frustrating.

# TRANSPORTATION

## The Métro

The Paris Métro (RATP) has been in existence since the turn of the century. It truly plays an essential role in the life of the city and is filled with its own character, energy, and mythology. The system has 13 lines that reach 321 stations. You can get nearly everywhere in a relatively short period of time for a reasonable price in relative safety and security on the Paris Métro. Don't be afraid of it. At times it gets a bit overcrowded, odiferous, noisy, and confused but on the whole the Paris underground subway system is among the best in the world. It'll be one of your greatest resources.

Whether you live in Paris or intend to commute by train from the Paris suburbs, you should purchase a monthly pass, *une carte orange*, which allows unlimited travel within five specific zones. The five circular zones are organized in concentric circles with Paris-proper consisting of zones 1 and 2. The other three zones extend far into the suburbs. A single ride (one yellow magnetized ticket) costs 5 FF. If not buying the *carte orange* or the weekly equivalent, *coupon jaune* (49 FF), buy a *carnet* (pack of ten indivi- dual tickets) for 32 FF. This is a substantial savings. The same card is also valid on Paris buses and the Métro and on the Regional Express trains (R.E.R.). The *carte orange* costs 167 FF for two zones; three zones cost 216 FF, four zones 296 FF, and five zones 357 FF. This is a real bargain. Your first time, you need a photograph of yourself, easily obtained from the instant photo booths located in many stations, and the orange card with plastic sleeve that you get at any Métro station ticket window. A yearly *carte orange* ticket (*la carte intégrale*) is also available. You are supposed to carry the magnetized ticket in a little slot in the sleeve and inscribe the number of the card onto the ticket and sign the card. Failure to do either can cause you a fine upon verification. Periodically, controllers stake out Métro stations and selected cars. The same is true for the lack of a picture. The card is strictly for the use of the person whose name and picture appear on the card.

First Class tickets are offered at a higher rate. It may seem odd that there is a class system on public transportation, but it's true. Each train has one bright yellow first class car marked with a big number 1. You can get a fine for riding First Class—except in rush hour—without a first class ticket. Always save your ticket until back out on the street.

One Métro phenomenon you're likely to observe is gate-hopping. A fair amount of people duck under or jump over the turnstiles to avoid payment. RATP officials have reduced some of this by installing quick-moving stop gates that make cheating harder. Often people sneak in for free behind someone who has paid. So, if someone pushes in behind you or asks to pass through the turnstile with you don't be alarmed. One student who was caught without a ticket, claims it's better to speak English, play dumb, and when asked for your name and address, say you're from Oshkosh.

Be aware of the "last Métro" phenomenon. The Métro runs till about 0h50, and you must keep this in mind if you want to get home the easiest and cheapest way. Be careful about catching the Métro but missing your transfer. If you miss the last Métro you'll have to either find a taxi, walk, "stay over" or when completely desperate sleep in a Métro station (which is funky but tolerated) until the first train at 5h45. The disco scene revolves around the first Métro concept. Otherwise, you can try the *Noctambus* (see Buses).

## How to Use the Métro

The Métro is easy to use, once you've mastered the symbols used to indicate exits, transfers, and train directions. First of all, Métro lines are named after their end points, i.e. the Porte de Clignancourt line is called *Direction Porte de Clignancourt*, and the same line traveling in the opposite direction is called *Direction Porte d'Orléans*. Naturally, it serves all the stations in between. Signs indicating direction are white. For transferring from one line to another, orange signs on the *quai* (platform) marked *correspondance* indicate the path to other *quais* and other directions. Blue signs marked *sortie* point you in the direction of the exit, and often you'll have a choice of exits, all emerging onto different streets or different sides of the street.

## The Bus

The sign of a real Parisian is the mastery of the bus system. Many new residents take a long time

before attempting to use buses. The Parisian Bus System is excellent, although its efficiency suffers from the generally congested traffic situation. The bus does have the advantage of allowing you to see more of the city than traveling underground by Métro. And there are still some lines with buses that have open, trolley-like back sections. Aside from the pollution, these are fun. *Paris par arrondissements* has maps of individual bus routes, otherwise stops are indicated on maps inside the Métro, at bus stops, and in large black letters on the side of each bus. Buses use the same tickets as the Métro, which are cancelled in the machine located at the front of the bus. Don't cancel your *carte orange!* Just flash it by the driver. The driver also sells individual tickets which must be punched *(oblitéré)* upon boarding and are only good on the bus. When standing at a bus stop, signal the driver if you want to be picked up. Inside the bus, there are red stop request buttons located on the aisle posts. Several lines have incorporated new vehicles which you can enter via the middle doors without showing your card to the driver.

Most buses, whose numbers are indicated at stops by black numbers on a white circle, run every day of the year from about 5h30-0h30. Buses whose emblem is a white number on a black circle generally run only from about 6h00-20h30 Monday through Saturday except holidays.

When the number on the front of the bus has a slash through it, the bus runs through only half of the route. This short range service usually happens only at rush hours and on certain routes.

If you're a late nighter, familiarize yourself with the *Noctambus* which leave the Châtelet-Hôtel de Ville area (avenue Victoria) every hour from 1h30-5h30 for 15 FF and traverse Paris in every direction. The mob scene to get on these can be intimidating. Here's a complete list of night buses, all marked with the sign of a black owl in a yellow circle:

**A**: Pont de Neuilly
**B**: Levallois Mairie
**C**: Clichy Mairie
**D**: Saint Ouen Mairie
**E**: Pantin Eglise
**F**: Les Lilas Mairie
**G**: Montreuil Mairie
**H**: Vincennes Château
**J**: Porte d'Orléans
**R**: Rungis Mareé

For more information contact:

**RATP Info**
53ter, quai des Grands Augustins
75006 PARIS
tel: 40.46.41.41

## Taxis

In general, Paris taxis are readily available and reasonably priced. However, finding a taxi in Paris is different from finding one in, for example, New York. Paris taxi drivers frequently do not feel obliged to stop for you if they don't have a passenger. When you do get them to stop, if your destination doesn't appeal to the driver, he will tell you so and drive off. Although relatively orderly, taxi stands can be competitive scenes—stand your ground. When ordering a taxi between 18h-21h, don't be surprised to find 20 or 30 FF already on the meter. French taxis, when ordered, start counting from the moment they set out to fetch you. It's always a better idea to find the number of the taxi stand closest to where you live, work, or usually need taxis.

Here is a partial list of taxi stands and their numbers:

| | |
|---|---|
| Pl Châtelet, 1e | 42.33.20.99 |
| Pl André Malraux, 1e | 42.60.61.40 |
| Pl de l'Opéra, 2e | 47.42.75.75 |
| 19 Bd. St. Denis, 2e | 42.36.93.55 |
| rue Bretagne, St. Denis, 3e(Square du Temple) | 42.78.00.00 |
| Métro rue Rambuteau, 4e | 42.72.00.00 |
| Métro St. Paul, rue de Rivoli, 4e | 48.87.49.39 |
| Pl St. Michel, 5e | 43.29.63.66 |
| Pl Monge, 5e | 45.87.15.95 |
| 26 rue Soufflot, 5e | 46.33.00.00 |
| rue du Four, 6e | 43.29.00.00 |
| 72 Bd Montparnasse, 6e | 42.22.13.13 |
| Métro Odéon, 91 Bd St. Germain, 6e | 43.26.00.00 |
| 2 av Bosquet, 7e | 47.05.66.86 |
| 12 rue Solferino, 7e | 47.05.06.89 |
| 110 rue de l'Université, 7e | 47.05.03.14 |
| 1 av Georges V, 8e | 43.59.58.00 |
| 8 Bd Malesherbes, 8e | 42.65.00.00 |

| | |
|---|---|
| 1 av Friedland, 8e | 45.61.00.00 |
| 81 Bd Clichy, 9e | 42.85.00.00 |
| Pl Etienne d'Orves, 9e | 48.74.00.00 |
| 2 rue Faidherbe, 11e | 43.72.00.00 |
| 1 av République, 11e | 43.55.92.64 |
| 6 Pl Bastille, 12e | 43.45.10.10 |
| 1 Pl Edouard Renard, 12e | 46.28.00.00 |
| Pl d'Italie, 13e | 45.83.34.93 |
| 5 av Porte de Choisy, 13e | 45.85.40.40 |
| 73 Bd Montparnasse, 14e | 42.22.13.13 |
| 297 Bd Raspail, 14e | 43.35.01.00 |
| 45 av Félix Faure, 15e | 45.58.15.00 |
| 3 Bd Pasteur, 15e | 47.34.00.00 |
| 12 Pl Victor Hugo, 16e | 45.53.00.11 |
| 5 Pl Porte St Cloud, 16e | 46.51.19.19 |
| 11 Chaussée Muette, 16e | 42.88.00.00 |
| rue Batignolles, 17e | 43.87.00.00 |
| 1 Bd Berthier, 17e | 46.27.00.00 |
| 42 Bd Gouvion St Cyr, 17e | 45.74.00.00 |
| 1 av Porte de Clignancourt, 18e | 42.58.00.00 |
| 34 Bd Chapelle, 18e | 42.08.00.00 |
| 185 rue de Crimée, 19e | 40.35.28.27 |
| 211 av Jean Jaurès, 19e | 46.07.21.10 |
| 5 rue Lassus, 19e | 42.08.42.66 |
| Pl Gambetta, 20e | 46.36.00.00 |
| 1 av Porte des Lilas, 20e | 42.02.71.40 |

## TRAVEL & TOURISM

### Traveling After You Get to Paris

Paris is an excellent point of departure for international as well as domestic travel. The French travel considerably and spend sizeable portions of their savings on travel. As residents or students in Paris you'll undoubtedly want to capitalize on the excellent opportunities to visit the diverse regions of France, as well as other European countries. For travel information of all sorts concerning Paris and its environs consult:

**Tourist Office of Paris**
127, av. des Champs-Elysées
75008 PARIS
tel: 47.23.61.72

Other regions have their own information centers in Paris. Local information on rentals, hotels, sports, *gîtes* (inexpensive, rural farmhouse and vacation house rentals), festivals, etc. can be obtained at the following addresses for each region:

**Bretagne**: 17 rue de l'Arrivée, 15e, 45.38.73.15

**Savoie**: 31 av de l'Opéra, 1e, 42.61.74.73

**Lozère**: 4 rue Hautefeuille, 6e, 43.54.26.64

**Pyrénnées**: 1 rue Berger, 1e, 42.33.73.82

**Auvergne**: 194 rue de Rivoli, 1e, 42.61.82.38

**Hautes Alpes**: 4 av de l'Opéra, 2e, 42.96.05.08

**Limousin**: 18 bd Haussmann, 9e, 47.70.32.63

For students to benefit from special student travel reductions, an International Student Identification Card is needed. This can be obtained by bringing your passport, student card, a photo and 35 FF to:

**Council on International Educational Exchange** (CIEE)
16, rue de Vaugirard
75006 PARIS
tel: 46.34.02.90

Another organization specializing in student travel:
**Jeunes Sans Frontières**
5, rue de la Banque
75002 PARIS
tel: 48.24.29.29

Additionally, Paris is well connected to numerous locations around the Mediterranean as well as points in Africa. Charter flights are readily available to Corsica, Greece, Yugoslavia, the Canary Islands, Spain, Turkey, Tunisia, Sicily, and others. Here is a list of travel agencies that offer students reasonable trips, charters, and inexpensive flights to North American and European destinations:

**Access Voyages**
6, rue Pierre-Lescot
75001 PARIS
tel: 40.13.02.02

**Australie Tours**
129, rue Lauriston
75016 PARIS
tel: 45.53.58.39

**Blue Marble Travel**
(organizes bicycle trips)
3, rue Clotaire
75005 PARIS
tel: 46.33.02.00

**Discount Flight Services (DFS)**
157 rue Vercingétorix
75014 PARIS
tel: 40.44.58.58
Contact: Alain BESANÇON

**Voyageur du Canada**
5, Place André Malraux
75001 PARIS
tel: 40.15.06.60

**Carrefour des Etats-Unis**
5, Place André Malraux
75001 PARIS
tel: 42.60.32.51

**Club Méditerranée**
Place de la Bourse
75002 PARIS
tel: 42.61.85.00

**Forum Voyage, USA**
55, Av. Franklin Roosevelt
75008 PARIS
tel: 42.89.07.07
Minitel: 3514 FV

**Go Voyages**
22, rue de l'Arcade
75008 PARIS
tel: 45.22.08.50
Minitel: 3615 GO VOYAGES

**Nouvelles Frontières**
87, Bd. de Grenelle
75015 PARIS
tel: 42.73.05.68
Minitel: 3615 NF

# TOURIST OFFICES

Here is a list of official tourist offices in Paris which provide travel information and documentation:

**Austria**
47, av de l'Opéra
75002 PARIS
tel: 47.42.78.57

**Belgium**
20, Bd des Capucines
75002 PARIS
tel: 47.42.41.18

**Cyprus**
15, rue de la Paix
75002 PARIS
tel: 42.61.42.49

**Czechoslovakia**
32, av de l'Opéra
75002 PARIS
tel: 47.42.38.45

**Denmark**
142, av. des Champs-Elysées
75008 PARIS
tel: 42.25.12.64

**Finland**
13, rue Auber
75009 PARIS
tel: 42.66.40.13

**Great Britain**
63, rue Pierre Charron
75008 PARIS
tel: 42.89.04.75

**Greece**
3, av de l'Opéra
75001 PARIS
tel: 42.60.65.75

**Ireland**
9, Bd. Madeleine
75001 PARIS
tel: 42.61.84.26

**Israel**
14, rue de la Paix
75009 PARIS
tel: 42.61.01.97

**Italy**
23, rue de la Paix
75002 PARIS
tel: 45.66.66.68

**Monaco**
9, rue de la Paix
75002 PARIS
tel: 42.96.12.23

**Morocco**
161, rue St Honoré
75001 PARIS
tel: 42.60.633.50

**Netherlands**
31-33, av des Champs-Elysées
75008 PARIS
tel: 42.25.41.25

**Norway**
88, av Charles-de-Gaulle
92200 NEUILLY-SUR-SEINE
tel: 47.45.14.90

**Poland**
49, av de l'Opéra
75002 PARIS
tel: 47.42.07.42

**Portugal**
7, rue Scribe
75009 PARIS
tel: 47.42. 55. 57

**Spain**
43ter, av. Pierre 1er de Serbie
75008 PARIS
tel: 47.20.90.54

**Sweden**
146, av. des Champs-Elysées
75008 PARIS
tel: 42.25.65.52

**Switzerland**
11bis, rue Scribe
75009 PARIS
tel: 47.42.45.45

**Tunisia**
32, av de l'Opéra
75002 PARIS
tel: 47.42.72.67

**Turkey**
102, av des Champs-Elysées
75008 PARIS
tel: 45.62.78.68

**West Germany**
9, rue de Téhéran
75008 PARIS
tel: 43.59.46.50

**Yugoslavia**
31, bd des Italiens
75002  PARIS
tel: 42.68.07.07

# Air Travel

Leaving Paris or meeting someone's plane at either Charles-de-Gaulle or Orly, make sure you are clear as to which airport and which terminal you're supposed to be at. General airport information and message services can be obtained by calling:

**Aéroport Charles-de-Gaulle**: 48.62.22.80
**Aéroport Orly**: 49.75.15.15

Minitel service is also available for flight information/departure and arrival times by dialing on your telephone: 3615, and HORAV on your Minitel unit. (See Minitel under Communications).

Here is a list of major airlines, with ticket office addresses and phone numbers:

**Aer Lingus**
47, av. de l'Opéra
75002 PARIS
res: 47.42.12.50

**Air Canada**
31, rue Falguière
75015 PARIS
res: 43.20.12.00

**Air Europe**
45, rue de Richelieu
75001 PARIS
res: 49.27.91.00

**Air France**
119, av. des Champs-Elysées
75008 PARIS
res: 45.35.61.61

**Air Inter**
54, rue Père Corentin
75015 PARIS
tel: 45.39.25.25

**American Airlines**
109, rue du Fbg. St.-Honoré
75008 Paris
res: 42.89.05.22

**Biman Bangladesh Airlines**
90 av. des Champs-Elysées
75008 PARIS
res: 42.89.11.47

**British Airways**
38, av. de l'Opéra
75002 PARIS
res: 47.78.14.14

**Canadian Airlines International**
15, rue de la Paix
75002 PARIS
res: 42.61.72.34

**Continental Airlines**
92, av. des Champs-Elysées
75008 PARIS
res: 42.25.31.81

**Delta Airlines**
Immeuble Lavoisier
4, Pl. des Vosges
92052 PARIS Cedex 74
res: 47.68.92.92

**Northwest Airlines**
16, rue Chauveau Lagarde
75008 PARIS
res: 42.66.90.00

**Pan American World Airways**
1, rue Scribe
75009 PARIS
res: 42.66.45.45

**Qantas Airways Limited**
7, rue Scribe
75009 PARIS
res: 42.66.53.05

**Republic Airlines**
6, rue Chaussée d'Antin
75009 PARIS
tel: 48.24.32.24

**Trans World Airlines (TWA)**
101, av. des Champs-Elysées
75008 Paris
res: 47.20.62.11

**United Airlines**
40, rue Jean Jaurès
93170 BAGNOLET
res: 43.62.14.14

**UTA**
3, Bd. Malesherbes
75008 PARIS
res: 40.17.44.44

**Wardair**
24, av. Hoche
75008 PARIS
res: 49.53.07.07

## Other Airlines (Res. & Info.)

**Aeroflot**
tel: 42.25.43.81
**Aerolineas Argentinas**
res: 42.56.31.16
**Aéromexico**
res: 47.42.40.50
**Air Afrique**
res: 45.61.96.20
**Air Algérie**
res: 42.60.30.62
**Air Gabon**
res: 42.66.13.72
**Air India**
res: 42.66.13.72
**Air Lanka**
res: 42.97.43.44
**Air Madagascar**
tel: 42.60.30.51
**Air Malta**
tel: 45.49.06.50
**Air Mauritius**
tel: 47.42.75.02
**Alitalia**
res: 40.15.00.21
**Austrian Airlines**
res: 42.66.34.66
**Cameroon Airlines**
res: 47.42.78.17
**Cathay Pacific Airways**
res: 42.27.70.05
**Ceskoslovenske Aerolinie**
res: 47.42.38.45
**China Airlines**
tel: 42.25.63.60
**Egypt Air**
res: 42.66.08.86
**El Al**
res: 47.42.41.29

**Ethiopian Airlines**
tel: 42.66.16.26
**Finnair**
tel: 47.42.33.33
**Gulf Air**
res: 47.23.70.70
**Iberia**
res: 47.23.00.23
**Icelandair**
tel: 47.42.52.26
**Iran Air**
tel: 43.59.01.20
**Iraqi Airways**
tel: 45.62.62.25
**Japan Air Lines**
res: 42.25.85.05
**Kenya Airways**
tel: 42.61.82.93
**K.L.M. (Dutch Airlines)**
res: 47.42.54.40
**Korean Airlines**
res: 42.61.51.74
**Kuwait Airways**
tel: 42.60.31.21
**Libyan Arab Airlines**
tel: 45.62.33.00
**L.O.T. Polish Airlines**
tel: 47.42.05.60
**Lufthansa**
res: 42.65.37.35
**Olympic Airways**
res: 42.65.92.42
**Pakistan International Airlines**
tel: 45.62.92.41
**Royal Jordanian**
tel: 42.61.57.45
**Sabena**
res: 47.42.47.47
**Scandinavian Airlines (SAS)**
res: 47.42.06.14
**Singapore Airlines**
tel: 42.61.53.09
**Swissair**
tel: 40.78.10.00
**TAP (Portugal)**
tel: 42.96.16.09
**Thai Airways**
res: 47.20.64.50
**Varig**
tel: 47.20.03.33

# TRAIN TRAVEL

The French rail system, the SNCF, is, on the whole, extremely extensive and efficient. You may have heard of the TGV, *le train à grande vitesse* or high speed train, that has cut the traveling time in half between Paris and, for example, Marseille, 900 kilometers away, to a little over four hours instead of eight. The TGV currently serves the Paris, Lyon, Marseille line to the south and the Bordeaux line to the southwest. Additionally, the TGV goes to Geneva and Lausanne, and a new ultra high speed western line to the Atlantic has recently been inaugurated. High speed train travel is expanding rapidly in Europe with a network being prepared to tie in with London (via the Eurotunnel) and several German cities within the next two years. The TGV requires reservations, which can be made in most travel agencies, all train stations, and at home with the Minitel (see Communications).

Paris has six main rail stations, all of them on Métro lines. All offer a wide range of services: bars and restaurants, refreshment stands, newsstands and information booths (sporadically staffed).

**SNCF Train Info.**
Information: 45.82.50.50
Reservations: 45.65.60.60
Open daily from 8h-20h

---

## PARIS TRAIN STATIONS & DIRECTIONS SERVED:

**Gare du Nord:** Serves the north, including the Channel ports, where trains connect with ferries and hovercraft from Britain; also services Belgium, Holland and the Scandinavian countries.
**Gare de l'Est:** Serves the east, Nancy and Strasbourg, and Germany and Eastern Europe, including Moscow.
**Gare d'Austerlitz:** Serves the southwest; Bordeaux, Toulouse, and Spain and Portugal via Orleans, Tours, Poitiers and Angouleme.
**Gare St. Lazare:** Serves Normandy and boat trains to/from Dieppe.
**Gare Montparnasse:** Serves western France, especially Bretagne.
**Gare de Lyon:** Serves southeastern France, Switzerland, Italy, Yugoslavia and Greece.

---

When leaving Paris by train, make sure you know from which station your train leaves. Before boarding your train make sure you *compostez* (punch) your ticket and reservation stub in one of the automatic cancellation machines located at the head of each platform. Failure to do so may result in a stiff fine—train travel within France is essentially based on the honor system. In most cases a conductor will check your tickets anyway.

Persons under 26 are eligible for discounts of up to 50% on train travel in Europe. These special tickets—B.I.G.E.—can be purchased at the following agencies:

**Transalpino**
14, rue Lafayette
75009 PARIS
tel: 48.24.29.29

**Tours 33**
85, Bd St Michel
75005 PARIS
tel: 43.29.69.50

The most advantageous and inexpensive way to travel extensively in Europe is with the INTER RAIL card. This offers students (under age 26) unlimited train travel in second class during one month from the date of the first part of the journey for the fixed sum of 1290 FF. The Inter Rail Card is valid in all of western Europe, Yugoslavia, Greece, Hungary, Romania, and Morocco. It gives a 50% reduction in the country of purchase.

Two other discounts exist for students under the age of 26. The *Carré Jeune* (140 FF) gives you a 50% reduction in France during the low period days *(période bleue)* on four one-way tickets, and/or a 20% discount during the peak period *(période blanche)*. The *Carte Jeune* (also 140F) is valid during the summer only and offers a 50% reduction on tickets in France, as long as the departure is in a *période bleue*. Both cards can be purchased at all train stations.

Other reductions are posssible at certain times of the year for destinations more than 1000 kilometers from Paris. Information can be obtained from:

**SNCF**
127, av des Champs-Elysées
75008 PARIS
tel: 47.23.54.02

For train information on other national railroads for other countries:

**U.K.**
**Chemins de Fer Britanniques**
57, rue St Roch
75001 PARIS
tel: 42.60.36.92

**Germany**
**Chemins de Fer Féd. Allemand**
13, rue Alsace
75010 PARIS
tel: 42.49.13.40

**Spain**
**Chemins de Fer Espagnols**
1, av Marceau
75016 PARIS
tel: 47.23.52.01

**Amtrak Railways**
c/o Wingate
19 bis, rue du Mt. Thabor
75001 PARIS
tel: 42.60.39.85

**Canadian National Railway**
1, rue Scribe
75009 PARIS
tel: 47.42.76.50

**Venise Simplon Orient Express**
11, rue de Surène
75008 PARIS
tel: 47.42.91.81

A few notes on long distance train travel. Aside from the ultra-modern TGV, the SNCF uses primarily two models of train cars. The older ones are divided into compartments of six moderately uncomfortable seats, while the newer ones are merely organized into rows of comfortably reclining seats. Trains are always divided into Second Class and First Class, Smoking and Non-Smoking. Most trains offer snacks and drinks and many are equipped with dining cars. Having your dinner on a train, elegantly seated at a table with linen tablecloth and real silverwear can be a lot of fun, but be prepared to spend close to 150 FF per person for the meal. Otherwise, bring along your own provisions, especially a bottle of water.

The overnight trains to Amsterdam, Copenhagen, Frankfurt, Venice, Athens, Rome, Madrid, etc. can make for highly memorable experiences. The least expensive sleeping arrangement on a night train is the *couchette* or six-bunk compartment. Depending who you get in your compartment, you may be able to sleep well or not at all. Each bunk comes with a blanket, pillow, and sleeping-bag shaped sheet which comes sealed in a plastic wrapper to insure hygiene. When crossing international borders at night, the train con-ductor will keep your passport until morning to be able to show it to the border police and customs inspectors. This is totally normal. Don't be alarmed.

## Bus/Coach Travel

There are some very cheap bus excursions from Paris to London, Amsterdam, and other European cities. In the days prior to the Islamic Revolution in Iran, there were weekly buses originating in London and passing through Paris on their way across Europe to Istanbul, Tehran, Kabul, and finally India. For $30 a rugged individual could get from Paris to Bombay. The route changed in the Seventies, passing through Pakistan instead of Afganistan on its way to India. There are still bus excursions, but few foreigners risk going through Iran anymore. Bus information can be obtained from:

**Eurolines**
3, av. Porte de la Villette
75019 PARIS
tel: 40.38.93.93
**Nouvelles Frontières**
166, Bd. Montparnasse
75014 PARIS
tel: 43.35.40.91
**Trans-Channel**
24, rue Saint Quentin
75010 PARIS
tel: 42.09.01.00
**Fédération Nationale des Transports Routiers**
6, rue Paul-Valéry
75016 PARIS
tel: 45.53.92.88

## Boats/Ferries
**Irish Ferries**
8, rue Auber
75009 PARIS
tel: 42.66.90.90
**Hoverspeed** (hydrofoil to U.K.)
11, rue de Surène
75008 PARIS
tel: 47.42.03.03
**Sealink Ferries**
16, Bd. des Capucines
75009 PARIS
tel: 47.42.86.87/47.42.00.26
**Bell Lines**
8, rue Estérel
94633 RUNGIS Cedex
tel: 46.87.22.31
**Norfolk Line**
Tour Franklin Cedex 11
PARIS LA DEFENSE
tel: 47.76.42.02
**P. & O. Lines**
9, Pl. de la Madeleine
75008 PARIS
tel: 42.66.40.17

# Student Excursions

The following student organizations have planned domestic and international excursions at reasonable rates. Write or call for their programs and schedules. Traveling with French students can be an excellent way to meet new friends, improve your French and see new parts of the world.

**L'Autobus**
4bis, rue St. Sauveur
75002 PARIS
tel: 42.33.86.72

**Bureau des Voyages de la Jeunesse**
20, rue Jean-Jacques Rousseau
75001 PARIS
tel: 42.33.55.00
(Italy, Austria, Yugoslavia)

**Centre de Coopération Culturelle et Sociale**
26, rue Notre-Dame-des-Victoires
75002 PARIS
tel: 42.61.53.84
(England, Sweden, Germany, Israel, Austria, Russia, Greece, Denmark)

**Centre Touristique des Etudiants et de la Jeunesse**
20, rue des Carmes
75005 PARIS
tel: 43.25.00.76
(charter flights)

**Fédération Unie des Auberges de la Jeunesse**
27, rue Pajol
75018 PARIS
tel: 42.41.59.00
(issues student hostel cards for all of Europe)

**Office du Tourisme Universitaire (OTU)**
137, Bd. St. Michel
75005 PARIS
tel: 43.29.12.88
(cheap charters, good bulletin board. International Student Card required)

# Hitchhiking

It's rare to see people *faire du stop* (hitchhike) in Paris itself, but you may see hitchhikers (with signs) at the entrance ramps to the beltway around Paris called the *Périphérique*, especially at the Porte d'Orléans and Porte d'Italie, where the *Autoroute du Sud* feeds in. Hitchhiking is illegal on the *autoroute* ramps themselves. This is essentially the only route to Lyon, Orleans, and the rest of central France (*Midi*) and the south of France. Hitchhiking is not ill-advised but it tends to be slow in that Europeans are rather cautious and slightly distrustful about letting strangers into their cars, or houses for that matter.

A much better solution exists in most European countries: an organized hitchhiking agency that dispatches riders with drivers for a small fee. For 60 FF Allô-Stop will find you a seat in a car leaving for most destinations at around the same time you want to leave. Participation in the expenses for gas and tolls depends on the driver but tends to be standard. Weekend bus trips to Amsterdam for 230 FF and London for 360 FF are also organized by Allô-Stop.

**Allô-Stop**
84, Passage Brady
75010 PARIS
tel: 42.46.00.66

# ADMINISTRATIVE MATTERS

France's international reputation represented by those three great words: *Liberté, Fraternité, Égalité* tell only a part of the story. Anyone who has lived in France for at least a year will be able to confirm the same thing: French bureaucracy can be enough to provoke fits of rage. You have to learn to flow with the tide, to figure out the inner logic and, when applicable, use it to the ends that you're after. Don't panic. Everything administrative in France takes time, and most things, you will learn, are *en cours* (in process). There are, nonetheless, a number of practical pointers that can ease you through the administrative labyrinth.

The fact that you're not just visiting France, you're no longer a passing visitor, means your legal and administrative status in France takes on new proportions. As a tourist, one is allowed to remain in France for a maximum of three months—and is forbidden to work, of course. As a student, you'll need a student visa before entering France. This will be your first step towards obtaining the infamous *carte de séjour* (extended visitors card).

French administration is famous for its own sense of logic, the long lines, the eternal delays, the mammoth frustrations. So be prepared. Aside from your battery of papers, documents, certificates, photocopies, letters, receipts, statements, etc. always be equipped on your person with stamped envelopes, pictures of yourself, bank statements, electric and gas bills (EDF-GDF) (the only reliable and widely accepted proof of address in France), a stack of one, two, five, and ten franc coins for photocopies, instant photos, envelopes, etc. And remember, in France it's the written document that matters. Everything must have an official stamp on it (*tampon*) so the more *tampons* the better your documents will be received. The document carries more weight in France than the spoken word. And, don't forget, as well prepared as you think you are for your administrative procedures you will have to come back at least once. *C'est comme ça*, and it's like that for everyone. In some cases, your university may have established regular inside contacts, *pistons*, as they're called in French, with the local authorities and will proceed to procure your papers for you. The system or practice of having a *piston* is inherent in the centralized bureaucracy. Don't get moralistic about this; if you have a good contact and are really in need of help call your *piston*, but don't waste a favor on a small and banal matter. In other cases, you'll be on your own. And you'll complain. But that's okay; the French complain all the time; it's built into the national charm.

Some contend that living legally in France is not as difficult as most foreigners tend to think. The key is learning the ropes fast. Problems only arise when students decide to remain in France after having entered as a visitor or tourist. The French take illegal immigration quite seriously, although most cases of severe legal action being taken usually have been directed toward North Africans, black Africans, and Asians. North Americans are usually dealt with more leniently. But nonetheless French employees of the State, *fonctionnaires* (Federal employees—a term you will hear a lot), don't appreciate broken laws.

To repeat, all foreigners residing in France for more than three months must have either a visa allowing them to do so, or a *carte de séjour*. Until the age of 16 (18 for full-time students) minors may reside in France without a *carte de séjour* but they must still enter the country legally. Many foreigners who want to stay in France for more than three months, but do not want to start the administrative process in motion for regularizing their long term status, simply take the train to Brussels or Geneva or London at the end of each three-month period to have their passports stamped and thus reinitiate another three-month period. This is feasible but somewhat impractical and of course not a real solution for those who think they might want to stay longer or hope to study or work legally in France. However, if you don't need to work and you're sure you're only staying 6-12 months, this may be your best option.

A student falls into a slightly different category than a foreigner coming to work or reside in France. Students can be in France on either a short or long term basis, and the visa they solicit reflects the length of their stay. Students who are nationals of EEC (European Economic Community) countries (with the exception of Spain and Portugal) do not require student visas, but must still follow French requirements to obtain the temporary resident permit or *carte de séjour* through the year 1992. After that—we'll see. Nationals from Andorra and Switzerland fall under the requirements for EEC nationals. Spanish and Portuguese students must first solicit a student visa in their home countries and then the *carte de séjour*.

## Student Visa Procedures & Residence Permits

Most students who are planning to pursue university-level studies in France are required to obtain a student visa (not a tourist visa) before leaving their country of residence. Visas are a strict requirement of French law and may be issued to you only in your country of residence. The French police refuse to "normalize" students who enter France without visas. Once you have arrived in Paris, your university may assist you in completing the necessary formalities which allow you to reside legally in France.

### Who Must Obtain a Visa?

All students who intend to enroll at an American university program in France, and of course in the French university system, must obtain a visa except: those already holding a valid *carte de séjour* and citizens of Andorra, Belgium, Denmark, Germany, Greece, Ireland, Italy, Luxembourg, Netherlands, Switzerland, the U.K. and French nationals. It is not possible to obtain a visa after arriving in France. If you do not already have one, you will be told to return to your home country for a visa.

# To Whom is the Application Made?

For student visas and more information, contact the French Consulate nearest you. Here is a list:

## French Consulates for Those Residing Outside the U.S.

**AUSTRIA**
Technikerstrasse 2
A-1040 Wien
Tel: (43-222) 65.47.47 or 65.51.00

**BAHRAIN**
Diplomatic Area 319
Road 1901
P.O. Box 26134
Manama
Tel: (973) 29.17.34

**BELGIUM**
4, Avenue des Arts
1040 Brussels
Tel: (55.21) 210.12.72

**DENMARK**
Ny östergade
1101 Copenhagen K
Tel: (45.1) 15.51.22

**EGYPT**
2, place Ahmed Orabi
P.O. Box 474
Alexandria
Tel: (20.3) 800.207 to 800.488

**FINLAND**
Itaïnen Puistotie 13
00140 Helsinki 14
Tel: (358.0) 171.1521

**GERMANY**
Kappellenweg 1 A.
5300 Bonn 2
Tel: (49.228) 36.20.31 or 36.20.35

Cecilienallee 10
4000 Düsseldorf 30
Tel: (49.221) 49.90.77/78

Bettinastrasse 62
6000 Frankfurt-am-Main
Tel: (49.69) 74.01.37 to 39

Pöseldorferweg 32
2 Hamburg 13
Tel: (49.40) 44.14.07 to 09

Möhlstrasse 5
8000 München 80
Tel: (49.89) 47.50.16 or 47.98.00

**GREECE**
36, Blvd. Amalias
Athens 10558
Tel: (30.1) 322.71.63 or 323.04.76/79

**HOLLAND**
Vijzelgracht 2
P.O. Box 20018
1000 HA Amsterdam
Tel: (31.20) 22.58.11 to 13

**ISRAEL**
Immeuble "Migdalor"
1-3, rue Ben Yehouda
63801 Tel-Aviv
Tel: (972.3) 65.15.25 to 27

**ITALY**
Via Giulia 251
00186 Roma
Tel: (39.6) 656.52.41

1, Piazza Ognissanti
50123 Firenze
Tel: (39.55) 21.35.09 or 21.83.80

Via del Vecchio
Politecnico 3
20121 Milano
Tel: (39.2) 79.43.41/42

Torino & Genova
95, Corso Vittorio Emanuele - 11
10128 Torino
Tel: (39.11) 51.74.86 to 88

**JAPAN**
Obhayashi Building 24th floor
37 Kyobashi 3 Chome Higashi-ku
Osaka 540
Tel: (81.78) 946.6181/82

**JORDAN**
Djebel Amman, rue Mutanabi
P.O. Box 374
Amman
Tel: (962.6) 41.273/74

**KUWAIT**
Bloc N° 12
Lot N° 156/158
Jabriya-Kuwait
P.O. Box 1037 Safat
Tel: (965) 531.98.50 to 53

**LEBANON**
Mar-Takla
Beyrouth
Tel: (961) 450.580 or 451.611

**MEXICO**
Havre N°15
06600 Mexico 6 D.F.
Tel: (52.5) 533.1360 to 64

**MONACO**
Immeuble Monte-Carlo Sun
74, Blvd. d'Italie
P.O. Box 345
Tel: (16) 93.50.51.67

**MOROCCO**
Rue du Prince Moulay Abdallah
B.A. 15810 Casablanca Principal
Tel: (212.9) 27.14.18 or 27.99.81

49, Avenue Allal Ben Abdallah
P.O. Box 139, Rabat
Tel: (212.7) 248.24 or 309.36

**NORWAY**
Drammensweien, 69
0271 Oslo 2
Tel: (47.2) 44.18.20

**PORTUGAL**
123, Calçada
Marquês de Abrantes
Lisboa 1200
Tel: (351.1) 60.81.31 to 33

**SAUDI ARABIA**
Immeuble Saoud Al Fayan
Quartier Olaya
Riyadh
Tel: (966.2) 642.12.33 or 642.14.47

Cheikh Mohammed Bin Abdul
Wahab Street, Sharafiah - P.O. Box 145
Jeddah
Tel: (966.2) 642.12.33 or 642.14.47

**SPAIN**
Paseo de la Castellana N°79
Edificio U.A.P.
Tel: (34.1) 455.54.50

11, Paseo de Gracia
08007 Barcelona
(34.3) 317.81.50 or 317.82.08

**SWEDEN**
Linnégatan 78
115-23 Stockholm
Tel: (46.8) 630.270

**SWITZERLAND**
11, rue Imbert-Galloix
P.O. Box 1205 Geneva
Tel: (41.22) 29.62.11 to 15

Muhlebachstrasse 7
P.O. Box A 112
CH 8008 Zurich
Tel: (41.1) 251.85.44

**TURKEY**
8, Istiklâl Caddesi (Taksim)
Istanbul
Tel: (90.1) 143.1852/53

**UNITED ARAB EMIRATES**
Street Cheikh Khalifa
P.O. Box 4014
Abou Dhabi
Tel: (971) 33.11.00

**UNITED KINGDOM**
24 Rutland Gate
London SW7
Tel: (44.1) 581.52.92 to 99

# What Type of Visa is Necessary?

The type of visa you request depends on two factors: your nationality and the amount of time you plan to spend at a university in France.

**1**. If you will be attending a university program for just one semester, a *"visa d'étudiant pour six mois avec plusieurs entrées"* should be requested. This releases you from *"carte de séjour"* or temporary residence permit formalities as the visa is, in itself, your temporary permit.
PLEASE NOTE THAT THIS VISA IS NOT GRANTED TO ALL NATIONALITIES. CONSULT YOUR LOCAL FRENCH CONSULATE FOR FURTHER INFORMATION.
**2**. If you are applying for at least one year, a *"visa de long séjour pour études"* should be requested.

# How is the Application Made?

The French Consulate nearest you will require the following:
**1**. A certificate of admission from the university in Paris that has accepted you. Most Consulates will not issue a visa without a certificate of admission or some proof of official contact. The visa is valid if you matriculate as a full-time student.
**2**. A financial guarantee as specified by your Consulate. In most countries, this will be a letter from your parents or your bank, signed in the presence of a notary public. It will certify that you will have an income of at least 1,800 FF per month for the duration of your stay in France. This figure is subject to change.
**3**. A statement proving that your health insurance covers you in France. This is also required to apply for a residence permit and to register at the university you've selected. (See Health).
**4**. Authorization by a parent or guardian if you are under 18 years of age.
**5**. Several photographs as specified by the Consulate.
**6**. Your valid passport
In order to avoid unnecessary delays, it is recommended that you write or telephone the Consulate, requesting exact details concerning the documents required. Since different procedures are in effect for students seeking admission to French universities, if you're attending an American program you must clearly request visa information for study in France outside the French university system. Since the time required to issue a visa will vary from Consulate to Consulate and from country to country, you are urged to apply for your student visa as far in advance of your departure date as possible.

# French Consulates in the United States

In order to find out where to apply for your student visa, consult the columns on the next page. The number which follows your state of residence indicates the reference number of the Consulate you should contact. The Consulates are listed below.

# ADDRESSES OF FRENCH CONSULATES IN THE U.S.

| | | | |
|---|---|---|---|
| Alabama | 7 | Montana | 9 |
| Alaska | 9 | Nebraska | 2 |
| Arizona | 5 | Nevada (c) | 5 |
| Arkansas | 7 | Nevada (d) | 9 |
| California (a) | 5 | New Hampshire | 1 |
| California (b) | 9 | New Jersey | 6 |
| Colorado | 5 | New Mexico | 5 |
| Connecticut | 6 | N. Carolina | 10 |
| Delaware | 10 | New York | 6 |
| D.C. | 10 | N. Dakota | 2 |
| Florida | 11 | Ohio | 3 |
| Georgia | 7 | Oklahoma | 4 |
| Hawaii | 9 | Oregon | 9 |
| Idaho | 9 | Pennsylvania | 6 |
| Illinois | 2 | Puerto Rico (e) | 8 |
| Indiana | 2 | Rhode Island | 1 |
| Iowa | 2 | S. Carolina | 10 |
| Kansas | 2 | S. Dakota | 2 |
| Kentucky | 2 | Tennessee | 7 |
| Louisiana | 7 | Texas | 4 |
| Maine | 1 | Utah | 9 |
| Maryland | 10 | Vermont | 1 |
| Massachussetts | 1 | Virginia | 10 |
| Michigan | 3 | Washington | 9 |
| Minnesota | 2 | W. Virginia | 3 |
| Mississippi | 7 | Wisconsin | 2 |
| Missouri | 2 | Wyoming | 9 |

**1)Boston, MA 02116**
3 Commonwealth Avenue
(617) 266-1680
**2)Chicago, IL 60611**
444 No. Michigan Avenue
Suite 3140
(312) 787-5359
**3)Detroit, MI 48143**
100 Renaissance Center
Suite 2975
(313) 568-0990
**4)Houston, TX 77019**
American General Tower
Suite 867
2727 Allen Parkway
(713) 528-2181
**5)Beverly Hills, CA 90211**
8350 Wilshire Blvd.
(213) 653-3120

**6)New York, NY 10021**
934 Fifth Avenue
(212) 606-3600
**7)New Orleans, LA 70115**
3305 St. Charles Ave.
(504) 897-6381
**8)Hato Rey, PR 00918**
Mercantil Plaza Blvd.  Suite 719-720
Stop 27-1/2 Ponce de Leon Ave.
(809) 753-1700 or 3414
**9)San Francisco, CA 94115**
540 Bush Street
(415) 397-4330
**10)Washington, DC 20007**
4101 Reservoir Road NW
(202) 944-6000
**11)Miami, FL 33131**
One Biscayne Tower
2 S Biscayne Blvd
(305) 372-9798

**a:** Counties of Imperial, Inyo, Kern, Kings, Mono, Orange, Riverside, San Bernardino, San Diego, San Louis Obispo, Santa Barbara, Ventura.
   **b:** All counties excluding those listed in (a).
   **c:** Counties of Clark, Lincoln, Nye, Esmeralda, Mineral only.
   **d:** All counties excluding those listed in (c).
   **e:** Also: Viegues, Virgin Islands (US), Turks and Caicos Islands, Montserrat, Virgin Islands (UK), Cayman Islands, Antigua, Barbuda, Redonda, Dominica, St. Christopher, Nevis, Anguilla, St. Lucia, St. Vincent, Beli.

Since September 1989, students intending to study in France for only six months have been issued a six month or 180 day student visa which enables them to stay in France without having to complete *carte de séjour* procedures. The visa in itself is the temporary residence permit. However, it must say this *("le titulaire de ce visa est dispensé de solliciter une carte de séjour," or "le présent visa vaut autorisation de séjour")*. If these magical words are not found somewhere on the visa, you have to follow the *carte de séjour* routine like everybody else.

## How to Get the *Carte de Séjour*

Students entering certain programs in Paris, such as those of The American University of Paris, benefit from a group procedure which makes obtaining a *carte de séjour* a simple routine. This is obviously the easiest for you. The only thing demanded of the student is that he or she: a) comply with the basic physical examination required by the French Government for the first card (not required for EEC nationals) and b) pick up the card on the required date and submit a copy to the indicated office.

If you're a returning student living in Paris you may submit requests for renewals at the same office in your university.

Legally enrolling at a university in France entails showing proof that the student has entered France legally and has completed, or is in the process of completing, *carte de séjour* formalities. So, don't take these instructions too lightly. Listed below are the basic documents required by the *Préfecture de Police* when soliciting a *carte de séjour*. This list is in no way definitive as *Préfecture* requirements can undergo modifications and can vary from *département* to *département*.

## *Carte de séjour*—List of Requirements

**1**) Valid passport and a photocopy of the page that has your name, address, and picture and the page on which your visa is found (if applicable).

**2**) Three black and white identity photos.

**3**) Results of medical visit from the OMI *(Office des Migrations Internationales)*. This you will get once you have done the exam at the date requested by the *préfecture*. It is taken with you when you go to pick up your card, and thus it is extremely important that you do not miss this.

**4**) Proof of domicile in France (ie: electric and gas bill—EDF/GDF— in your name or your rent contract, or a letter from the person who is housing you, a copy of their electric and gas bill and a copy of their *carte d'identité française* or *carte de séjour*.

**5**) A self-addressed stamped envelope (2,30 FF stamp).

**6**) Proof of financial means: financial guarantee letter from your parents which has been stamped by the French Consulate in your country of residence will do. In subsequent years, you should keep receipts of bank transactions or bank statements from your French bank to prove that you have been receiving funds regularly from abroad to support you.

**7**) *Certificat de scolarité* from your school or university.

**8**) Proof of adequate insurance coverage in France with specific mention of medical repatriation. This should be in French, and clearly state the exact coverage for which the student is insured.

**9**) Some *préfectures* require birth certificates, while others request originals as well as copies of all documents listed above.

In Paris, all students applying for the *carte de séjour* must present themselves at the *Préfecture de Police*. Students have been uniformly siphoned off to the *Préfecture de Police* in the 19th *arrondissement*, at 222 rue d'Aubervilliers, which has cut down but not eliminated the waiting time. At certain times of the year, September and October, for example, lines can be four to five hours long. Arriving early, curiously enough, is often but not always the best strategy, because everyone else will have had the same idea. The *carte de séjour* service closes at 16h. Bring a good book and a picnic, however, because even with the best strategies, lines are inevitable. All others go to their local *préfecture* (each *arrondissement* has its own).

It is always useful to request a complete list of all necessary documents before making your *demande* (request) for the *carte de séjour*. This will minimize the number of trips to the *préfecture*, the time spent in lines, the frustrations, etc. Sometimes it's hard getting your questions answered. State employees handling these requests can be impatient, short-tempered, and seemingly spiteful. They are as stuck in the system as you. Remember to be as organized and efficient and as polite and pleasant as possible, even when you really want to scream and punch. You might not get very far by charming the clerk, but you certainly will slow down the procedure if you create an adversary relationship. Nothing at all administrative can be done over the phone so don't even give it a thought. And don't ask for the clerk's name or to see the supervisor. French employees never give out their names, will rarely call over a supervisor, and will only be vexed by your attempt to overpower them. Don't get huffy; just learn how to maneuvre.

## Renewal of the *Carte de Séjour*

In the years that follow your first student *carte de séjour*, you no longer need to solicit a new student visa. The card must never expire in order to avoid having to repeat all the above steps. Renewals are simple, but you should be aware that you have to justify your student status of the past year. You have to take the same documents listed above with the exception of the medical results. In addition, you need a *certificat d'assiduité* (letter from school or university you attended stating that you attended classes and passed your exams) and a copy and the original of the *carte de séjour*.

Renewal of the *carte de séjour* costs 160 FF payable by *timbre fiscal* (government tax stamp) that can be purchased at a Tax Office or, easier, in any *tabac* (tobacco shop). Sometimes they're out of stock, so you'll have to hunt down another.

The first student *carte de séjour* is free; the medical exam costs 270 FF.

## *Carte de Résident*

The *carte de résident*, created in 1984, permits its holders to live and work in France. It is valid for 10 years and is automatically renewed, and it replaces a former system of *carte de séjour* and *carte de travail,* both of which were valid for periods of one, three or ten years. According to the *Office National d'Immigration*, you can request the ten-year *carte de résident* if you have a *carte de séjour temporaire* and have been present in France for at least three years. Additionally, you need to prove that you have regular and sufficient revenue to support yourself and your dependents. This proof takes the form of a work contract or promise of contract. Foreign students are considered to be a valuable asset to their country of origin and for this reason the French government tends to discourage the awarding of the ten-year card to students who want to remain in France after their studies.

There are other legal means of working in France for both short and long-term periods. Aside from the short-term possibilities, it is advised that you consult a lawyer. The first step is to obtain a *visa de long séjour* (one year) from a French consulate in your home country. This will give you access to your first *carte de séjour*. Once in France and having obtained the card you can proceed to request status as a *travailleur indépendant,* or self-employed person. This cannot be done as a student. The initial visa requires your ability to prove a minimum of $1000 per month for the year in France on deposit in your home country. And with *travailleur indépendent* status you'll be obliged to pay monthly sums to the URSSAF, the Social Security administration for self-employed individuals.

## Doing Business/Forming a Company

This is potentially complicated—for assistance, consult the US Embassy Foreign Commercial Service at 2, av Gabriel, 75382 PARIS CEDEX 8, tel: 42.96.12.02, FAX: 42.66.48.27. Additionally, information and support can be obtained from the American Chamber of Commerce in France, 21, av Georges V, 75008 PARIS, tel: 47.23.70.28. The Chamber of Commerce publishes a business directory and a magazine called *Commerce in France*. A third resource is the French-American Chamber of Commerce located at 7, rue Jean Goujon, 75008 PARIS, tel: 42.56.05.00. Most likely you'll need to consult a lawyer for administrative and tax issues. Each *mairie* (city hall) has free legal assistance one evening a week. For English speaking lawyers consult *Paris-Anglophone*. Sam Okoshken, an American lawyer in Paris, specializes in setting up small companies and preparing tax returns. Levine & Okoshken, 53, av. Marceau, 75008 PARIS, tel: 42.56.34.92.

# LANGUAGE

## The Spoken Word

Speaking the language is absolutely essential and clearly one of the most significant prerequisites for participating in the life of the society that surrounds you. And in France this is particularly true. So much of French culture and so many French attitudes are present in the language—the verbal and facial gestures, the syntax, the vocabulary, the role of dialogue. You may find it difficult at first, especially when you realize that what you say and what you mean may not be the same thing. You may feel a sense of loss in that expressing yourself in another language means losing the comfort of the personality through which you have learned to define yourself. But making the effort will pay off in ways that are incalcul-ably enriching—learning French will open your eyes to a different way of thinking and living in the world, and enable you to share the concerns and feelings of fifty-five million people.

The French in general like to talk, and the language in all its richness gains much of its melodic quality from the long and circular phrases needed to express what could be said in a word or two in English or German. This love of words, though, is reserved for specific places and contexts...the *café*, the dinner table, the *table ronde*, the conference. You might notice that people don't talk very loudly in subways, buses, streets or public places. This comes from the French distinction between public and private life. Personal life is private and is handled discreetly.

The French will not openly talk about or be overheard discussing family matters, emotions, or money. With this silent backdrop it's not surprising that tourists seem remarkably loud and obnoxious.

On the other hand, the French can be highly vocal and overt when in the public mode— partaking in a *manifestation* (demonstration) or *grève* (strike), for example—and these are regular institutions in Parisian life.

## The Written Word

The French attention to form is primordial. When it comes to written French there are no short cuts; you must abide by the set forms for addressing someone or some problem even in the most banal circumstances. Salutations and forms of *politesse* (politeness) may strike you as longwinded and even hypocritical but their absence may very well be read as an insult. The best bet here is to memorize one of the following and use it to close all your letters of official or administrative nature. Otherwise, purchase a small and inexpensive book called *La correspondance pratique* by Jean-Yves Dournon (Livre de Poche) which, although a bit dated, provides models for all necessary forms of correspondence.

# le mot

# Some Standard
## *formules de politesse* for Letters

For formal letters addressed to someone you don't know well here are polite but neutral ways to close, roughly equivalent to the English sincerely yours; yours very truly, or yours truly. Remember that *Monsieur* can be changed to *Madame*. When you're not sure, it's best to write *Madame, Monsieur*, instead of the more traditional *Messieurs*, which is now not highly appreciated by some women.

—*Je vous prie de recevoir, Monsieur, l'assurance de mes sentiments distingués.*

—*Veuillez croire, Monsieur, en l'expression de mes sentiments les meilleurs.*

In writing to a "superior" (i.e. cover letters to possible employers, etc):

—*Veuillez croire, cher Monsieur, à mes sentiments cordiaux et respectueux.*

—*Veuillez agréer, Monsieur, l'expression de ma respectueuse considération.*

For friends and parents:

*N'oublie pas d'embrasser Jeanine pour moi.*

*Meilleurs/Affectueux souvenirs*

*Amicalement*

*Bien cordialement à vous/toi*

*Grosses bises!*

*Salut!*

**Note**: the French have a high regard for the handwritten letter. In France you are judged by your handwriting. Telephone skills tend to be less than proficient, spotty at best, but the way the hand constructs words on a page in even the individual with the most basic level of education is taken seriously. And the skills are surprisingly high. The handwriting you may find difficult to decipher at first, but this is no fault of the writer (See Handwriting). Even the occasional *clochard* (beggar) or down-and-out street person in the subway station or along the street often takes the trouble to write out his or her story in chalk on the sidewalk or on a piece of cardboard. "I am 56 years old, unemployed, recently released from the hospital. Can't you help me?" Or the more direct and classic: *"J'ai faim. S.V.P."* When applying for a job or responding to a classified ad, it is always appropriate to reply with a handwritten letter, neatly formulated, beginning with your name and address, the city you're writing from and the date. All documents and contracts require that you close with *"Lu et approuvé"* in your handwriting.

Handwriting is often analyzed professionally as an indicator of character and stability. Often the most inoffensive and slightest error will provoke the average French person to start all over. Don't send messy letters.

The letter plays an important role in France for a number of historic reasons. Whereas Americans often prefer the quickness and effectiveness of a telephone call, the French opt for the *courrier* (correspondence) especially in business, financial, and official matters. A letter creates a *trace* or proof of the exchange and everything done in France must be backed up by a signed piece of paper, as you will soon learn (if you haven't already). The French are *méfiant* (distrustful) of the spoken word, banking everything on the signed contract, whereas the English sense of honor relies deeply on the spoken word and the handshake; the Gentleman's Agreement. So don't be overly casual when leaving a note for even the gas company, let alone your banker or the owner of the apartment you are renting. And, yes, penmanship counts a lot.

The typewriter kind of got skipped over in the history of French communications. The French jumped from the handwritten page to the computer. Many young people in Paris own personal computers, whereas the typewriter has been a far rarer item in the French household. Not surprisingly, most French students cannot type and those who study at American universities or business schools complain bitterly when required to type academic papers. French university professors never require that papers be typed.

## *Ça va*

Even if it was only French 100 or some light-weight course in rudimentary *français* at night- or summer-school, chances have it that you probably know at least that one great French catch-all: *"Comment allez-vous?"* or its familiar counterpart *"Comment ça va?"* (How goes it?) simplified as *ça va?* (It goes?). But, did anyone tell you that you can't just prance down the *pâté de maisons* (block) and sputter to complete strangers, *ça va?* You just can't ask any random person how he or she is doing, the way you'd toss into the air a friendly or mechanical "Hi!" "Howdy!" "What's up?" "What's happening?" or "How ya doin?" Make eye contact and ask a passerby how he or she is doing and in most cases the person will look behind him to see if you're addressing someone else, ignore you totally, or stop in his tracks with a perplexed glaze on his face, lower lip pursed, and inquire: *On se connaît?* Have we met? Do we know each other?

The textbooks back home often forget in their first lessons on "Greetings" to discuss language as a function of culture. And face it, understanding a culture foreign to your own is precisely what's needed to assure a rewarding and meaningful *séjour* (stay) in your new, albeit temporary, country. The more you absorb about the social relations and interactions of the French and the cultural underpinnings of French society, the more you will not only enjoy being part of Parisian life but begin to comprehend better your own culture and language. The world doesn't grow, but your conception of it does. So, if you're ignored on Day One or you let yourself be influenced by the derogatory comments of cursory travelers who lambast the French for alleged rudeness, arrogance, or chilliness, you're missing the much larger point and only widening cultural barriers.

A good rule of thumb is to suspend all judgments for at least a month! Admittedly, there is a certain formality and pace of interchange deeply engrained in French culture (as witnessed in both verbal and written expression) that is at first going to separate the friendly and direct

American from his new environs. This is par for the course. It shouldn't be distressing; it's interesting! As American or non-French students or newly-arrived residents in Paris, an openness to your surroundings in a French—not American—context will be your passport to an enriching and pleasurable time.

The following exchanges with the familiar *ça va* reveal several important attitudes.

—*Ça va?* the question, literally meaning How goes it?, is often answered with itself, *Ça va*, meaning "It goes."

This makes for easy language learning, but what in fact does it mean? Everything lies in the intonation of the response. *Ça va* could reflect a great enthusiasm for life, a pang of desperate depression, or a plain moment of daily mediocrity. The nuances abound. So learn to listen for them and use them yourself. These are rich words.

—*Ça va?* or the formal *Comment allez-vous?* are often answered directly with the question *Et vous?* (And you?)

The first few times you get involved in this interchange you are liable to get annoyed. Don't ignore me, that's not an answer, you'll want to complain. The repetition of the answer for the question simply demonstrates the French love of form. It's the asking of the question that counts, not the answer. There is nothing I can do if you aren't doing well; the best I can do is to ask you how you're doing. Soon, you'll see that this little tidbit of dialogue is really very adorable and convenient.

## Les Bises

When greeting someone they know, the French shake hands and/or give a quick succession of impersonal kisses on alternating cheeks called *les bises*. There are lots of nuances here that only experience can sort out, but here are a few. Some people give two kisses, some three, and others four. It there are six people in the room and you give four *bises* each, that calls for a lot of kissing. Remember this is just a form of saying *bonjour*. What's interesting to note here is that the French are used to and comfortable with close personal contact. They are not bothered (*gênés*) by human proximity or touching. They don't require the same distance Anglo-Saxons insist upon when talking. So get used to *les bises*. Even French people have cute little moments when two people are unsure if it'll be two, three, or four *bises*. Two is the most common, four is more classical; three is for those who want to be a bit different without abandoning tradition. People from the south of France tend to kiss more. *Les bises* are usually for men and women or women and women, but good male friends *font la bise* also. Start on the left cheek and don't really kiss, just touch cheeks and steer your lips inwards.

Handshakes are required particularly when men greet each other equally for the first time or the zillionth time. When you arrive at work, for example, you shake your co-workers' hand and say *bonjour*. It may seem highly repetitious, but it's a very pleasant way for people to acknowledge each other. Similarly, the handshake and *les bises* are repeated when leaving.

# Telephoning

Those first few calls can be traumatic. It's especially difficult to integrate your French into dialogue when you cannot see the other person and can't rely on gestures. Here are a few simple telephone dialogue patterns for the uninitiated:

**How to ask for someone:**
—*Bonjour, est-ce que je peux parler avec..?* (Hello, can I speak with...?)
—*Bonjour, puis-je parler avec..?* (Hello, can I speak with...?)
—*Bonjour, est-ce que Monsieur (Mademoiselle, Madame)...est là?* (Hello, is...there?)

**Answering the telephone:**
—*Ne quittez pas.* (Don't hang up, or hang on.)
—*Il/Elle n'est pas là.* (He/she is not here.)
—*Vous vous êtes trompé de numéro.* (You have the wrong number.)
—*Qui est à l'appareil?* (Who's calling?)
—*Est-ce que je peux laisser un message.* (Can I leave a message?)
—*C'est* (your name) *à l'appareil.* (It's...calling.)
—*Comment ça s'ecrit?* (How is that spelled?)
—*Je suis desolé(e).* (I'm sorry.)
—*Répétez, s'il vous plaît.* (Please repeat that.)
—*Lentement, s'il vous plaît.* (Slowly, please.)

# Language Schools

In the last few years there has been a dramatic increase in the number of language schools in Paris for both French and English. Much of this is in anticipation of 1992 and all the transpollenation that is expected to follow. Here is a broad selection of schools where French is taught in Paris:

**Alliance Française**
101, Bd. Raspail
75006 PARIS
tel: 45.44.38.28

**An American in Paris**
25, Bd. de Sébastopol
75001 PARIS
tel: 40.26.22.90

**Berlitz France**
29, rue de la Michodière
75002 PARIS
tel: 47.42.46.54

**Bibliothèque Publique
d'Information
Centre Pompidou (Language Lab)**
75181 PARIS Cedex 04
tel: 42.77.12.33

**British Institute**
11, rue de Constantine
75007 PARIS
tel: 45.55.71.99

**Chambre de Commerce et
d'Industrie de Paris-Enseignement**
42, rue du Louvre
75001 PARIS
tel: 45.08.37.34

**Centre d'Echanges Internationaux**
104, rue de Vaugirard
75006 PARIS
tel: 45.49.26.25

**Centre Linguistique Bouchereau**
116, av. des Champs-Elysées
75008 PARIS
tel: 45.63.17.27

**Clé International**
27, rue de la Glacière
75013 Paris
tel: 45.87.44.00

**Cours de Civilisation Française de la Sorbonne**
47, rue des Ecoles
75005 PARIS
tel: 40.46.22.11 ext. 2664 or 2675

**Dialangues**
7, rue de Surène
75008 PARIS
tel: 42.68.18.54

**French Language Instruction for Anglophones**
34, rue Alphonse Bertillon
75015 PARIS
tel: 48.28.03.21

**Institut Catholique**
21, rue Assas
75006 PARIS
tel: 42.22.63.49

**Institut de Langue Française**
15, rue Arsène Houssaye
75008 PARIS
tel: 42.27.14.77

**Institut Parisien de Langue et de Civilisation Françaises**
87, Bd. de Grenelle
75015 PARIS
tel: 40.56.09.53

## Self-Taught French

**Assimil**
(wide selection of books, cassettes, and PC software)
11, rue des Pyramides
75001 PARIS
tel: 42.60.40.66

## Sample of French Handwritten Letters & Numbers

A B C D E F G H I J
K L M N O P Q R S
T U V W X Y Z

a b c d e f g h i j k l
m n o p q r s t u v
w x y z
1 2 3 4 5 6 7 8 9 10

# EDUCATION

## The French System

Formal education in France begins for many at the age of three months in the state-run *crèches* (nurseries). These tend to be remarkably well-organized and pedagogically-sound institutions. Aside from the shared colds and minor illnesses, the *crèches* seem to offer only positive factors for French society. Mothers reassume their secure jobs and the kids tend to become very well-adjusted. Education of the French palate begins in infancy, too, as the tiny ones begin to be fed everything from sole to brains, artichokes to Port Salut cheese. Between the ages of three and six years; the child can attend his neighborhood *école maternelle* (pre-school) which is also state-run. Education is compulsory from six to sixteen and is free in state schools. 83% of children are in state education; the remainder go to private schools, most of which are run by the Catholic Church. The French educational tradition emphasizes encyclopedic knowledge and memorization. The rigidness of former years, however, has loosened somewhat. In general, all children attend the same kind of state day schools, and the tenacious go on to study for the *baccalauréat*, which is roughly equivalent to a level of studies one to two years beyond the American high school diploma. This *bac* is a highly important indicator of a student's potential choices in life. At age 15 or 16 the more academic children go to a *lycée* (high school) to prepare for the *bac*, usually taken at age 18 or 19. The *bac* is more of a means to get into a university than a job qualification in itself. Passing the *bac* is essential for access to all upper-level jobs. Failure is a negative status symbol and source of shame in some socially well-placed families. (Note: *passer* is to take an exam, *réussir* is to pass, *rater* to fail.)

There are almost a million university students in France. Unlike the United States, admission to a state-run university is not selective, but guaranteed to everyone who has passed the *bac*. Student/teacher ratios are high. There is little personal contact between professors and students. The system is centralized and tightly-controlled. The Sorbonne's international reputation stems from the quality of the minds who teach there. The archaic organization of the university, however, may dissuade you from enrolling. University structure has been the focus of many political debates and upheavals in the past two decades.

In brief, the French university system is organized into three cycles: the 1er, 2e, and 3e. The first is usually two years, and comprises the *DEUG* and the *Licence*. The second cycle, or *Maîtrise*, is roughly equivalent to the American Master's degree. The third cycle, and clearly the most prestigious in the French system, is the Doctoral program, which not long ago offered three different doctoral diplomas. More recently the long and serious *doctorat d'Etat* has been replaced by the *doctorat d'université* modelled after the American Ph.D. A unique, although disruptive, quality of the university cycle system is the fact that prescribed programs are subject to modification with governmental and ministerial changes. For all questions of recognized transferable credits, you must submit in writing a *dérogation* (appeal) to the universities' *Service des équivalences*. Remember to bring not only transcripts but all original diplomas. French Universities need to see the stamped document.

In 1968, in keeping with the international climate, there were a series of nationwide demonstrations, walk-outs and riots staged by French University students demanding an overhaul of the dated and archaic university system. Since then the scene has relaxed somewhat and universities have now been split up into smaller, more manageable units. Thus the Sorbonne is now simply a building which houses a part of the amorphous *Université de Paris* system. There are a number of programs in Paris run by American colleges which include the possibility of study at one of the Paris campuses. They can also be contacted directly. A complete list of all universities and schools in France, public and private, is published by *L'Etudiant* magazine, called *Le Guide des Etudes Supérieures 1990*. Another source of information are French Consulates in the United States, which provide information on specific areas of study in France through their Cultural Services office.

# MAJOR PARIS UNIVERSITIES:

## Université de Paris

### Université Panthéon Sorbonne - Paris 1
12, place du Panthéon
75231 PARIS Cedex 05
tel: 46.34.97.00

### Université de Paris 2
(Droit, Economie et Sciences Sociales)
12 place du Panthéon
75231 PARIS Cedex 05
tel: 46.34.97.00

### Université de la Sorbonne Nouvelle - Paris 3
17, rue de la Sorbonne
75005 PARIS
tel: 45.87.40.00

### Université de Paris- Sorbonne - Paris 4
1, rue Victor Cousin
75230 PARIS cedex 06
tel: 40.46.22.11

### Université René Descartes - Paris 5
12, rue de l'Ecole-de-Médecine
75270 PARIS cedex 06
tel: 40.46.16.16

### Université Pierre et Marie Curie - Paris 6
4, place Jussieu
75230 PARIS cedex 05
tel: 43.36.25.25

### Université de Paris 7
2, place Jussieu
75251 PARIS cedex 05
tel: 43.36.25.25

### Université de Paris Dauphine - Paris 9
Place du Maréchal-de-Lattre-de-Tassigny
75775 PARIS cedex 16
tel: 45.05.14.10

### Institut National des Langues et Civilisations Orientales
2, rue de Lille
75007 PARIS
tel: 49.26.42.00

# Art Schools

**Ecole du Louvre**
34 quai du Louvre
75041 PARIS cedex 01
tel: 42.60.25.50 or 42.60.39.26

**Ecole Nationale Supérieure des Arts
Décoratifs (ENSAD)**
31, rue d'Ulm
75005 PARIS
tel: 43.29.86.79

**Ecole Nationale Supérieure des
Beaux-Arts (Beaux-Arts)**
17, quai Malaquais
75272 PARIS cedex 06
tel: 42.60.34.57

**Les Ateliers-Ecole Nationale
Supérieure de Création Industrielle**
48, rue Saint-Sabin
75011 PARIS
tel: 43.38.09.09

# Architecture Schools

**Ecole d'architecture Paris-Belleville**
78-80, rue de Rebeval
75019 PARIS
tel: 42.41.33.60

**Ecole d'architecture Paris-la Seine**
14, rue Bonaparte
75006 PARIS
tel: 42.61.81.11

**Ecole d'architecture Paris-La Villette**
144, rue de Flandre
75019 PARIS
tel: 40.36.79.70

**Ecole d'architecture Paris-Tolbiac**
5, rue du Javelot
75013 PARIS
tel: 45.82.27.27

**Ecole d'architecture Paris-Villemin**
11, quai Malaquais
75006 PARIS
tel: 42.60.34.57

**Ecole spéciale d'architecture**
254, bd Raspail
75014 PARIS
tel: 43.22.83.70

# Grandes Ecoles

The difference between a university and one of the *Grandes Ecoles* is vast. There are about 250 small, autonomous, and elite *Grandes Ecoles*. They train high-level specialists in engineering, applied science, administration and management studies. The entrance exam for French students requires two or three years' rigorous preparatory study in special post-bac classes at the *lycées*. Extremely few foreigners are admitted to the *Grandes Ecoles*. Only 10% of the students are women. These schools turn out a high proportion of senior civil servants and industrial and business leaders. One of most prestigious is the *Ecole Polytechnique*, founded by Napoleon to train engineers for the armed forces. It is still run by the Ministry of Defense and headed by a general. Other *Grandes Ecoles*: *Ecole Centrale*, *Ecole des Hautes Etudes Commerciales*, and *Ecole Nationale d'Administration*, which trains future high-level political types.

# L'Institut d'Etudes Politiques

More than 800 of the 5000 students at *L'Institut d'Etudes Politiques de Paris*, or *Sciences-Po*, are foreign. You must speak and write French to be admitted. Several possibilities for courses of study:

Those who already have a master's degree in a related field (Political Science, Economics, History, etc.) can enter the *troisième cycle* and obtain a *Doctorat* for further research work in the field or a *Diplôme d'Etudes Supérieures Spécialisées* (DESS) for preparation for more professional work.

Those who already have three years of university work can enter the *deuxième cycle* by passing an entrance exam. They receive the *Diplôme de l'Institut* in two years of study.

Students having completed some university work: the *Cycle d'Etudes Internationales* is suitable for those on Junior Year Abroad in American University programs; no preparation for diploma.

*Certificat d'Etudes Politiques*: this is a one-year program for international students which concentrates on studies of modern France, and prepares those who wish to enter the *deuxième cycle*.

Further information can be obtained by contacting:

**Fondation Nationale des Sciences Politiques**
27, Rue Saint Guillaume
75341 PARIS Cedex 07
tel: 45.49.50.50
FAX: 42.22.31.26

## Foreign & Exchange Programs in Paris

Presently, there are more than fifty university exchange and foreign study programs in Paris and a handful in the rest of France. Additionally, there are a number of English-language universities based in or with campuses in Paris, the largest and most complete being The American University of Paris with its 1000 students and 275 courses each semester. The complete list of higher education programs (in alphabetical order) is found below and is followed by a list of schools and alumni associations.

## University Programs

**Academic Year Abroad**
Reid Hall
4, rue de Chevreuse
75006 PARIS
tel: 43.20.91.92

**Alma College**
c/o Alliance Française
35, rue de Fleurus
75006 PARIS
tel: 45.49.08.16
Director: Mme. ZIEGLER

**Allegheny College in Paris**
49, rue de la Glacière
75013 PARIS
tel: 43.31.10.80

**American Business School**
15, av. de la Grande Armée
75016 PARIS
tel: 45.01.96.01

**American Institute for Foreign Study**
Reid Hall
4, rue de Chevreuse
75006 PARIS
tel: 43.22.11.91
Director: Mrs. Marthe B. COOPER

**American School of Modern Music**
117, rue de la Croix-Nivert
75015 PARIS
tel: 45.31.16.07

**American University of Paris, The**
31, av. Bosquet
75007 PARIS
tel: 45.55.91.73
telex: 205 926
FAX: 47.05.33.49
President: Ms. Catherine W. INGOLD
Academic Dean: Mr. William CIPOLLA
Registrar: Ms. DeeDee PEASE
Acting Dean of Students: Larry PODELL
Assist. Dean: Ms. Charlotte KESSLER
(American university education; B.A./B.S. degree)
**Admissions/Development Office**
165, rue de l'Université
75007 PARIS
tel: 45.55.91.73
Dir. of Admissions: Mr. John NISSEN
V. P. for Development: Mr. John McKEE

**American University of Paris, The**
Division of Continuing Education
34, av New York
75116 PARIS
tel: 47.20.44.99
Director: Ms. Susan R. KINSEY
Dir. of Summer Program: Ms. Camille
  HERCOT

**American University of Paris, The**
80 E. 11th St., Suite 434
New York, N.Y.  10003
tel: (212) 677-4870

**Boston University in Paris**
49, rue Pierre Charron
75008 PARIS
tel: 42.56.18.64
(offers Masters degrees in International
Relations)

**Boston University Paris Internship**
725 Commonwealth Avenue B2
Boston MA  02215
tel: (617) 353-9888

**Center for University
Programs Abroad**
19/21, rue Cassette
75006 PARIS
tel: 42.22.87.50
tel: (315) 853-6905 Clinton, N.Y, USA
Directors: Elliot CHATELIN, Pascale
BESSIERES

**Central College (Iowa)**
214, bd Raspail
75014 PARIS
tel: 43.20.76.09
Director: Inge DRAPPIER

**Centre Nord Américain**
11, rue Pierre et Marie Curie
75005 PARIS
tel: 43.25.25.45

**Collège Irlandais**
5, rue Irlandais
75005 PARIS
tel: 47.07.31.33

**Columbia University**
Reid Hall
4, rue de Chevreuse
75006 PARIS
tel: 43.20.24.83
Architecture Program: 42.78.53.44
Director of Studies: Mrs. Danielle
HASSE-DUBOSC

**Earlham/Kenyan**
Centre F.A. Odéon
1, Pl de l'Odéon
75006 PARIS
tel: 46.34.16.10

**Ecole Européenne des Affaires
European Master's in
International Business**
108, Boulevard Malesherbes
75017 PARIS
tel: 47.54.65.78
Director: Bruno LEBLANC

**EDUCO/Duke/Cornell**
23, rue du Montparnasse
75006 PARIS
tel: 42.22.34.66
Director: Marianne DEVAUX

**European University**
35, rue des Chantiers
78000 VERSAILLES
tel: 46.44.39.39
Director: Mme. TOAN

**European University of America**
17/25, rue de Chaillot
75016 PARIS
tel: 40.70.11.71
Director: Mr. FORGET

**Hamilton College**
Reid Hall
4 , rue de Chevreuse
75006 Paris
tel: 43.20.77.77

**Hollins College**
4, Pl de l'Odéon
75006 PARIS
tel: 46.34.59.85

**Indiana University**
Public Adm. Program
C/O ENA
13, rue de l'Université
75007 PARIS

**Institute Franco-Américain
de Management**
19, rue Cépré
75015 PARIS
tel: 47.34.38.23
Director: Ms. Marie-France JOSEPH
(Associated with Hartford University,
Northeastern University, Boston
University and Pace University)

**MBA Insead**
Bd. de Constance
77305 FONTAINEBLEAU Cedex
tel: 60.72.40.00
Director: M. Philippe NAERT
(10 month graduate MBA program)

**MBA Institute**
38, rue des Blancs-Manteaux
75004 PARIS
tel: 42.78.95.45
Director: M. GEORGEL

**MICEFA**
*Mission Interuniversitaire de Coordina-
tion des Echanges Franco-Américains*
101, bd Raspail
75006 PARIS
tel: 45.49.20.38
(CUNY, Brown, Cornell, UVA, Mt. Holyoke, Bates,
Amherst, Tufts, Berkeley, Stanford, Johns Hopkins,
Sweet Briar, U. of Michigan, U. of Texas-Austin, U. of
Louisiana, Tulane, Waterloo, Cal. State, New Jersey
Statem, Indiana U., U. of Illinois, U. of Wisconsin,
Ohio State, U. of Minnesota, U. of Iowa, Colorado
State)

**Middlebury College**
Reid Hall
4, rue Chevreuse
75006 Paris
tel: 43.20.70.57

**New York University**
56, rue de Passy
75016 PARIS
tel: 42.88.52.84
Director: Mme WALTHER

**New York University**
Experimental Theater Wing
77, rue de Charonne
75011 PARIS
tel: 40.27.81.85

**Paris American Academy**
9, rue des Ursulines
75005 PARIS
tel: 43.25.08.91
and
Pavillon Val-de-Grâce
277, rue St. Jacques
75005 PARIS
tel: 43.25.35.09
Director: Richard ROY

**Paris Internship Program/Lake
Forest College**
43, rue Lacépède
75005 PARIS
tel: 45.87.20.51

**Parsons Paris School of Design**
10-14, rue Letellier
75015 PARIS
tel: 45.77.39.66
FAX: 45.77.10.44
Director: Samuel HOI

**Reid Hall Centre Universitaire
Americain**
4, rue Chevreuse
75006 PARIS
tel: 43.20.33.07
(eight American Academic Year Abroad
programs located here)

**Sarah Lawrence College**
Reid Hall
4, rue Chevreuse
75006 PARIS
tel: 43.22.14.36
Director: Mme MIDDLETON

**St. Xavier of Chicago**
(MBA Night School)
71, rue du Faubourg St Honoré
75008 PARIS
tel: 42.66.99.44
Director: Mary Bea BOUCHET

**Southern Methodist University**
Reid Hall
4, rue Chevreuse
75006 PARIS
tel: 43.20.04.86
Director: Dr. Catherine HEALEY

**Schiller International University**
103, rue de Lille
75007 PARIS
tel: 45.51.28.93

**Scripps College**
26, rue des Carmes
75005 PARIS
tel: 43.54.91.89

**Skidmore College**
142, rue de Rivoli
75001 PARIS
tel: 42.36.02.55

**Smith College**
Reid Hall
4, rue de Chevreuse
75006 PARIS
tel: 43.21.65.54

**Stanford University**
1, Pl de l'Odéon
75006 PARIS
tel: 45.48.95.57

**SUNY Brockport/SUNY Oswego**
Centre Franco-Américain
1, Pl de l'Odéon
75006 PARIS
tel: 46.34.16.10

**University of California**
Paris Center for Critical Studies
1, Place de l'Odéon
75006 PARIS
tel: 46..33.85.33
Director: Ms. Debbie GLASSMAN
(undergraduate and graduate)

**SUNY Stony Brook**
4, rue St Nicolas (c/o NYU)
75012 PARIS
tel: 42.47.06.04

**Tufts University**
2, rue des Taillandiers
75011 PARIS
tel: 43.21.35.85

**Tulane/Newcomb**
Reid Hall
4, rue de Chevreuse
75006 PARIS
tel: 43.21.35.85

**University of Illinois at Chicago**
Centre Franco-Américain
1, Pl de l'Odéon
75006 PARIS
tel: 46.34.16.10

**University of Hartford Business School**
8, Terrace Bellini
92807 PARIS LA DEFENSE
tel: 49.00.19.61
Office of Graduate Studies
Paris MBA Program
200 Bloomfield Avenue
West Hartford, CT USA 06117
tel: (203) 243-4641

**Wesleyan University**
Reid Hall
4, rue de Chevreuse
75006 PARIS
tel: 43.22.12.47

# Schools

**American School of Paris**
41, rue Pasteur
92210 SAINT CLOUD
tel: 46.02.54.43
Headmaster: M. Jim MORIARTY

**American School-Harriet Bonelli**
1, rue Crébillon
75006 PARIS
tel: 43.25.10.22

**British School of Paris**
38, Quai de l'Ecluse
78290 CROISSY-SUR-SEINE
tel: 39.76.29.00
Headmaster: M. Livingston SMITH

**Ecole Active
Bilingue Jeannine Manuel**
Ecole Internationale de Paris
70, rue du Théâtre
75015 PARIS
tel: 45.75.62.98
Director: Ms. Jacqueline ROUBINET
and
39, av. de la Bourdonnais
75007 PARIS
tel: 45.51.20.84
and
141, av. de Suffren
75007 PARIS
tel: 47.34.27.72

**Ecole Jeanne d'Albret**
1, rue Denis Poisson
75017 PARIS
tel: 45.74.10.95
Director: M. BERBEZY

**International School of Paris**
Grades K-5
96 bis, rue du Ranelagh
75016 PARIS
tel: 42.24.43.40
Grades 6-12
7 rue Chardin
75016 PARIS

**Lycée Int'l de Saint-Germain-en-Laye**
230, rue du Fer-à-Cheval
78104 SAINT-GERMAIN-EN-LAYE
tel: 34.51.94.11
Headmaster: M. Edgar SCHERER
Director (American Section): Mme
Nancy MAGAUD

**Marymount School**
72, Bd. de la Saussaye
92200 NEUILLY-SUR-SEINE
tel: 46.24.10.51
Headmistress: Sister Maureen VELLON

**United Nations Nursery School**
40 rue Pierre-Guerin
75016 PARIS
tel: 45.27.20.24
(international bilingual school for
children 2-6; summer school in July)

**Women's Institute for Continuing
Education (WICE)**
20 Bd. Montparnasse
75007 PARIS
tel: 45.66.75.50
President: Carol ALLEN
(offers courses in Teaching English as a
Foreign Language, Career Development, Self-Development, Living in
France, Arts, Humanities. Has career
services, a monthly newsletter, a
volunteer service, a health referral
service, and open houses)

# Exchange Programs

**Aspect Foundation
Exchange Programs**
53, rue du Fbg. Poissonnière
75009 PARIS
tel: 48.00.06.00
FAX: 48.00.05.94
Representative: M. Peter SPIER

**Council on International
Educational Exchange (C.I.E.E.)**
Centre Franco-Américain Odéon
1, Pl. de l'Odéon
75006 PARIS
tel: 43.59.23.69 or 46.34.16.10
Dir. of Programs: Ms. Andrea MASON

**Cultural Crossing**
60, rue de Varennes
75007 PARIS
tel: 45.48.62.51
Director: Ms. Polly PLATT

**Experiment in International Living**
89, rue Turbigo
75003 PARIS
tel: 42.78.50.03
Director: M. Gilbert GUILLEMOTO

**Fondation des Etats-Unis**
15, Bd. Jourdan
75690 PARIS Cedex 14
tel: 45.89.35.77 (admin.)
tel: 45.89.35.79 (students)
Director: M. Terence MURPHY
(residence and cultural center)

**Fondation Franco-Américaine**
38, av. Hoche
75008 PARIS
tel: 45.63.28.30
FAX: 42.56.09.75
Director: M. Marceau LONG
(awards, scholarships, and grants)

**Franco-American Commission for
Educational Exchange**
(Fulbright Commission Scholarships)
9, rue Chardin
75016 PARIS
tel: 45.20.46.54
FAX: 42.88.04.79
Director: M. COLLOMBERT

# Student Loans

Citizens of the United States who have been accepted by certain American university programs overseas, such as AUP, are eligible to participate in the Stafford Loan Program (formerly the GSL) and the Supplementary Loan for Students Program (obtained directly through a bank in the United States). All Stafford Loan applicants will have to demonstrate need and must complete the FAF form (obtained through the College Board). Parents also have the possibility of borrowing through the PLUS Program. Student loans are made by banks in the United States. Students should first consult with the prospective lender, with the student loan agency of his or her state of residence, or with the nearest regional office of the U.S. Office of Education.

Students who are residents of France are eligible to participate in special loan programs with French banks. The Financial Aid Coordinator of your school or university can assist applicants in obtaining further details.

(Visiting students attending the AUP for a semester or a year, with the intention of returning to their home institution to complete degree requirements, are not eligible for Financial Aid from AUP. However, they may be able to use their federal and state financial aid while in Paris). Because individual college or university policies differ, students are urged to contact the financial aid or study-abroad office of their home institution for detailed information.

## The Working Student

As a student in France with a valid student card, you are eligible to legally work part time *(mi-temps),* up to 20 hours per week. To obtain the little blue work permit *(autorisation de travail),* you must present your student card, passport, *carte de séjour,* letter or contract of employment which states the specific hours, days and times, photos, and a stamped envelope to the following address:

**Ministère du Travail**
80, rue de la Croix Nivert
75015 PARIS
tel: 40.56.60.00

You will probably also be required to prove that you are not a French *boursier* (French State Scholarship Recipient) by picking up a waiver form at: CNOUS, 6 rue Jean Calvin, 5e, Métro Censier. Open 13h30-16h.

Otherwise, three-month work permits are issued to students at IEEC at 1, Place de l'Odéon 75006 PARIS for the fee of 500 FF.

# Museums /Galleries

There are nearly one hundred museums in Paris, dedicated to just about every subject, from wine to history to anthropology, transportation, new technology and, of course, art. Many of the major museums are free or half-price on Sundays, and some offer student discounts (a valid Student ID helps). Teachers are admitted free to all museums upon presentation of faculty identification. You can also buy a card called the *Carte musées et monuments* good for one day (50 FF), three consecutive days (100 FF), or five consecutive days (150 FF) which gives you admission to over 60 museums and monuments in Paris and surrounding areas and eliminates the need to wait in line for tickets. These cards are for sale in museums and monuments, the Métro, and tourist offices. *Pariscope* and *Officiel des Spectacles* have extensive museum and gallery listings, with informa-

tion on current exhibitions. Of the numerous Paris guides available, the *Michelin Guide to Paris* and the *Hachette Guide Bleue* are the best for background and history. In general, national museums are open 9h45-17h every day except Tuesday. The following is a list of the major museums with days and schedules.

*Le Louvre*: rue de Rivoli, 75001, PARIS (Métro: Palais-Royal-Musée du Louvre). Information: 40.20. 51.51. Open every day except Tuesday. Hours: permanent exhibitions 9h00-18h00, Wednesday until 21h45; temporary exhibitions 12h00-20h00. Price: 25 FF, 13 FF for those under 25 years of age (proof of age is required), free for those under 18.

*Musée d'Orsay*: 1, rue Belle-chasse, 75007 PARIS, (Métro: Solférino). 40.49.48.14; recorded message: 45.49.11.11; program information: 40.49.48.48 or

40.49.48.34 or 40.49.48.84. Open daily except Monday: 10h00-18h00; Thursday until 21h15; Sunday 9h00-18h00. Price: 23 FF, 12 FF; Sunday 12 FF; free for those under 18.

**Musée Rodin**: 77, rue de Varenne, 75007 PARIS (Métro: Varenne). 47.05. 01.34. Open daily except Monday: 10h00-17h45. Price: 20 FF.

**Musée Picasso**: Musée Hôtel Salé, 5, rue de Thorigny, 75004 PARIS, (Métro: Chemin Vert or Saint Paul). 42.71.25.21. Open daily except Tuesdays: 9h15-17h15; Wednesday until 22h00; Price: 28 FF, 16 FF.

**Musée d'Art Moderne**: 11, av du Président Wilson, 75016 PARIS, (Métro: Iéna). 47.23.61.27. Open daily except Monday: 10h00-17h30; Wednesday until 22h30. Price: 20 FF.

**Centre Georges Pompidou**: 19, rue Rambuteau, 75001 PARIS, (Métro: Châtelet-Les Halles). 42.77. 12.33. Open weekdays: 12h00-22h00; Saturday, Sunday and holidays: 10h00-20h00; closed Tuesday. Museum: 23 FF (17 FF for those under 25). The library keeps the same hours.

**Cité des Sciences et de l'Industrie**: Parc de la Villette, 30, av. Corentin-Cariou 75019 PARIS (Métro: Porte de la Villette). 46.42. 13.13. Open daily except Monday: 10h00-18h00. Price: 30 FF, 23 FF.

**Musée des Arts Décoratifs**: 107-109, rue de Rivoli, 75001 PARIS, (Métro Palais-Royal). 42. 60.32.14. Open Wednesday-Saturday: 13h30-18h00; Sunday: 11h00-18h00. Closed Monday and Tuesday. Price: 20 FF, 14 FF.

**Musée de Cluny**: 6 rue Paul-Painlevé, 75005 PARIS, (Métro: St. Michel). Open 9h45-12h30, 14h00-17hh15. Closed Tuesdays. Price 15 FF, 8 FF on Sundays.

**Musée du Petit Palais**: av. Winston-Churchill, 75008 PARIS, (Métro: Champs-Elysées-Clemenceau). Open 9h45-17h00, closed Mondays. Admission: 15 FF, 8 FF on Sundays.

**Musée de la Publicité**: 18 rue de Paradis, 75010 PARIS, (Métro: Château d'Eau). Open 12h00-18h00. Closed Tuesdays. Admission: 18 FF, 10 FF for the unemployed, for students and over 65s with passport. Price of admission includes the *cinéma-thèque* (movie theater).

**Musée des Arts Africains et Océaniens**: 293, av Daumesnil, 75012 PARIS, (Métro: Porte Dorée). Open every day 10h00-12h30; 13h30-17h30. Admission: 22 FF, under 18 free. 13 FF on Sundays.

**Musée Guimet**: 6, place d'Iéna, 75016 PARIS, (Métro: Iéna). Admission: 15 FF, 8 FF on Sundays. The Asiatic Art Collection of the Louvre.

**Musée de l'Homme**: Palais de Chaillot, place du Trocadéro, 75016 PARIS, tel: 45.53.70.60, (Métro: Trocadéro). Open 9h45-17h15 Monday, Wednesday, Sunday. Admission 16 FF, 8 FF for students.

**Musée de l'Orangerie**: Place de la Concorde, 75001 PARIS, (Métro: Concorde). Open 9h45-17h15, Monday, Wednesday, Sunday. Admission 15 FF, 8 FF for those 18-25. Under 18 free. Houses Monet's gigantic Water Lilies.

# Galleries

There are essentially three major gallery districts in Paris: St Germain-des-Près, Les Halles/Beaubourg and the Bastille. Consult *Paris Beaubourg, Paris Rive Gauche* (semi-monthly gallery and exhibition listings), *Canal* (publication specializing in listings of current exhibitions), *Pariscope* or *l'Officiel des Spectacles* (at newstands) for current exhibitions. For those just beginning to tune in to the gallery scene, here are a handful of the more interesting and pace-setting galleries for contemporary art: Isy Brachot, Daniel Templon, Yvon Lambert, Galerie Lelong, Durand-Dessert, Antoine Candau, Claire Burrus, Crousel-Robelin-Bama, Blondel, Claude Bernard, Caroline Corre, J.J. Donguy, Adrien Maeght, Darthea Speyer, Trigano, Zabriskie, La Hune and Galerie 10. For photography, visit Galerie Samia Saouma and Galerie 666. The word for art opening is *vernissage*. The FIAC (*Foire International d'Art Contemporain*) in the Grand Palais each year is definitely worth a visit. For info call 45.62.84.58.

## BOOKSTORES

Paris is a sheer delight in its proliferation of small bookshops. Additionally, Paris wouldn't be Paris without its rows of *bouquinistes* (book stalls) most of which line the Left Bank *(rive or quai)* of the Seine. These are independently-owned, mainly by individuals who have a passion for used or rare books. In recent years the quality of the offering has dwindled to include tacky postcards and cheap prints, but fortunately the integrity of the traditional buying, selling, and browsing on nice days along the Seine has remained intact.

The book as object plays a sacred role in Parisian life. In general, the quality of book production is higher in France than in the US with serious covers reserved for quality literature. The most prestigious literary publishing houses in France are Gallimard, le Seuil, and Grasset, but there are scores of excellent publishers of literary, political, social and pure science books. Despite contemporary economic pressures, much effort is made in France to protect the life of the small bookshop and the small publisher. The retail prices of books are regulated so that large outlets, department stores, and supermarket chains cannot simply slash prices. The most you'll ever find a new book marked down is 5%. The FNAC (see department stores) has the most exhaustive collection of French books in Paris, and is particularly well-equipped in travel books.

As English-speaking and -reading students you'll probably be more directly interested in sources of English books in Paris. Fortunately, there are a lot of resources at hand. If you're not already aware you should be—Paris has an illustrious and important tradition of English and American expatriate writers, poets, and artists, as well as editors and publishers who have made fabulous contributions with their work in

Paris. Although this tradition may not be the source of your inspiration for coming to live or study in Paris, it certainly does generate much of the aura and myth about Paris that attracts tourists and long term visitors each year. And if this glorious past is what drew you to Paris, you might be disappointed to find a changed Paris. For in-depth discussion of Paris' expatriate literary and artistic history see: Ernest Hemingway's *A Moveable Feast*, Noël Riley Fitch's *Sylvia Beach and the Lost Generation*, and *Literary Cafés,* Brian Morton's *Americans in Paris*, Maurice Girodias' *The Frog Prince*, Hugh Ford's *Published in Paris*, and Dougald McMillan's *Transi-tion*, among others.

There are a few things to remember regarding books. First, new ones in most cases are a lot more expensive than back home. The price in francs is not a simple conversion from dollars or pounds; each bookstore has its own conversion mark-up rate to compensate for shipping and customs charges. So, you might want to carry or have books shipped to you from home. And there are always libraries (see Libraries).

Students, writers, or researchers will not be able to anticipate in advance all of their reading needs. Here is an up-to-date and annotated list of English-language bookstores in Paris:

**The Village Voice**: 6, rue Princesse, 75006. Métro: Mabillon. Tel: 46.33.36.47. Closed Sunday. Monday open from 14h-20h, Tuesday-Saturday 11h-20h. Founded in 1983 by French owner Odile Hellier, the Village Voice (no connection to the newspaper) has evolved into one of the most significant literary English book-shops in Europe. Tucked into a small street just off the Boulevard Saint Germain, the store hosts a lively reading series that has included some of the most important American, Canadian, British, and French authors writing today, including William Kennedy, Raymond Carver, Alison Lurie, Mavis Gallant, and Louise Erdrich. These readings are free and often conclude with wine and discussion. Odile, assisted by her nephew Jan, diligently attempts to stock a rich collection of the newest literary titles from both the US and the UK in her bright and modern store. Additionally, the collection is vast in modern and contemporary fiction, poetry, and translations as well as works in the social and political sciences, philosophy, the environment, and women's studies. The store also has a wide variety of literary journals and intelligent maga-zines—*The Village Voice, Times Literary Supplement, New Yorker, Harper's, Paris Review, Frank, Granta*, etc. Ask to get on the mailing list. Offers 5% discount to students.

**Shakespeare & Company**: 37, rue de la Bûcherie, 75005. Métro: St. Michel. No telephone. Open daily from noon until midnight. George Whitman's Shakespeare & Company is by far the most celebrated single bookshop on the continent. Much of this reputation comes from Sylvia Beach's original Shakespeare & Company which was located on the rue de l'Odéon in the Twenties and Thirties. It was there that James Joyce's *Ulysses*, published by Beach in 1922, first saw the light of day. Ernest

Hemingway, Gertrude Stein and a whole stable of luminous literati congregated there. Beach's store was shut by the Germans at the beginning of the Occupation. George Whitman, the self-acclaimed illegitimate grandson of Walt Whitman (his father was also Walt, but a writer of science books in Salem, Massachusetts) resurrected the name in the spirit of the original enterprise, tagging on "the Rag and Bone Shop of the Heart." Everything you hear about Shakespeare & Co. is true. It's unruly, chaotically organized, overrun at times by weirdos and dubious writers, but the bookshop is a living legend and a wealthy storehouse of fabulous first editions and signed copies of novels and volumes of poetry whose authors came through Paris and gave a reading or book party under the supervision of poetic and iconoclastic George. He is often offering tumblers of iced tea or chipped plates of Irish stew to visiting writers, wanderers, and the mildly down and out. The store has thousands of used books and a spotty selection of new titles. It's impossible to predict what you'll find. The prices are high for the new stuff, but can be excellent for used and obscure hardcovers. George will buy your used books and pay you cash if you bring identification. In the warm months, the sidewalk in front of the store—exquisitely set in the Latin Quarter opposite Notre Dame—becomes a favorite hang-out for visitors, backpackers, and local riff-raff, a scene which will give you a good whiff of the state of contemporary Bohemia. And if you are writing poetry or fiction ask George to be slotted into the Monday night reading series. A good way to test your voice. The shop sells its own mag called *Paris Magazine*, and is now preparing its fourth issue in twenty two years.

**The American University of Paris Bookstore**: located in the basement of the American Church, 65, Quai d'Orsay, 75007, tel: 45.55.91.73 (ask for bookstore) principally serves the university community. Under the management of Bill Gadsby, the bookstore has expanded its operations to function as a vital and effective source of academic and trade titles for the public at large. Gadsby can order bulk loads of new titles from the US or UK at highly competitive prices and surprisingly fast. Although a university bookshop, it's open to walk-ins.

**The Abbey Bookshop**: 29 rue Parcheminerie 75005 tel: 46.33.16.24. One of the newer additions to the English literary scene in Paris, this Canadian-owned, small but well-organized and pleasant shop in the Latin Quarter is making a serious go at it. One of its real advantages is the owner's ability to procure titles from North America in record time. The store offers its clients plenty of service. Strong in fiction, poetry, and the humanities. On occasion, the Abbey also has readings.

**Attica**: 34, rue des Ecoles, 75005. Métro: Maubert-Mutualité. Tel: 43.26.09.53 and 84, Bd. St. Michel, 6th. Métro: Port Royal. Tel: 46.34.16.30. Closed Sunday and Monday morning. Attica is an old standby for English books in Paris. More British-oriented than American, Attica on the rue des Ecoles is a densely packed space for new fiction, poetry, journals, and guides. The store also caters to

French students looking for English titles for their university English courses, thus a lot of classics and 19th century fiction. Students get a small discount upon request. The Attica collection of language books, and language method techniques is found at their second location on Bd. Michel, near the Port Royal.

**Nouveau Quartier Latin**: 78, Bd. St. Michel, 75005. Métro: Luxembourg. Tel: 43.26.42.70. Closed Sunday. Only new titles. Here's a store that you can call to find out if they have what you need. Well organized and highly modern, NQL specializes in Anglo-American literature and guidebooks.

**W.H. Smith**: 248, rue de Rivoli, 75001. Métro: Concorde. Tel: 42.60.37.97. Closed Sunday. Part of the major British bookstore chain. Anglo-American literature, cookbooks, guidebooks, maps, magazines and newspapers. This store is large and commercial, but its selection of contemporary titles and gift books is vast, and its display of English-language publications is among the best. The upstairs tearoom no longer exists.

**Brentano's**: 37, av de l'Opéra, 75002. Métro: Pyramides. Tel: 42.61.52.50. Closed Sunday. Anglo-American literature, art books, magazines, and newspapers. Brentano's rides on a long and illustrious reputation. Today it greatly serves the French anglophile market and business and tourist crowds interested in English paperbacks and bestsellers. It's less connected to the literary anglophone population than some of the other bookshops but it's the only English bookshop in the neighborhood of the Opéra. The back entrance area hosts a large selection of English-language periodicals.

**Albion**: 13, rue Charles V, 75004. Métro: St. Paul. Tel: 42.72.50.71. Closed Sunday and Monday morning. Classical and contemporary Anglo-American literature, some history and science.

**Galignani**: 224, rue de Rivoli, 75001. Métro: Tuileries. Tel: 42.60.76.07 Closed Sunday. Books, guidebooks, maps, newspapers, and magazines. This bookshop is actually the oldest English bookstore on the continent. It has for many years enjoyed a fine reputation as a supporter of the anglophone literati. Its selection of fiction, travel, and art books is extensive.

**Cannibal Pierce Australian Bookshop**: 7, rue Samson 93200 SAINT DENIS, tel: 48.09.94.59. This is Paris's only Australian bookshop. Although it's a bit out of the way, it's worth the trip. The collection is eclectic and stimulating. There are regularly scheduled readings and performances in the store led by resident Australian poet June Shenfield.

**Golden Books**: 65, rue Lhommond, 75006. Métro: Luxembourg. Tel: 43.31.73.17. Open afternoons. Psychology, health and New Age books.

**Librarie de l'Unesco**: 9, pl. de Fontenoy, 75007. Métro: Ségur. Tel: 45.68.10.00 Closed Saturday and Sunday. Newspapers and UNESCO publications (Education and Science).

**Librairie Internationale de Sèvres**: 82, Grande Rue, 92310 SEVRES, 45.34.18.70

**Tea and Tattered Pages**: 24, rue Mayet 75006 PARIS tel. 40.65.94.35. The newest of the English bookshops, this cozy spot near Métro Duroc specializes in used and inexpensive paperbacks. The selection is still limited, but it's growing. The prices warrant a visit—so do the brownies and fudge, and believe it or not, pastrami!

# French Bookstores

As for French bookshops, there are scores of excellent ones, with a high concentration in the fifth and sixth *arrondissements*. A few well-known ones include La Hune, 170, Bd. St. Michel, and Le Divan at 37, rue Bonaparte, near the Place St. Germain-des-Près in the 6th *arrondissement*, and Flammarion at the Pompidou Center. The *l'Oeil de la Lettre* group of literary bookstores are first class, one of which is Librarie Compagnie on the rue des Ecoles next to the Sorbonne.

The FNAC, the largest retail cooperative of electronic, stereo, and photographic equipment, also has the most extensive collection of books and records in France and is planning to open up a new international bookstore on Bd. St. Michel near Cluny. And Virgin Records, the new mega record store on the Champs-Elysées, has a well-stocked bookstore in the basement.

**FNAC Forum Halles**
1 rue Pierre Lescot
75001 PARIS
tel. 40.41.40.00

**FNAC Montparnasse**
136 rue de Rennes
75006 PARIS
tel: 49.54.30.00

An especially useful address for students is the Parisian institution, Gilbert Jeune and Gilbert Joseph, a three-store operation that specializes in academic and university texts and school supplies, and buys back used books on the fourth floor. Bring your student I.D.

**Gilbert Jeune**
26 Bd. St. Michel
75006 PARIS
tel: 46.34.21.41

As for specialized bookshops these may come in handy:

**Cinema**
**Acacias Librairie Ciné Reflé**
3bis rue Champollion
75005 PARIS
tel: 40.46.02.72

**La Chambre Claire**
14 rue St. Sulpice
75006 PARIS
tel: 46.34.04.31

**Photography/Theater**
**Association Liko**
161 rue Rennes
75006 PARIS
tel: 45.48.69.49

**Women**
**Femmes Savantes**
73bis av. Niel
75017 PARIS
tel: 47.63.05.82

**Librairie des Femmes**
74 rue Seine
75006 PARIS
tel: 43.29.50.75

**Science Fiction/*Bande Dessinée* (Comic Books)**
**Cosmos 2000**
17 rue Arc de Triomphe
75017 PARIS
tel: 43.80.30.74

**Music**
**La Librairie Musicale de Paris**
68bis rue Réaumur
75003 PARIS
tel: 42.72.30.72

**Politics**
**Librairie des Sciences Politiques**
30 rue St. Guillaume
75007 PARIS
tel: 45.48.36.02

**Third World**
**Librairie Harmattan**
16 rue des Ecoles
75005 PARIS
tel: 43.26.04.52

**Cuisine**
**Librairie Gourmande**
4 rue Dante
75005 PARIS
tel: 43.54.37.27

**Government Publications**
**La Librairie de la**
**Documentation Française**
29/31 Quai Voltaire
75007 PARIS
tel: 40.15.70.00

**Spanish/Latin American**
**Ediciones Hispano-Americanas**
26 rue Monsieur
75006 PARIS
tel: 43.26.03.79

**Librairie Espagnole**
72 rue Seine
75006 PARIS
tel: 43.54.56.26

**Russian**
**Librairie du Globe**
2 rue Buci
75006 PARIS
tel: 43.26.54.99

**Arabic**
**Al Manar Librairie**
220 rue St. Jacques
75005 PARIS
tel: 43.29.40.22

**German**
**Calligrammes Librairie**
8 rue Collégiale
75005 PARIS
tel: 43.36.85.07

**Marissal Bucher**
42 rue Rambuteau
75003 PARIS
tel: 42.74.37.47

**Indian**
**Adi Shakti Tapovan**
9 rue Gutenberg
75015 PARIS
tel: 45.77.90.59

**Italian**
**Librairie Italienne**
Tour de Babel
10 rue Roi de Sicile
75004 PARIS
tel: 42.77.32.40

**Librairie Italienne**
54 rue Bourgogne
75007 PARIS
tel: 47.05.03.99

**African**
**Présence Africaine**
25bis, rue des Ecoles
75005 PARIS
tel: 43.54.15.88

**Japanese**
**Tokyo Do**
8 rue Ste. Anne
75001 PARIS
tel: 42.61.08.71

**Polish**
**Librairie Polonaise**
123 Bd. St. Germain
75006 PARIS
tel: 40.51.08.82

**Portuguese**
**Librairie Portugaise Michel**
**Chandeigne**
10 rue Tournefort
75005 PARIS
tel: 43.36.34.37

# LIBRARIES (*BIBLIOTHEQUES*)

You may find, in dealing with the libraries in Paris, the same sort of inconvenience as you did in other areas of daily life, such as shopping. The inconvenience in this case stems from a certain degree of inaccessibility and inherent lethargy which takes a little time to get adjusted to. If you are coming from a small university where you had your own desk at which you could camp out until early morning hours, you may find the adjustment difficult. You may have to keep a more civilized schedule when it comes to your treks to the library. The libraries frequently have quite limited hours. One exception is the *Bibliothèque Publique d'Information* at the Pompidou Center which is open until 22h.

Limited hours are not the only handicap in getting your term paper finished, for most libraries do not allow you to borrow books. So be prepared to take good notes. These libraries only offer *consultation sur place* (books don't leave the library). You may or may not find working photocopy machines. The machine in the Sorbonne library requires one franc per copy!

Some libraries require that you register and obtain a card. Be prepared to have to wait in a line when you go. You'll need some identification, such as your passport and proof of address and a couple of photographs. Another thing to be aware of is that in many libraries you are not free to browse through the stacks. Instead, you must go to the *salle de catalogues* and fill out a description of want you are looking for *(fichier)*. An employee, in one of those omnipresent blue smocks that sets workers apart from white collar employees, will look for the book and send it to the *centre de distribution*.

The library at the Sorbonne is a fascinating place to visit but a frustrating place to use. It can take up to twenty minutes to obtain each book, depending on which *guichet* your book is filed under. Of course, don't expect to do much research around lunchtime. Special permission must be obtained from the president of the *salle* for access to the reference section.

**American Library in Paris**: 10, rue du Général-Camou, 75007 PARIS, tel: 45.51.46.82. The largest collection of English language books in Paris. Open Tuesday-Saturday from 10h-19h. Membership is required and costs 300 FF a year and allows you to check out books. You need to bring a recent photo, student identification, proof of residency in Paris (such as telephone bill) and another piece of identification. If you do not want to be a member, you may spend the day in the library for 30 FF but you cannot check out books. AUP students are automatically members. This library owns over 80,000 volumes and over 700 periodicals and journals.

**American University of Paris Library**: 9, rue de Monttessuy, 75007, tel. 45.51.46.82. This library is physically connected to the American Library in Paris. It is open more hours than any other library in France—seven days a week for a total of eighty hours per week. It has over 50,000 titles and adds close to 3000 titles every year. Reserved for AUP students only.

**Benjamin Franklin Documentation Center**: 2, rue St.-Florentin, 75001 PARIS, tel: 42.96.33. 109,000 volumes in English. Housed in the US Consulate building, Talleyrand at Place de la Concorde. Open 13h-18h Monday-Friday. Extensive documentation on the USA. Open to university students. Bring your passport.

***Bibliothèques et Discothèques de la Ville de Paris***: 31, rue des Francs Bourgeois, 75004 PARIS, tel: 42.76.67.60. This is the main branch of the City of Paris' 55 municipal public libraries.

***Mairie du 5ème***: 21, pl. du Panthéon, 75005 PARIS, tel: 43.26.85.05. Feminist library.

***Bibliothèque Nationale***: 58, rue de Richelieu, 75002 PARIS, tel: 47.03.81.26. Known as the BN, this library houses one of the world's most important and complete collections of books, periodicals; manuscripts and archives. Dark, dense, and serious, the BN is accessible to graduate students and researchers with letters of accreditation.

***Bibliothèque Publique d'Information***: Centre Pompidou, 19, rue Beaubourg, 75004 PARIS, tel: 42.77.12.33. Open Monday, Wednesday, Thursday and Friday from noon to 10h. Saturday, Sunday, and public holidays from 10h to 22h. Closed Tuesday. *Consultation sur place*. Free access to books. No inscription required.

***Bibliothèque Sainte Geneviève***: 10, pl. du Panthéon, 75005 PARIS, tel: 43.29.61.00. Open Monday-Saturday from 10h-22h. Personal library card is required, which you can obtain Monday-Friday before 17h30 and on Saturday between 14h-17h30. Bring a photo and identification, no charge. *Consultation sur place*. Distribution service.

**English Language Library for the Blind**: 35, rue Lemercier, 75017 PARIS, tel: 42.93.47.57.

**British Council Library**: 9-11, rue de Constantine, 75007 PARIS, tel: 45.55.95.95. Open Tuesday, Thursday and Friday from 10h30-18h. Wednesday from10h30-19h. Saturday from 10h30-16h. Membership costs 200 FF a year (with passport and photo) and allows you to check out books. Otherwise you may use the library at 25 FF a day. Mainly books from or about Britain.

***Université de la Sorbonne***: 13, rue Santeuil, 75005 PARIS, tel: 43.31.53.94 Open Monday from 13h-19h. Tuesday-Friday from 9h30-19h. Saturday from 10h-17h30. Membership is required unless you are enrolled at Paris III. Cost is 75 FF. Distribution service, which always closes one hour before the library does. You are allowed to borrow two books for 15 days.

## Other Libraries

***Agence Culturelle de Paris***: 12, rue François Miron, 75004 PARIS, tel: 42.71.84.93.

***Bibliothèque Internationale de Musique Contemporaine***: 52, rue Hôtel de Ville, 75004 PARIS, tel: 42.78.67.08.

***Bibliothèque Service Métier d'Art***: 107, rue de Rivoli, 75001 PARIS, tel: 42.61.46.36.

***Bibliothèque de Géographie***: 191, rue St. Jacques, 75005 PARIS, tel: 43.29.42.04.

***Bibliothèque de l'Opéra***: Pl. Charles Garnier, 75009 PARIS, tel: 47.42.07.02.

**Bibliothèque de l'Union des Arts Décoratifs**: 109, rue Rivoli, 75001 PARIS, tel: 42.60.32.14. Open Tuesday-Saturday, 10h-17h30; Monday 13h45-17h30. Closed Sunday. No registration is needed. More than 100,000 works, from the origins to contemporary art.

**Bibliothèque des Arts**: 3, pl. Odéon, 75006 PARIS, tel: 46.33.18.18.

**Bibliothèque Musicale Gustav Mahler**: 11 Bis, rue Vézelay, 75008 PARIS, tel: 42.56.20.17.

**Bibliothèque Polonaise**: 6, quai Orléans, 75004 PARIS, tel: 43.54.35.61.

**Bibliothèque Roumanie Pierre Sergesco Marya Kasterska**: 39, rue Lhomond, 75005 PARIS, tel: 43.37.82.74.

**Bibliothèque Russe Tourgenev**: 11, rue Valence, 75005 PARIS, tel: 45.35.58.51.

**Bibliothèque Ukrainienne Simon Petlura**: 6, rue Palestine, 75019 PARIS, tel: 42.02.29.56.

**Centre Information Documentation Israël Proche Orient**: 134, rue du Fbg. St. Honoré, 75008 PARIS, tel: 42.25.55.80.

**Centre Protestant d'Etudes et de Documentation**: 46, rue Vaugirard, 75006 PARIS, tel: 46.33.77.24.

**Institut de France, Bibliothèque Thiers**: 27, pl. St. Georges, 75009 PARIS, tel: 48.78.14.33.

**Institut des Hautes Etudes Cinématographiques**: 9, av. Albert de Mun, 75016 PARIS, tel: 47.27.06.32.

**Institut des Hautes Etudes de l'Amérique Latine**: 28, rue St. Guillaume, 75007 PARIS, tel: 45.48.00.98.

**La Joie Par Les Livres**: 8, rue St. Bon, 75004 PARIS, tel: 48.87.61.95.

**Métrolire**: 6, pl. Nation, 75012 PARIS, tel: 43.43.32.17.

**Service Information Documentation Juifs-Chrétiens**: 73, rue Notre Dame des Champs, 75006 PARIS. Open Monday to Friday from 14h30-18h.

**Société Asiatique de Paris**: 3, rue Mazarine, 75006 PARIS, tel: 46.33.28.32.

**Université Paris I, Bibliothèque Centre Pierre Mendès-France**: 90, rue Tolbiac, 75013 PARIS, tel: 40.77.18.14.

**Ville de Paris**: 2, rue Guadeloupe, 75018 PARIS, tel: 42.38.38.25.

# HOUSING

## Street Signs & Addresses

In French, your address and phone number are your *coordonnées*. Some addresses may seem strange at first but you'll learn these nuances rapidly. You can live on a *rue*, an *avenue*, a *boulevard*, an *impasse*, a *cour*, a *passage*, a *parc* or a *chemin*. The street number may be a regular whole number like 34 or 7 or 178, but it may also have an extra bit, *bis* or *ter*, which means that the house is attached or adjacent to the property that takes the whole number. Other aspects of the address: *bâtiment* (building name or number), *escalier* (stairway), *étage* (floor), *code*, (door code), *à droite* or *à gauche* (side of the floor). When visiting someone, always get as much of this information as possible. People usually will tell you something like this: *J'habite au 35 Boulevard du Montparnasse, escalier C au fond de la cour, quatrième étage à gauche*. If you see *Cedex* at the end of an address, it simply means that the address is a post office box and the mail is kept at the post office. Most buildings have either a door code which is activated at night or a buzzer system called an *interphone*. There will always be a button to activate the door and, on the inside, a lit button to turn on the timer for the lights in the stairwell.

## Short Term Housing Options

Miles Turner's *Pauper's Paris* is a great resource for good value hotels and student hostel listings. Here are a few:

**Café Couette**
8, rue d'Isly
75008 PARIS
French "bed and breakfast" association which has rooms throughout France. 90 FF for single and 120 FF for double room.

**Maubisson Hôtel des Jeunes**
12, rue des Barres
75004 PARIS
Métro: Hôtel de Ville
Group of four historic converted houses in the Marais which has rooms available for students.

**Ligue Française des Auberges de Jeunesse (LFAJ)**
38, Bd. Raspail
75007 PARIS
Métro: Sèvres-Babylone
Limited to three-day stays for holders of the YHA (Youth Hostel Assocciation) card, but very cheap.

**Hôtel Studia**
51, Bd. St. Germain
75005 PARIS
tel: 43.26.81.00
Excellent location at Place Maubert

## Searching

Probably the most frustrating aspect of living in Paris is the hassle of searching for a place to live. The options are numerous, from finding other people to live with to cloistering yourself in your own small room. Remember, however, that the competition at certain times of the year can be extremely tough and that only those who rise early and call first will have a chance. The competition is at its worse during the month of September when the Parisians come back from a month of vacation and students need to find accommodations.

# Finding an Apartment

The simplest and cheapest way to find accommodations is to look for individuals who have apartments or rooms to rent. Avoiding the agencies will save you from paying high fees (as much as four month's rent, one of which is nonrefundable) and, in some cases, a lot of paper work. There are several newspapers you can consult which list housing ads *(petites annonces)* from individuals. *J'annonce* comes out weekly on Wednesday morning and *De Particulier à Particulier* comes out every Thursday morning. These two papers also have Minitel services which are updated daily. The French daily *Le Figaro* also has extensive listings. To recognize ads not placed by agencies, look for the words *propriét. loue.*

*France-USA Contacts*, a twice monthly give-away, and the monthly *Paris Free Voice* list housing opportunities as well as all sorts of services and some job opportunities. These are available at most English language bookstores, public places and restaurants. *The International Herald Tribune* also advertises apartments but these tend to be rather costly. *Passion* has listings but since the magazine comes out monthly things get out of date quickly.

Here is a sample housing ad followed by a translated explanation.

---

*17ème ROME. 4p. cuis. bns. ref.nf. 2.300 44435111*

17th *arrondissement* near Métro Rome, 4 rooms kitchen, bathroom, newly remodelled.  2300FF a month.  Call 44.43.51.11

---

## Column Headings in the Newspaper

| | |
|---|---|
| *Immobilier* | Real Estate |
| *Achats et Ventes* | Wanted/Offered for Sale |
| *Location Offres/Demandes* | Offered/Wanted to Rent |
| *Meublé* | Furnished |
| *Vide* | Unfurnished |

## Helpful Terms

| | |
|---|---|
| *agences s'abst.* | no agencies |
| *asc. (ascenseur)* | elevator |
| *bns. (bains)* | bathrooms |
| *bal. (balcon)* | balcony |
| *boxe* | parking space |
| *calme* | quiet street, building |
| *carac. (caractère)* | with character |
| *caution* | security deposit |
| *chgs. (charges)* | supplementary monthly fee in addition to rent; |
| *chb. (chambre)* | bedroom |
| *chambre de bonne* | maid's room |
| *chambre indépendante* | independent room |
| *charm.* | charming |
| *chauf. cent.* | central heating |
| *com.* | agent's commission |
| *cft. (confort)* | "comfort"—i.e. private bath, carpeted rooms, equipped kitchen |

| | |
|---|---|
| *coq. (coquette)* | cute |
| *cour* | courtyard |
| *dche. (douche)* | shower |
| *ét. él. (étage élevé)* | high floor |
| *éq. (equipped)* | equipped with major appliances |
| *except.* | exceptional |
| *garconnière* | bachelor's apt; small studio or room |
| *grenier* | attic, room under roof |
| *imm.* | building |
| *imm. mod.* | modern building |
| *imm. nf.* | new building |
| *imm. p de t* | cut stone building |
| *imm. rec.* | recent building |
| *imm. anc.* | old building |
| *interméd.* | agent |
| *jar./jdn.* | garden |
| *kit.* | kitchenette, usually not windowed |
| *loue, je loue* | I am offering for rent (i.e. no agency) |
| *lux.* | luxurious (carpeting) |
| *loyer* | rent |
| *m² (metre carré)* | square meter (about 10 square feet) |
| *moq.* | wall-to-wall carpeting |
| *part à part* | private party to private party; no agency |
| *p. (pièce)* | room, not including bathroom |
| *poss. (possibilité)* | possibility of |
| *pr. cpl.* | for a couple only |
| *poutres apparentes* | beamed ceilings |
| *rav. (ravissant)* | delightful |
| *ref. nf. (refait neuf)* | newly remodeled |
| *r. (rue)* | street |
| *slle. (salle)* | large or formal room |
| *salle de réception* | large living room |
| *salle à manger* | formal dining room |
| *salle d'eau* | sink |
| *salle de bains* | with shower or bath |
| *ss. (sans)* | without |
| *stdg. (standing)* | "status" or "high class" building |
| *gd. stdg., tr. gd. stdg.* | more of the above |
| *studio* | one room apartment, usually with bath and kitchenette |
| *s/ (sur)* | on |
| *tél* | telephone |
| *terr.* | terrace |
| *ttc (toutes charges comprises)* | all charges included |
| *w.c.* | toilet, in room separate from bath |

There are also many bulletin boards scattered all over Paris. Try the following for finding housing:

**The American Church in Paris**: 65, Quai d'Orsay. 75007. Métro: Alma-Marceau, Invalides. Tel: 47.05.07.99 Open Monday-Saturday 9h-22h30; Sundays 9h-19h30.

**FUSAC (France-USA Contacts) Bulletin Board**: (*Centre d'annonces et bureau*): 40, rue de Boulanger, *sous-sol* (basement), 75005, open from Monday to Saturday 10h-19h. Tel: 43.26.87.83.

**The American Cathedral**: 23, Ave. Georges V, 75008. Métro: Georges V, Alma-Marceau. Tel: 47.20.17.92.

**Shakespeare and Company**: 37, rue de la Bûcherie, 75005. Métro: St. Michel. No telephone. Open noon-midnight seven days a week.

**Canadian Cultural Center**: 5, rue de Constantin 75007. Métro: Invalides.

*Centre d'Information et de Documentation Jeunesse*: 101, quai Branly, 75015. Métro: Alma-Marceau.

Many *laveries* (laundromats), *boulangeries*, and large grocery stores (Prisunic, Monoprix, etc.) also have bulletin boards.

## Paperwork

First, consider the amount of time you are planning to stay in Paris. When looking through rent ads, note whether the apartment is furnished or unfurnished. If you are only staying for a short time, a furnished place will be much more suited to your needs, even though the rent may be higher. If you plan to stay for a while, however, consider taking an unfurnished place since you can most likely obtain a standard three-year lease and will want to get set up with your own stuff (*un bail de trois ans*). The advantages to having a three-year *bail* (lease) include a set percentage over which your rent may not increase annually, the right to sublet for one year, and the right to break your contract if you give your landlord three months notice by registered letter (*lettre recommandée avec accusé de réception*). On the other hand, you have the right to six months notice from the landlord before having to move out.

When you do find an apartment, the *propriétaire* (landlord) will want a *caution* (security deposit) as well as some proof that you are financially able to pay the rent. A letter from a parent or sponsor stating financial support will normally suffice. So will a bank statement or pay slip. You will probably be asked to sign a lease. Under French law, minors (under 18) cannot sign contracts, and if you are under this age the landlord or his agent may insist that your parents or some responsible adult sign for you. If you must sign a lease, ask for an *inventaire détaillé* (detailed inventory) of the apartment and its contents, and make two copies. This way the landlord can't hold you responsible for any damage done to the apartment before you moved in.

## The French Apartment

*L'entrée*: Often the best apartments are in the most unlikely places, so don't be influenced by the building's street-side appearance; the grungiest looking building may have a beautiful garden and an entirely different look behind the front door.

**La Cour**: Most French urban structures are built in a square, around a courtyard. The Paris everyone can see is but a portion of what it contains: behind the average front door may be a formal garden complete with fountain, a stone-paved walkway leading to a private residence, hidden behind the walls of the *bâtiment* (building), or a parking lot. It may also be just a play-ground for the children of the *concierge* and a passageway to the back section of the building.

**Le/La concierge**: The *concierge* in Paris, almost always a Portuguese or Spanish wife and husband team crammed into a tiny apartment in the entranceway of the better Parisian apartments, plays a unique role in daily French life. He or she is the on-site representative of the organization or group of owners in an apartment building (*syndic*). He/she knows all, hears all, tells all, and is a great person to get along with. Their principal tasks include shining the brass in the entranceway, distributing the mail in the building, cleaning the stairwells, doing minor repairs, carting out the garbage cans, receiving packages, etc. When you move in, and at Christmas, it is a good idea to tip your concierge as much as you can afford (100 FF is normal) and according to the amount of extra work you make for them. *Concierges* are very valuable allies and very powerful enemies. If problems arise over such things as noise after 22h, your *concierge* can often prevent or instigate much unpleasantness.

**Le WC (les toilettes)**: WC means "water closet," and that's what it is, a closet-sized space with a toilet. The WC (also called *le water*, pronounced as if the word was French) is very often its own separate room. Although this may seem odd at first, it's rather practical. The WC is colloquially referred to as *les chiottes* (the crapper). Other classic bathroom functions are performed in the *salle de bains*.

### La salle de bains

**Bidet**: you may be perplexed on your first trip to a French bathroom to find this little fixture. Historically designed to serve aristocratic women as a hygienic aid, today the *bidet* can be used for lots of things, relieving the pain of hemorrhoids, hand-washing delicate clothing, bathing a baby, or soaking your feet. Fresh water enters the fixture through a vertical spray in the center of the bowl, through a flushing rim or integral filler or through a pivotal spout that delivers a horizontal stream of water. A pop-up drain allows you to fill it with water.

**Le bain/La douche**: Consider yourself lucky if you end up with a shower curtain. This seemingly essential bathroom fixture is not seen as essential to the French. Invariably the shower is improvised via a metal hose running from the bathtub spout, and dexterity is a must to prevent splashing, especially since you will probably not have a place to hang the nozzle on the wall. But washing your hair with one hand has got to be character-building. In the older buildings you'll have to get used to tiny tubs, sitting tubs, and other microscopic means of washing. It's all great fun.

**La Cuisine**: Parisian kitchens tend to be an exercise in space utilization. They often have tiny but efficient appliances, especially refrigerators *(le frigo)* and gas stoves. Rented apartments almost never come with appliances, and often don't even have kitchen cabinets.

## Moving In

When you have found your apartment and are ready to move in, keep in mind that the electricity and gas will probably have been turned off. Contact your local EDF-GDF office *(Electricité de France /Gaz de France)* to reactivate the service. Bring proof of address—your rental agreement, for example. To obtain a telephone, call *renseignements téléphoniques* (information—dial 12) to find out at which PTT *(Postes-Téléphones-Télégraphes)* office you must make your request. The best bet is to go in person to have the service and number activated. If you want an itemized bill of all calls you must request this from the start. It's 20 FF a month. The bill comes every two months and you have two weeks to pay. Expect a wait of seven to ten days. If there is already a phone, the landlord may insist that you list the number under your name. If the phone is under the name of the landlord or previous tenant, your access to 19, calls out of the country, may be blocked.

## Moving Out

Before leaving, ask for a *relevé spécial* (special reading) of the electricity, gas and telephone from the local EDF-GDF and PTT center listed on your bills. Allow fifteen days.

## Room with a French Family

You can also rent a room in an apartment with a French family or, more often, an individual *propriétaire*. This housing arrangement usually consists of a private room with limited access to the kitchen, telephone, and bathroom facilities. Each situation offers varying degrees of privacy. Some landlords have more than one room to rent in their apartments, making it possible for two students to live together. Others have large rooms that can be shared by two people. There are varying degrees of comfort (private or shared bathroom, television, personal phone) and the price fluctuates accordingly. Landladies and couples are usually interested in some cultural exchange, which can help enable the student to ease his/her way into daily French life. This is an arrangement that can often be made through your particular school's housing office. AUP makes extensive housing arrangements.

**Room with Breakfast and Some Evening Meals**: similar to the above, with the addition of some meals which encourages more conversation. Breakfast is provided every day while the number of dinners varies. The most common arrangement is two to three dinners per week. Arrangements can usually be made for additional meals.

### *Chambre de bonne*

The most inexpensive accommodation is usually a *chambre de bonne* (maid's room). This is usually a converted maid's room on the top floor of a once-bourgeois apartment building. It often has a separate entrance from that of the landlord (very often a 6th floor walk-up). It is usually a small room for one person with a sink and a hotplate. Many independent rooms do not have private showers or full kitchens, but shared shower and bathroom facilities are usually available in the hallway. Some landlords offer the use of the shower in their apartment. This doesn't sound too glamorous but it can have its charm for a while.

## Au Pair

Another alternative to finding an apartment is to look for an *au pair* job. *Au pair* arrangements are usually available only for female students. This work often consists of baby-sitting, housework, English lessons, mother's helper chores, collecting children at school, or any combination thereof in exchange for room and board and a small salary. It often entails some evening or weekend work. Students must generally have some knowledge of French and be willing to work a regular schedule. Though the conditions of such positions can vary, the following agencies will arrange *au pair* positions. Though they require that the student be under 30 years of age, have a valid student visa and be enrolled in classes, they will ensure that the student be paid about 1,000 FF a month plus room and board in exchange for 30 hours a week of work. You should keep in mind that *au pairs* are often treated as paid help rather than members of the family. The quality of this experience depends wholly on the household that you work in.

**Accueil Familial des Jeunes Etrangères**: 23, rue du Cherche-Midi, 75006. Métro: Sèvres-Babylone. Tel: 42.22.50.34. Open Monday-Friday from 10h-16h and Saturday from 10h-noon.

**Arche**: 7, rue Bargue, 75015. Métro: Volontaires. Tel: 42.73.34.39. Open Monday-Friday from 9h-17h.

**Géolangues**: 75, rue d'Amsterdam, 75008. Métro: Place Clichy. Tel: 45.26.14.53. Open Monday-Friday from 10h-19h.

**Inter Séjour**: 4, rue de Parme, 75009. Métro: Liège. Tel: 48.74.04.98. Open Monday-Friday 9h30-17h30.

**Relations Internationales**: 20, rue de l'Exposition, 75007. Métro: Ecole Militaire. Tel: 45.51.85.50. Open Monday-Friday from 9h-12h30 and from 14h-18h30.

## Cité Universitaire

This Paris has rooms available at very reasonable rates in 30 different *maisons* (houses) for university students (under 30) studying in Paris. If you are an architecture buff, you might want to investigate the two maisons designed by Le Corbusier: the Swiss Foundation and the Franco-Brazilian Foundation. Make sure to call or write far in advance of your arrival date if you are considering this option. Rooms go fast, and can only be booked for a year-long period. A single room goes for 1050-1400 FF, and a double room for 750-900 FF per month, depending on the maison. This could also be a good alternative to a hotel while you are looking for other accommodations—rooms are available to anyone with an International Student Identity Card at 80-100 FF per night during the summer and in September before the beginning of the school year. A list of all the houses is available from the central office at the following address:

**Cité Universitaire**
19 Bd. Jourdan
75014 PARIS
tel: 45.89.13.37

Or try contacting one of the following directly:

**Fondation des Etats-Unis**
Cité Universitaire
15 Bd. Jourdan
75690 PARIS Cedex 14
tel: 45.89.35.77 (administration)
45. 89.35.79 (students)
Director: Terence MURPHY

**Maison des Etudiants du Canada**
31, Bd. Jourdan
75014 PARIS
tel: 45.89.67.59

## Neighborhoods

To give you an idea in advance of the difference between neighborhoods, the general location of Paris' principal areas and a brief subjective description of each of the 20 *arrondissements* has been included. Use the enclosed map to locate these areas. Note that 75005, or 5e, means Paris, 5th *arrondissement*.

Opéra: 1e, 2e, 9e *arrondissements*
Les Halles: 1e
Le Marais: 3e, 4e
Ile Saint-Louis: 4e
Quartier Latin: 5e
Saint Germain: 6e
Champs de Mars/Invalides: 7e
Etoile/Faubourg St-Honoré: 8e
Chinatown: 13e
Parc Monceau: 17e
Montparnasse: 14e, 15e
Victor Hugo/Palais de Chaillot: 16e
Montmartre: 18e
Belleville/Ménilmontant: 19e, 20e.

# Paris by
*Arrondissement*

Here are a few comments on the character of each *arrondissement*. There are of course charming finds in every *quartier*, but the following comments should be useful when having to select a neighborhood sight unseen. One of your first purchases in Paris should be a small square red or black book called *Plan de Paris par Arrondissements*, which includes detailed maps, a street and Métro index, and bus routes. This is indispensible for finding your way around Paris. Trust this advice, you'll need one. Carry it at all times.

**1er**—Central Paris, well connected by Métro and bus. Tends to be pricey and very busy. Not a great place if you have a car. Châtelet is very congested. But very central. Chic and trendy around Les Halles. The park Palais-Royal is a bastion of undisturbed Parisian elegance.

**2e**—Also central but more commercial in the sense of wholesale outlets. Sentier is the core of Paris' garment district. You may find unusual places to live here but it's more the exception than the rule. The parts near the Opéra and Madeleine are very high rent districts and not especially inviting in terms of daily Parisian neighborhood life. The streets between Les Halles and the Grands Boulevards are some of the oldest, truly Parisian, and enchanting you'll find. The rue Montourgeuil, the oldest market street in Paris, is worth a detour. Also contains the fashion-chic Place des Victoires.

**3e, 4e**—Very central with many lovely little streets, *cafés,* shops, etc. Congested, but worth it. Expensive. The Marais has lots of living advantages. One of the most desireable areas of Paris, for those who insist on old buildings with character and cultural exposure.

**5e**—Left Bank, the Latin Quarter. This is where you get both the chic and the classy. The areas down by St. Michel are tight and noisy but you can't beat the location. The areas up closer to the 13e are more residential, well connected to the center of Paris and very pleasant. You can't go wrong in the 5e. Tends to be expensive, but great little finds are not impossible.

**6e**—Left Bank, St. Germain des Près, Odéon. This is for the wealthy and artistic. Many bookshops, galleries, cinemas, classy *cafés*, restaurants and publishers. Between St. Germain and the Seine, prices are sky high. The 6e extends up to Montparnasse and over to Duroc. Lots of wonderful little streets. Very desirable.

**7e**—Tends to be expensive, high class, and residential. Also houses many of the government ministries. Not very lively at night, although very pleasant and pretty. The street behind Les Invalides, the avenue de Tourville, is the most expensive property in the French version of Monopoly. The Esplanade des Invalides offers sprawling lawns that are not off-limits for frisbee-playing and picnicking.

**8e**—Right bank. Financial and corporate territory. Champs-Elysées. Very high rents and a lot of pomp. Lots of motion and money. Some surprisingly quaint and quiet streets. The rue St. Honoré has to be a highlight for extravagant Sunday window shopping.

**9e**—This includes Pigalle and Clichy. More *populaire*, meaning working-class. This could be fun.

Depends on particular street and apartment. Don't exclude this. The covered passageways are to be discovered.

**10e**—There are some great spots near La République and along the St. Martin canal, although along the major boulevards and St. Denis, an element of tackiness and sleaze is present. Definitely worth checking out. Less expensive than nearby 3e and 4e.

**11e**—Not too far from things and yet still filled with great finds, but hurry up. Close to the Bastille on one end and Nation on the other. The 11e has a lot to offer without the pretentions of the Marais. Excellent for artists.

**12e**—Up and coming around Bercy and Gare de Lyon, areas that were rather run-down and depressed. Not the most beautiful district, but you may find more space for less francs here than elsewhere. The new construction tends to be hideous though.

**13e**—The heart of the new Chinatown. Here you can find quaint streets with little houses next to horrible rows of Miami Beach style high rises. Some excellent, authentic Chinese restaurants. The parts near the 5th are very desirable.

**14e**—Denfert, Montparnasse, Porte d'Orleans. On the major north south axis. Many popular neighborhoods and great markets. Without a doubt some of the best residential living in Paris.

**15e**—Highly sought after residential district among Parisians. Less interesting than the 14e but comfortable and not without its share of trees. The parts near the Seine host an unlikely outcrop of Japanese tourist hotels. To be avoided. Check carefully on map before accepting the 15e. The rue de Commerce, however, captures the essence of daily Parisian family life.

**16e**—Etoile, Trocadéro, etc. Definitely the most boring and bourgeois area of Paris, yet one of the richest spots on earth. Many students end up here, attracted by the nearby Champs-Elysées, prestigious address and safety. A mistake. The streets, although pretty, are dead quiet at night and there is nothing to do. Street life is absent except around the rue de Passy.

**17e**—The most schizophrenic district of Paris. Half is worse than the 16e, although the Parc Monceau is absolutely lovely—to stroll around. The other half is *populaire*, real and even funky. A bit far from the heart of things but this could be worth it if you want to really experience Paris life. Prices vary dramatically.

**18e**—Kind of far from central districts, although this depends if you're on a good Métro line. More immigrants than elsewhere. Less expensive, but you definitely can get more for your money. Lots of things to discover. Touches Montmartre. Some great markets.

**19e**—Probably the least known of all the Paris districts. Not very convenient in most cases, but again, you may find a great space near a Métro. Check it out.

**20e**—A lively mix of races and ethnics, Africans, Antillean, etc. Some excellent work spaces and artists' *ateliers*. Less expensive than the middle of town, working class, and less prestige, but it all depends on what you want.

## A Word on the *Banlieue*

You may find yourself living in the Parisian suburbs, which can be either pleasant or grim, depending on your expectations and the actual town you're in. The closest suburbs which touch Paris, and are well-served by Métro and bus lines, are called the *Proche-Banlieue*. The most "exclusive" and desirable include Neuilly, Boulogne and St. Cloud to the west, and St. Mandé and Vincennes to the east. The little towns in the *Vallée de Chevreuse*, served by the RER, are the most desirable southern *banlieues*. The towns to the north tend to be the poorest and what the French would describe as *triste*. The "Red Suburbs" signify the municipalities governed by the Communist Party and include Montreuil, Bobigny, Kremlin-Bicêtre, Malakoff, etc. These communities, although not very different from the others, tend in theory to cater to the needs of the working class. In towns like Montreuil, which houses the headquarters for the CGT (powerful left-wing worker's union), there are large Arab and African communities. Apartments and workspaces here can be cheaper and more spacious than anywhere in Paris. The more distant suburbs *(grandes banlieues)*, such as Versailles, St. Germain-en-Laye and Chantilly, are served by RER and commuter trains. The choice to live in the suburbs is a highly personal one depending on how important it is for you to be in the vicinity of Paris with its bridges, cafés and monuments. The suburbs tend to be quiet and provincial. Often there seems little difference in being 10 or 200 km from Paris.

## COMMUNICATIONS

France's sophistication in the field of communications is impressive. On the whole, you will see that the telecommunications field is one of the most dynamic areas of French industry. The Post Office *(La Poste)* will be, from January 1, 1991, separated administratively from France-Telecom, in an effort to increase efficiency. France has worked hard to bridge new technology and *la vie quotidienne* (daily life). FRANCE-TELECOM, the nationalized telephone company, has brought the latest technological developments into the home with the Minitel, a computer screen accessed through the telephone system which is at once a visual telephone book, reservation network, a research library, a home shopping tool, a direct means of written communication with other users, and more. Potential use of the Minitel as a Fax, printer, etc. is mind-boggling.

## The Public Telephone Booth (*Cabine téléphonique*)

Over the last several years most public coin-operated phone booths have been replaced with a new type that accepts only magnetized cards, called the *Télécarte*, which can be bought in post offices and *tabacs*, in units of 50 or 120 for 40 FF and 96 FF respectively. Buy one right away; they're very practical! Plus, it's getting increasingly difficult to find a public phone that takes coins (local calls require a one franc coin).

All Paris and the close suburbs have numbers beginning with 4 (the more distant suburbs begin with 3 or 6). Calls to other parts of France require the code 16. International calls must be preceded with 19. In both cases, wait for a new dial tone and then dial your number. On the coin phones, you'll get a round blinking sign on the phone when your money is about to run out. Shove in more coins—one, two, or five franc pieces are accepted.

In the Sixties and Seventies, broken phones were occasionally discovered which allowed free unlimited international calls to go through undetected. When the word got around, lines would form with foreign students at all hours of the night to call families and friends around the world at no charge. These wonderful little finds have all but disappeared with the new telephone card. The advantage of the card is that there is no money to deal with. Each unit costs 80 centimes and units are deducted automatically from the silicon chip embedded in the card at a rapidity which depends on where and when you're calling. One minute to the United States costs about 10,26 FF from 14h-20h, 7,86 FF from noon to 14h, 20h-2h, and 6,26 FF from 2h to noon.

To use *Télécarte* phones, pick up the receiver, slide in the card, arrow facing forward, close the *volet* (sliding mechanism), wait for a dial tone, and make your call. After hanging up, wait about five seconds; the volet will open. Don't forget to take your card. See chart on the next page for telephone country codes.

**Calling the French provinces from Paris**: Dial 16, wait for the tone, dial the number.

**Calling between the provinces**: Dial the number; no 16 needed.

**Calling the Paris area from the provinces**: Dial 16, wait for the tone, dial 1, and then the number.

**Making an international call from France**: Dial 19, wait for the tone, dial the country code, city code and the number (for the USA, 11 instead of 1).

**Getting international information**: Dial 19, wait for the tone, dial 33-12 and the country code.

**Lodging complaints**: Dial 13.

**International operator**: Dial 19, wait for the tone, dial 33 and the country code (11 for the USA).

# Country Codes:

| | | |
|---|---|---|
| Afghanistan: 93 | Ecuador: 593 | Lesotho: 266 |
| Albania: 355 | Egypt: 20 | Liberia: 231 |
| Algeria: 213 | El Salvador: 503 | Libya: 218 |
| American Virgin Is.: 1809 | Ethiopia: 251 | Liechtenstein: 41 |
| Angola: 244 | Falkland Islands: 500 | Luxembourg: 352 |
| Antilles (Dutch): 599 | Faroe Islands: 298 | Martinique: 596 |
| Argentina: 54 | Fiji: 679 | Macao: 853 |
| Australia: 61 | Finland: 358 | Madagascar: 261 |
| Austria: 43 | Gabon: 241 | Madeira: 351 |
| Azores: 351 | Gambia: 220 | Malaysia: 60 |
| Bahamas: 1809 | German Dem. Rep.: 37 | Malawi: 265 |
| Bahrain: 973 | Ghana: 233 | Maldives: 960 |
| Bangladesh: 880 | Gibraltar 350 | Mali: 223 |
| Belgium: 32 | Greece: 30 | Malta: 356 |
| Belize: 501 | Greenland: 299 | Mauritania: 222 |
| Benin: 229 | Grenada: 1809 | Mauritius Island: 230 |
| Bermuda: 1809 | Guadeloupe: 590 | Mexico: 52 |
| Bolivia: 591 | Guam: 671 | Mongolia: 976 |
| Botswana: 267 | Guatemala: 502 | Montserrat: 1809 |
| Brazil: 55 | Guinea: 224 | Morocco: 212 |
| British Virgin Is.: 1809 | Guinea Bissau: 245 | Mozambique: 258 |
| Brunei: 673 | Guinea Equatorial: 240 | Namibia: 264 |
| Bulgaria: 359 | Guyana: 592 | Nauru Islands: 674 |
| Burkina Faso: 226 | Haiti: 509 | Nepal: 977 |
| Burma: 95 | Hawaii: 1808 | Netherlands: 31 |
| Burundi: 257 | Honduras: 504 | New Zealand: 64 |
| Cameroon: 237 | Hong Kong: 852 | Nicaragua: 505 |
| Canada: 1 | Hungary: 36 | Nieves: 1 |
| Cape Verde: 238 | Iceland: 354 | Niger: 227 |
| Cayman Islands: 1809 | India: 91 | Nigeria: 234 |
| Central African Rep.: 236 | Indonesia: 62 | Norfolk Island: 6723 |
| Chad: 235 | Iran: 98 | Norway: 47 |
| Chile: 56 | Iraq: 964 | Oman: 968 |
| China: 86 | Ireland: 353 | Pakistan: 92 |
| Colombia: 57 | Israel: 972 | Panama: 507 |
| Comores: 269 | Italy: 39 | Papua/New Guinea: 675 |
| Congo: 242 | Ivory Coast: 225 | Paraguay: 595 |
| Cook: 682 | Jamaica: 1809 | Peru: 51 |
| Costa Rica: 506 | Japan: 81 | Phillipines: 63 |
| Cuba: 53 | Jordan: 962 | Poland: 48 |
| Cyprus: 357 | Kenya: 254 | Portugal: 351 |
| Czechoslovakia: 42 | Korea: 82 | Puerto Rico: 1809 |
| Denmark: 45 | Kuwait: 965 | Qatar: 974 |
| Djibouti: 253 | Laos: 856 | Romania: 40 |
| Dominican Rep.: 1809 | Lebanon: 961 | Rwanda: 250 |

Samoa US: 684
Samoa Western: 685
San Marino: 39
Sao Tome e Principe: 239
St Vincent: 1809
St Kitts: 1809
St Helena/Ascension: 247
St Lucia: 1809
Saudi Arabia: 966
Senegal: 221
Seychelles: 248
Sierra Leone: 232
Singapore: 65
Somalia: 252
Solomon Islands: 677
South Africa: 27
Spain: 34

Sri Lanka: 94
Sudan: 249
Surinam: 597
Swaziland: 268
Sweden: 46
Switzerland: 41
Syria: 963
Taiwan: 886
Tanzania: 255
Thailand: 66
Togo: 228
Tonga: 676
Trinidad/Tobago: 1809
Tunisia: 216
Turks/Caicos Is.: 1809 946
Turkey: 90

Uganda: 256
United Arab Emir.: 971
United Kingdom: 44
Uruguay: 598
U.S.S.R: 7
U.S.A.: 1
Vanuatu: 678
Vatican City 39
Venezuela: 58
Vietnam: 84
West Germany: 49
Yemen: 967
Yugoslavia: 38
Zaire: 243
Zambia: 260
Zimbabwe: 263

## Country Direct Services

For a direct connection with an operator in a country, dial 19, wait for the tone, and dial:

| | | | |
|---|---|---|---|
| Australian Direct | 00 61 | United Kingdon Direct | 00 44 |
| Canada Direct | 00 16 | United States: | |
| Hong Kong Direct | 00 852 | USA Direct (AT&T) | 00 11 |
| New Zealand Direct | 00 64 | CALL USA (MCI) | 00 19 |

## Minitel

The Minitel is a small, on-line computer connected to the French phone lines that is available free of charge to anyone possessing a telephone. Although the directory service, obtained by simply dialing 11, is free for the first two minutes, other services such as banking, shopping, research, and ticket reservations are charged by the minute directly to your phone bill. So be careful with this fascinating and vastly useful tool.

Throughout Paris you will see a strange host of billboards advertising Minitel services. These begin with the code numbers 36.14, 36.15 or 36.16 and include a code word or key. To use the Minitel, turn on the unit, dial the code number on your telephone, wait for the Fax-like tone, and then press *Connexion Fin* on the Minitel keyboard. The rest should be self-evident. Here are a few useful Minitel services:

**3615 AHP04**
Tourist activities and resources in the Haute-Provence Alps; cultural animation, leisure activities, thermal spas, etc. Accommodation guide.
**3614 AIRTEL**
National and international airline schedules and airfares.
**3614 CASE**
French health or thermal, seaside and tourist resorts: facilities, leisure activities, list of accommodations.
**11 FUAJ**
Specify FUAJ under *Nom* and Paris under *Ville* and you will find information on all youth hostels in France.
**3614 ED**
Administrative and emergency phone numbers and addresses.

### 3614 EVAZUR
Tourist guide to the Cote d'Azur and the Midi. Useful addresses: hotels, restaurants, camping sites, discos.

### 3614 NATURISM
Information on naturism and naturist holiday centers (nudist colonies).

### 3614 TMKT
Telemarketing. All the groceries, health and beauty aids and even soft and hard beverages you need. Delivered promptly for 40 FF. You can charge purchases to major credit cards.

### 3615 BBC
British and international news broadcast in English by the BBC.

### 3615 CAP 2
Municipal libraries in Paris.

### 3615 CORUS
Information concerning 150 mountain resorts.

### 3615 CUM
Direct dialogue and messages for singles. Horoscope, games, etc.

### 3615 FL
Information concerning river tourism.

### 3615 GAULT
Listing of 2500 selected Paris restaurants with Henri Gault's opinions on the best ones.

### 3615 HORAV
Airport guide: parking, services, hotels. Flight departure and arrival times.

### 3615 ITOUR
National directory of tourist bureaus by region, department and town.

### 3615 KITI
Guide to cultural sites, monuments, and castles.

### 3615 LIBE
American and international news in English direct from USA TODAY.

### 3615 METEO
Weather.

### 3615 PAT
Medical information for tourists.

### 3615 RANDO
Guide of walking trips in France. List of maps and guides.

### 3615 SNCF
French National Railway information. Train times, reservations, sleeping compartments, etc.

### 3615 TOTAL
Complete network of Total Stations with nearest lead-free gas.

### 3615 VOYAGEL
All the formalities, useful addresses and practical information (hours and days which banks, shops, etc. are open) for all regions.

### 3615 UPI
International news in English.

### 3616 ASFA
Traffic conditions and highway information.

### 3616 SEALINK
Times and prices for ferries to England and Ireland.

### 3616 VOYAGEL * FRANCE
Formalities, addresses and practical information (hours and days of banking, shopping,etc.) to enable foreign tourists to have trouble-free holidays.

# The Post Office (*PTT*) (*La Poste*)

Although the French postal service has been rated tenth among the twelve EEC countries in Europe, you will probably be both impressed and frustrated by your experiences concerning the mail. First, you will have to get used to longer lines than you're probably accustomed to. The French post office handles so many functions that sending a simple letter sometimes gets caught in the shuffle of all the rest. The PTT handles long distance telephone calls, telegrams, an express mail system called Chronopost, the entire array of letter and package possibilities, plus numerous financial and banking functions such as savings accounts, cables or wire transfers of funds, payment of phone bills, distribution of major mailhouse catalogs, savings accounts, retirement plans, checking accounts, tax consulting, investment plans, housing funds, mortgages, and more. The PTT is in direct competition with commercial banks. Of eight windows (*guichets*) open in an average post office, only two or three will be equipped for sending letters or packages, marked *Envoi de lettres et paquets*.

## La Poste

**Hours**: Monday-Friday: 8h-19h.
Saturday: 8h-12h.
Closed Sunday

The Main Post Office is open 24 hours a day, 7 days a week:
52, rue du Louvre
75001 PARIS
tel: 42.33.71.60

## A Few Helpful Terms:

*Une lettre recommandée* (registered letter): the French use this rather expensive means not so much for security as to have proof that a particular letter, document, bill, or administrative measure was executed. Post offices tend to be cheap with the forms so you often have to wait to get to the front of the line to fill in your registered letter form. When picking up a registered letter, you must bring (in person) your *avis* (notice) plus valid identification that has a picture.

*Avec accusé de réception* (return receipt requested): this can be added to the registered letter if you want proof that your letter was in fact received on a certain date. Note: there is no such thing as insuring your letters or parcels, however, items sent *recommandée*—if lost, stolen, or damaged—can be reimbursed up to 750 FF.

*Lettres*: All letters should be marked LETTRE to insure that they go first class. Aerograms are 4,20 FF for the whole world. The basic 10 gram air mail letter to the United States, Canada, and the Middle East is 3,50 FF. The price for post cards is the same. The French often send post cards in envelopes, a habit that seems bizarre to North Americans. In any case, they usually put on the same postage as a letter, so that it then goes as fast as a letter. Given that postal rates change periodically, it's a good idea to request a rate sheet upon arrival from your local post office.

*Pli Non Urgent* (*PNU*) (Second class mail): This is cheaper but much slower, especially near the end of the week in that PNU items do not travel on weekends.

**Parcels**: Packages require more work to send in France than in many other countries. First class letters and packages are limited to two kilos (4.4 pounds). Books and packages are limited to five kilos (11 pounds). For heavier items, you are obliged to take your wares to a special window at the main post office of any *arrondissement* or the Central Post Office at 52, rue du Louvre in the first *arrondissement*. This post office, it should be noted, is the only 24 hour/7 days a week postal facility in Paris. This is useful when you have applications and other materials that need to be postmarked by a particular date.

**Chronopost**: Chronopost is the French Post Office's Express Mail service. Letters sent to the US by Chronopost arrive in 48 hours, guaranteed. Packages can also be sent by Chronopost. A letter will cost you about 200 FF. Minitel provides information on everything you ever wanted to know about Chronopost—36.14. EMS.

**Poste Restante**: If you find yourself in France without a reliable address, remember that you can always receive mail by having it sent to the post office of your choice marked with your name and *poste restante*.

## Terminology

| | |
|---|---|
| *la/le destinataire* | addressee |
| *l'aérogramme* | aerogram |
| *par avion* or *poste aérienne* | |
| | airmail |
| *le carnet de timbres* | |
| | book of stamps |
| *le changement* | |
| *d'adresse* | change of address |
| *le timbre* | |
| *philatélique* | commemorative stamp |
| *le guichet* | counter window |
| *la déclaration de douane* | |
| | customs declaration |
| *la distribution* | delivery |
| *la réexpédition* | forwarding |
| *la poste restante* | general delivery |
| *la réclamation* | inquiry |
| *assuré* | insured |
| *le facteur* | letter carrier |
| *la poste* | mail |
| *la boîte aux lettres* | mail box |
| *le mandat* | money order |
| *le paquet* or *le colis* | |
| | package |
| *le bureau de poste* | post office |
| *boîte postale (B.P.)* | post office box |
| *le mandat* | money order |
| *l'imprimé* | printed matter |
| *le récipissé* | receipt |
| *recommandé* | registered |
| *l'avis de réception* | return receipt |
| *l'expéditeur* | sender |
| *la dimension* | size |
| *par express* | special delivery |
| *le poids* | weight |
| *emballages* | mailing boxes |

## Television

French television has progressively loosened up and expanded over the last five years. Some would argue that the quality has diminished. Not so long ago there was no programming before noon so that kids wouldn't be fixed to tv sets. And there were few emissions after midnight. This has changed, although there are no late-night talk shows or all-night movie channels.

There are principally five French television stations and one subscriber station currently available to Parisian viewers, although new cable options are being installed and some neighborhoods have already been connected. The channels are: TF1, Antenne 2, FR 3,

La Cinq, and M6. Channel 4 is Canal Plus which you must pay for, except for certain programs during the day which are transmitted *en clair* (unscrambled). One of these *en clair* moments includes a 8h transmission of Dan Rather's CBS Nightly News from the previous evening. Dan is of course speaking English, but subtitles have been added for French viewers. It can be fun to watch your shifting perceptions of American life and media as you live overseas and begin to see the world in a wider, more international scope.

TF1 has been privately owned for only several years after a rather major battle on the subject. The programming is solid but a bit conservative. The news gathering and reporting is generally untenacious.

Antenne 2 is wholly State-owned, more liberal and more progressive in its programming. It programs many special events, interviews, and cultural happenings. The news, however, isn't much better than TF1. There is an excellent film series on Friday nights in V.O. *(version originale)* —often in English.

FR3 shares much of its programming with Antenne 2 but adds many transmissions.

Canal Plus shows a lot of films, many of which are lousy. It also provides a fair amount of American sports coverage otherwise unavailable in France.

La Cinq is the most American of French channels. It has a lively presentation with a lot of embarrassingly weak shows. It shows reruns from outdated and not-so-successful American serials from the Sixties and Seventies. The graphics are flashy.

M6 has a lot of entertainment, show biz and video clips.

Rumor has it there's a seventh channel that is filled with wonderfully enriching cultural programming. This is one of the new stations available in a limited way on cable. CNN is also available via cable, and a number of Paris' better hotels receive it for their guests. Limited areas of the city do receive the package, which includes more than 20 other cable stations including MTV, BBC, SKY and stations from Germany and around Europe. This is an area of rapid development in Europe. If you buy a television in France don't forget that it can only receive French channels. A US or British video player will not work with a French set, which is in the SECAM standard. Britain and most of Europe uses PAL, while North America uses NTSC. While bi-standard (PAL/SECAM) systems are widely available, tri-standard video players and recorders *(magnéto-scopes)* are rarer and expensive. The FNAC carries both a tri-standard video and tv. French law used to require a special annual users tax for tv and video owners. Electronics stores were obliged to report all sales to the government, so quick-witted consumers paid in cash and gave fictitious addresses; the *redevance* or users' tax has been dropped for video, but remains for tv (533 FF per annum in 1989). The sales tax is still high—18,6% on tvs, 25% on video.

Prerecorded video films are readily available but expensive, with little in English. Reels-on-Wheels (tel: 45.67.64.99), however, both sells and rents English and American films at affordable prices and delivers and picks up!

# Radio

The French radio bands had been strictly controlled in the Seventies. The airwaves were certainly not free. Numerous unofficial pirate stations were hidden around the city. Most radio emissions come from one centralized building complex in the sixteenth *arrondissement* called the *Maison de la Radio*. When Mitterrand came into power, radio in France was decontrolled. Scores of little radio stations sprang up at once. Many represented ethnic groups or regions. The result was a glut on the airwaves; it became difficult to pick up clear signals except for the huge and powerful commercial radio stations: RTL, Radio Luxembourg, Radio Monte Carlo, NRJ, and a few others. So, new rules were clamped on. Things have leveled out now.

Radio programming can be quite original in France, and if you are used to turning the dial to hear a different style of music, you may be pleasantly surprised to hear a Chopin Nocturne followed by Led Zeppelin followed by John Coltrane. To the French, either quality transgresses the bounds of style or the art of the smooth segue is still to be learned.

Here is a list of Paris' major FM Radio Stations, thanks to expatriate New Jersey DJ Bart Platenga whose radio column appeared in *Passion Magazine* and whose show Wreck This Mess can be heard on Radio Libertaire on Tuesdays at 16h30. Platenga writes: "Paris radio is more open and unpredictable in general than American or British radio. Just spin the dial & one gets an amazing variety of sound. But Paris radio is formating fast. Their station *ids* are VERY inventive, often better than the music they play. While in America there is lots of talk about nothing, in Paris there is too much talk about significance. The French like to talk ABOUT music. That's why you'll hear five minutes of music & then fifteen minutes of discussion about it. Perhaps that's why jazz is popular."

### FRANCE INTER - 87.8
French variety & cultural chandelier chats. Unadventurous forays into culture Muzak from this state-run station.

### RADIO ORIENT - 88.6
Arab pop.

### KISS FM - 89.0
Wallpaper muzak demographically aimed at the spineless upward bound consumers who dance to Pink Floyd and Madonna with no discernible change in step.

### RADIO LIBERTAIRE - 89.4
Anarchist federation's Voice Without Master. Eclectic embrace of world's disinherited and disaffected. Some of Paris' best blues, jazz, and alternative info.

### FIP PARIS - 90.4
Commercial-free sublime simmer of soothing woogie music from Barbieri to Mingus, Lester Young to Neil. Mellifluous djs, casual traffic (26 updates daily), weather, news interruptions.

### CANAL 9 - 90.9
Leans heavy on plod-plod ballady pop. Best: *Intérieurs Nuits* (live personal column with secret, sexy and perverse announcements), Fri. 23h - 1h.

### FRANCE MUSIQUE - 91.7
Though this state-run station is mainly devoted to classical, it wanders into jazz, ethnic and

experimental sounds.

**RADIO CVS - 92.1**

Ding-a-ling songs that make you want to stuff Malobars in your ears.

**TROPIC FM - 92.6**

Truly one of the cream. Joyous equatorial notes that are eclectic and human. Great creole-juju-mambo-salsa-zulu-ethno-pop-reggae bubbling stew.

**ICI & MAINTENANT - 93.1**

Decent stuff, depending on the show. Unique dedication to listener call-ins. Best: Spiral Insana (experimental, cut-up), Tues. 17h-18h30. Shares frequency with Radio Aligre.

**FRANCE CULTURE - 93.5**

France Culture (perhaps the only station in the world exclusively concerned with culture) broadcasts serious cultural topics 24-hours-a-day.

**RADIO FRANCE MAGREB - 94**

Arabic music with an edge.

**FUTUR GENERATION - 94.4**

The pop future as seen from the cyber-souls of E.T. fans.

**RADIO SHALOM - 94.8**

Vegas comes to Tel Aviv.

**RADIO TOUR EIFFEL - 95.2**

Some good, cool jazz that is unfortunately hindered by incessant interruptions.

**RADIO COURTOISIE - 95.6**

This Catholic-oriented, interview-heavy station, shares its frequency with Radio Asie.

**SKYROCK - 96.0**

This giant describes itself as "chewing gum for the ears." Chain-talking DJS vaccinated with phonographic needles whack off crappy, headless recordings.

**PACIFIC FM - 97.4**

Describes itself as *"la radio évasion"* (escapism radio). Intriguing mishmash of junk and gems from all over the world: from gutwrenching segues of airhead nostalgia (John Denver) to real Delta blues.

**RADIO BEUR - 98.2**

Arab pop & ethno-music with integrity. Best: Raîkoum (Raî) Monday 16h30-18h:

**RADIO PORTUGAL - 98.6**

Is schmaltzy sentimentality just a universal affliction? French with a Portuguese accent.

**RADIO LATINA - 99.0**

Solid and adventurous jazz daily like Cecil Taylor compositions actually allowed to stretch and explore.

**REUSSIR FM - 99.6**

Why succeed when you can fail so effortlessly. Station of "professional info & business communication." Obviously looking for its niche among career-oriented. Shares frequency with Jazzland.

**RADIO CLASSIQUE - 101.1**

Commercial-free, 24-hour-a-day classical music. One exception is the financial news, Mon. - Fri. 7h - 8h30.

**NRJ - 100.3**

The giant which boasts 5 million listeners. A fair selection of pop, house and rock.

**RADIO NOVA - 101.5**

Everything from urban warfare rap, love funk and acid garage jazz to zulu. Easiest station to pop on anytime.

**FUN RADIO - 101.9**

Noisy like your worst pinball nightmare. Pop without pulp. Bump without bang.

**OUI FM - 102.3**

Overrated computer-generated rock format that's white as nose candy. Trendy guitars and a bit of self-serious rock NOOZ.

**RTL - 104.3**

News bulletins on the hour, every hour. The concept here is acccessible, popular and lively - in short, close to millions of hearts nationwide.

**EUROPE 1 - 104.7**

News, soft rock, festival coverage, almanacs and DJ-hosted variety and entertainment programming. Very informal tone.

**RADIO NOSTALGIE - 105.1**

Lots of dippy, purring come-on *chanteurs & chanteuses*. All the romantic squish of a sponge dipped in cheap perfume.

**FRANCE INFO - 105.5**

Around-the-clock, state-run, commercial-free, nationwide news. Broadcasts in all French cities, albeit on different frequencies. Almost as up-to-the-minute as a wire service.

**TABALA - 106.3**

Paris' Afro station plays mix of African, Caribbean and black American music and African news.

**RADIO TOMATE - 106.7**

Small "associative" radio, collective idealism, alternative info. Best: Konstroy (alternative rock) Sun 17h-19h; *Poévie* (*engagé*, dub & ghetto poetry) Fri 19h-20h30; Radio Mango (Antilles culture) Fri 20h30-0h.

For news and information in English you can tune in to a range of international English news services, each with its particular ideology. One American professor in Paris contends there is only one real way to learn what's really happening in the world: listen to BBC World Service, Voice of America, Radio Tirana (Albania) English Service, and Radio Moscow English Service and average them out. In any case, it's both revealing and amusing tuning in to alter-native sources of information.

# Press

For a foreign city, Paris has a healthy variety of English-language publications. Here is a descriptive listing of what's being published regularly here in English:

***International Herald Tribune***: international daily newspaper providing global coverage from staff reporters, wire services, the *New York Times* and the *Washington Post*. American financial markets, sports and comics. 8 FF at the kiosk or 210 FF for a three-month subscription for students or teachers.

**International Herald Tribune**
181, av. Charles-de-Gaulle
92200 NEUILLY
tel: 46.37.93.00
Publisher: Lee HUEBNER

Editor: John VINOCUR
Public Relations: Louise JENOC

***The European***: A new, English-language weekend newspaper, based in London, published by Robert Maxwell and concentrating on Europe as a "nation." Color photos and graphics à la *USA Today*. 10 FF every Friday.

**The European**
24, rue Sentier
75002 PARIS
tel: 42.21.14.48

*Passion Magazine*: Monthly city magazine, founded in 1981 by Canadian Robert Sarner, filled with glossy images and featuring topical articles, reviews and excellent listings on upcoming events and "in" spots. Offers internships to students and recent graduates. 20 FF at newstands. Currently being reorganized by new, English owners: *Time Out*.

**Passion Magazine**
23, rue Yves Toudic
75010 PARIS
tel: 42.39.15.80

*Paris Free Voice*: A monthly community-oriented free newspaper with a circulation of 15,000. Published for over 10 years by stoic Parsons professor of photography, Bob Bishop, out of his basement office in the American Church. Inexpensive and effective classified ads.

**Paris Free Voice**
American Church
65, Quai D'Orsay
75007 PARIS
tel: 47.05.07.99

*Frank: An International Journal of Contemporary Writing & Art*: Has been publishing fiction, poetry, literary interviews and contemporary art twice a year since 1983. Available at literary bookshops in Paris and North America. Edited by fiction-writer David Applefield. 150 FF/$25 for four issues. 50 FF/$7 sample copy.

**Frank: An International Journal of Contemporary Writing & Art**
B.P. 29
94301 VINCENNES CEDEX

*France-USA Contacts*: An innovative semi-monthly circular of classified advertisements and useful tips devised, produced, and distributed by John and Lisa Vanden Bos. Distributed free in both Paris and New York. Free bulletin-board center, 10h-19h, Monday-Saturday.

**France-USA Contacts (FUSAC)**
40, rue des Boulangers, au sous -sol
75005 PARIS
tel: 43.26.87.83

*Paris-Anglophone*: Annual directory of all English-speaking professional, commercial and cultural activities in Paris. A handy tool for job-seeking and an invaluable mailing-list for entre-preneurs. Published by Frank Books and sponsored by France-Télécom. 125 FF.

**Paris-Anglophone**
B.P. 29
94301 VINCENNES Cedex

*Paris Boulevard*: A new, ex-pertly-designed, glossy monthly with topical articles on the French corporate world and the upper echelons of French society.

**Paris Boulevard**
Mediatime France
8 rue Simon le Franc
75004 PARIS
tel: 40.29.95.55

*Vocable*: Geared towards French readers wanting to maintain and improve their foreign language skills. English edition available at many kiosks and bookstores.

**Vocable**
4, rue de Cérisoles
75008 PARIS
tel. 47.20.74.16

**Speak Up**: An attractive monthly magazine and cassette designed for French readers.
**Speak Up**
Editions Atlas
87-89, rue de la Boétie
75008 PARIS
tel: 45.63.04.14

**The Key**: Tabloid newspaper for French students of English.
**The Key**
12, rue Pavée
75004 PARIS
tel. 42.72.15.95

**Art International**: One of the world's finest quarterlies in English on contemporary art. Edited in Paris by Thomas West, Jill Lloyd, and Michael Peppiatt. Well researched and written articles with high-quality reproductions.
**Art International**
77, rue des Archives
75003 PARIS
tel: 48.04.84.54

## Other English-language Press in France

Here is a selected list of major networks, stations, newspapers and magazines in France. For purchasing English and American magazines and newspapers W.H. Smith and Brentano's are good sources. The monopoly press distributor NMPP, which runs all Paris kiosks and is owned by the multinational French publisher Hachette, has its own international press shop:
**NMPP**
111, rue Réaumur
75002 PARIS

(For French press, see Politics.)

# Radio & TV
**American Broadcasting Co. (ABC)**
tel: 45.05.13.73

**British Broadcasting Co. (BBC)**
tel: 45.61.97.00 (television)
    45.63.15.88 (radio)

**Central Broadcasting System (CBS)**
tel: 42.25.26.52

**Cable News Network (CNN)**
tel: 42.89.23.31

**Canadian Broadcasting Corp. (CBC)**
tel: 43.59.11.85

**National Broadcasting Co. (NBC)**
tel: 43.59.11.71

**New Zealand Press Association**
tel: 43.27.02.75

**Radio Canada**
tel: 43.59.11.85

**Radio France Internationale**
English Service
tel: 42.30.30.62

**Radio Canada International**
tel: 48.45.64.97

**Tokyo Broadcasting Systems**
tel: 42.66.15.55

# Newspapers
**Los Angeles Times**
tel: 42.56.11.75

**New York Times**
tel: 42.66.37.49

**The Observer**
tel: 42.74.60.86

**The Sunday Times**
tel: 47.42.73.21

**USA Today**
tel: 43.74.54.46

**The Wall Street Journal**
tel: 47.42.08.06

**Washington Post**
tel: 42.56.01.80

## Journals/Newsletters

**Association of American Wives In Europe Newsletter**
tel: 42.56.05.24

**Paris Traveller's Gazette**
Voyageur des Etats-Unis
tel: 42.60.32.52

## Magazines

**Business Week**
tel: 42.89.03.80

**European Travel & Life**
tel: 43.54.18.24

**Newsweek Magazine**
tel: 42.56.06.81

**Time Magazine**
tel: 43.59.05.39

**U.S. News & World Report**
tel: 47.20.84.83

# POLITICS

No matter where you are in France, you're never very far away from a *café*, a restaurant or politics. The French, as you may have noticed, have opinions on most everything and don't hesitate to voice them. This is particularly true in politics, where one is either on the Left or on the Right, and never, but never the twain shall meet.

Back in the early days of the French Revolution, the first National Assembly met with the radical revolutionaries seated to the left of the Speaker, the cautious conservatives to his right. The division has been maintained ever since. Today, even the Right bows to the ideals of the Revolution—if not its methods—which founded the modern republic. There are still a few die-hard monarchists left around, gathering cobwebs in the wealthier *quartiers* (the Count of Paris, an elderly gentleman, is the living descendant of the last deposed King, and remains ever ready to sit upon the throne again, should the need arise, but his phone isn't exactly ringing off the hook).

In the waning years of the 20th century, France's Socialist Party, led by President François Mitterrand, has emerged as the dominant political party. These are hardly the radical politicians of the early 80s when they first won the presidency and a majority in the *Assemblée Nationale*. Their early policies of nationalizing industry and intervening in the economy have been abandoned in favor of a lighter hand. Today, their policies are less radically Left, more attuned to *la France profonde* (something akin to "the silent majority" in America). One thing they do have in common with their conservative predecessors, though, is a large and strong central government, with a massive bureaucracy: The power of *l'Etat* in France is supreme.

# The Leaders

François Mitterrand has been the leader of the Socialist Party for the last couple of decades. His reelection to a second seven-year term as President in 1988 should assure him of being the longest serving president in French political history. He has a reputation as a clever and patient politician—his nickname is "The Sphinx." He has managed to stay relatively aloof and above the fray of everyday politics, which has strengthened his popularity. The French like their presidents with a bit of haughtiness that reminds one of the attitude of royalty, a quality that Charles de Gaulle, the most successful French leader of the Right, had in abundance. They also want to see visible signs of intelligence. Mitterrand, for instance, is the author of several books and has been known to surprise reporters with his wide knowledge of literature and the arts. The idea of a populist, "just one of the boys" president à la Ronald Reagan is unthinkable in French politics.

The big question of the early 90s is who will be Mitterrand's successor as Socialist Party leader and presidential candidate. The battle is presently raging between Michel Rocard, the dapper and articulate Prime Minister, the brash former Prime Minister Laurent Fabius and long time party boss Pierre Mauroy, also a former Prime Minister.

The leading figure of the French Right is Jacques Chirac, the Mayor of Paris, who lost the last presidential election to Mitterrand but is so firmly entrenched in the Hôtel de Ville he may hold the job of mayor well into the next century.

The Right, however, is suffering from internal arguments between the two major parties, Chirac's RPR and the more centrist UDF.

There are always extremes in French politics, too, which at least keeps things interesting. On the extreme Right is the Front National, the nationalistic, xenophobic party led by Jean-Marie Le Pen, a somewhat loutish and loud politician who has been charged with being racist and antisemitic. Although not a serious force on the national scene, Le Pen and his party have managed to win significant percentages of the local vote in various regions across the country. The most successful political cards they play deal with crime and violence and fear of foreigners, especially Africans and Arabs.

On the other extreme is the French Communist Party, the PCF, led for years by the aging party boss Georges Marchais. From the 1950s through the 70s, the French Communists were a significant force in national and local politics. During the years of the Nazi occupation of France (1940-1944), the Communists were especially active members of the French Resistance, and much of their popularity is founded on their exploits during this period. They have also been, historically, the party of the worker and the immigrant, and have always been good at grass roots political organization. In recent years, though, the PCF has lost a large percentage of its electorate, and the party has been seriously weakened, not least because under Marchais, the French Communists have closely, even slavishly, followed the Moscow party line, and have thus been branded as "Stalinist."

Labor unions in France have been strong since the end of the Second World War. It is rare to go more than six months without strikes at one or another of the public services, such as transportation, postal or civil service, and rarer still to go through the Spring without at least one major march through the streets of Paris by one or several of the major unions, the CGT (the Communist-led union), the CFDT (Left, more Socialist-oriented) or the FO (relatively independent). The right to strike is fundamental to the French conception of the relationship between workers and management in a democracy, and there is surprisingly little serious grumbling by the general public when the Métro or railways are shut down because of a strike.

The newspapers in France follow the general political divisions. The best and most respected is *Le Monde*, which is slightly Left of center, and the closest one can come to the unattainable goal of objectivity in the French press. Its tone is authoritative, intelligent and serious, and it has sometimes been called the best newspaper in the world. Further to the Left is the younger and more irreverent daily, *Libération*, which features some remarkably good cultural coverage and the occasional investigative piece. The two big newspapers of the Right are the morning daily *Le Figaro*, and its evening sister, *France Soir*, both owned by the same newspaper magnate, Robert Hersant. *Le Figaro* has softened its aggressive political tone in recent months, and has been hoping to gain more readers among the younger, upwardly mobile set. Its classified ads are the best and most complete. *Le Parisien* is a relatively neutral daily newspaper, politically, and looks something like *USA Today*, with its color photos.

# BANKING & MONEY

As 1992-3 approaches, the portentous date for the member countries of the European Economic Community (EEC) to coordinate and consolidate many aspects of their local economies and commercial and cultural sectors into one united entity, French banking laws and practices will be obliged to loosen up. Your reactions and experiences with French and international banks in France will undoubtedly vary depending on what you're accustomed to. Remember one thing—France has never really been a service-oriented society. Things do not run around the omnipresent, operating practice that the customer is always right. Although money and financial gain play an important role in France, as in all Western societies, the French are unwilling to sacrifice everything for the sake of profit. A shopkeeper may refuse to stay open slightly after closing time, even to make a sale. Businesses often don't answer phones at lunchtime. Real estate brokers will wait for you to call back. All this can be both enchanting and annoying. Learn to be enchanted—the quality of daily life wins out over more aggressive commercial practices. Take the longer meal.

In banks, you will probably not have a personal first-name-basis relationship with your banker. He or she will not close each transaction with a drippy but sincere "Have a Nice Day." You will experience this everywhere from banks to restaurants. If you receive moderately polite and efficient service in a bank consider yourself lucky. And don't expect toaster ovens or Walkmans for opening an account! Patience is not a commodity found in abundance when the thick plexiglass *guichet* (window) service is involved. No one in any particular branch of any bank will ever have the authority to credit your account one *centime* without first passing on your written request to *la direction* (management) of the bank. All operations, complaints, modifications, and verifications are slow and tedious and, when possible, should be avoided. It is a good idea to get yourself known by at least two bank employees at your branch. That way when one is *en vacances* (holiday) you still have a chance of better service if needed. This will save you time and aggravation in that a number of bank operations run smoother when you're recognized and don't have to provide identification each time.

Over the last five years, France has become highly *informatisée* (computerized) in everything from banking to dating. *Guichets automatiques* (automatic tellers) abound. Between his *Carte Bleue* bank payment card and the Minitel, the private citizen in France essentially has access to all sectors of commercial life. This computerization comes as much from the French love of form (systems and structures) and aesthetics (style) as from a search for greater efficiency. So, service is improving in business as less and less is required from human interaction.

As for banking you'll probably have a few early questions: How do I change money? How can I receive money from abroad? What do I need to open a bank account? Which banks are the best for students? Where can I cash travelers checks? And what about credit cards in France? These are all answered in the pages to come.

A society's relationship to money reveals much about that society. If you're coming from the United States, where banking (except currency conversion in small banks) is a relatively easy and flexible activity, you may be frustrated at first when even attempting simple transactions. In France, the banks are a highly-regulated industry. The State has played an increasingly present role in matters of banking since 1983, when Mitterand nationalized about ten banks, two of which have been re-privatised. There are a handful of huge and omnipresent banks that have hundreds of branches all over Paris and in a majority of towns in the provinces. The largest French banks, and thus the ones with the most branch offices, are *Crédit Agricole, Banque Nationale de Paris (BNP), Crédit Lyonnais,* and *Société Générale.* Here are a few key banking addresses well-adapted for foreigners, where you'll be able to change money and ask questions.

**American Express International**
11, rue Scribe
75009 PARIS
tel: 42.66.09.99
Open 9h-17h Monday-Saturday for clients mail, currency exchange and travelers checks, and 9h-17h30 Monday-Friday for travel agency. In cases of stolen credit cards during hours of closure, call 47.77.72.00. For lost travelers checks call AMEX in Brighton, England at telephone number (19).05.90.86.00 (free call—all 05 calls, *numeros verts,* are automatically collect).

**Crédit Commercial de France (CCF)**
115, av. des Champs-Elysées
75008 PARIS
Métro: George-V
Hours: Mondays - Saturdays, 8h30-20h and in July, August and September on Sundays from 10h15-18h.

**Banque Nationale de Paris (BNP)**
Place de l'Opéra at rue 4 Septembre
Métro: Opéra
24 hour VISA automatic cash machine and automatic changer for foreign bank notes.

**BNP France-Etranger**
2, Place de l'Opéra
75002 PARIS
tel: 42.66.35.15
(specialized service for foreigners)

**Barclays Bank**
33, rue 4 Septembre
75002 PARIS
Métro: Opéra
9h30-16h, Monday-Friday
and Rond-Point des Champs-Elysées
75008 PARIS
Métro: Champs-Elysées-Clemenceau
Barclay checks only, and travelers checks. 7,50 F commission on checks up to £100.

**Citibank**
30, av. des Champs-Elysées
75008 PARIS
Métro: George V
Mondays to Fridays 9h-18h45, Saturdays 10h30-13h15, 14h30-18h30.

**Banking Hours**: generally 9h00-16h30 or 17h00 on weekdays, closed on weekends. Foreign banks close at 16h00.

**Foreign Currency Exchange**: Open nightly on weekdays until 20h00 at the Gare St. Lazare and the Gare de L'Est, everyday at the Gare du Nord and Gare de Lyon until 21h00 and 23h00, respectively. Many banks also have exchange windows, usually open during select hours (never during lunch). Many private exchange services have opened all over the city, many in response to the five million tourists who came for the bicentennial and the flood of new Japanese visitors in France. A popular one is called Chequepoint (Head Office, 150, av des Champs-Elysées), another is CHANGE. These are both reliable and advantageous in terms of rates and commission. There is some room for negotiation. Be insistent.

## Opening an Account

There has been some ambiguity as to the procedures for foreigners to open accounts in France. Simply, this stems from the curious fact that rules, regulations and formalities vary greatly from not only bank to bank but between branches of the same bank. As a student or new resident, you'll want to remember that the way you're handled is highly discretionary. So, it's to your advantage to present yourself well, convey stability, respectability, and the certainty and regularity of deposits. If you hit a snag, don't fight or lose sleep; try another branch, or another bank—there are plenty.

In most cases, you'll be asked for a *carte de séjour* and proof of address (EDF/GDF strikes again). However, even this fluctuates. One Société Générale manager stated confidently "just a passport will do." The BNP, although one of the largest banks, tends to require a lot of paperwork. The Société Générale may ask for fewer documents to begin with, but tends to be cautious in issuing checkbooks and *Carte Bleue* bank payment cards. Some of the smaller banks like B.R.E.D. may prove to be the easiest in opening up accounts and offering services but have fewer branch offices. Many banks will only let you open

accounts if you live or work in the neighborhood of the branch.

For your first two years in France you will be entitled to a *compte non-résident* (non-resident account) unless you are from an EEC country. Previously, the *compte non-résident* limited you to making deposits originating outside of France. These regulations have been dropped. So essentially there is no difference between a *compte non-résident* and a *compte résident* for deposits up to 50,000 FF. You can withdraw and deposit funds of any currency without limit. Note that although it's easy to deposit foreign currency checks and cash, hefty and seemingly illogical fees and commissions may be debited to your account and a delay of up to four weeks may occur before payment is completed. In most cases, you'll receive your *chéquier* (checkbook) in 2-3 weeks, and, if you request one, your *Carte Bleue* bank payment card. When you leave France, you might want to maintain your account in that after two years you'll qualify for a *compte résident*. This is easier than starting everything over should you decide to return.

## Checking Accounts

The personal check plays a vast role in daily French life. You will most certainly want to get yourself *un compte-chèque* (a checking account) and *carnet de chèques* (checkbook), in that paying by check is the most widely accepted and easiest form of handling your affairs in French. Everywhere from restaurants to gas stations, the personal check is readily accepted. You can even pay for your monthly Métro pass with a check. All stores accept checks. The post office accepts checks, too. *La Poste* also offers an efficient banking system including savings and checking accounts; you must have *résident* status, however, to take advantage of this. You will often, but not systematically, be asked to show some form of identification when you pay by check. The reason for the widespread acceptance of checks stems from the fact that checks in France are not negotiable or even cashable as they are in the US. Most checks in France are *barrés*, meaning they have two lines or bars pre-printed across the front of each check. This simply signifies that the check cannot be signed and reendorsed for payment to a third party. All checks thus must be deposited into the bank account of the person whose name appears on the face of the check. So, be wary of accepting a personal check from someone if you do not have a bank account yourself. You will not be able to go the the maker's bank and cash the check. It must be deposited. This means that all payments by check are officially recorded and thus are easily controlled by bank inspectors, accountants, and eventually the *fisc* (tax collectors). Most salaries in France are paid directly into the employee's bank account via *virement* (wire). Similarly, bank mortgages are deducted automatically from the recipient's account. A *relevé de compte* is the statement of account, whereas the R.I.B. is the *relevé d'identité bancaire* which gives all the codes of your account, bank, and branch. Most banks put one at the end of every checkbook. These are demanded of you when payment is to be wired directly into your account. This obviously limits the mobility of money in French society, but it also restricts seriously the degree of fraud and the frequency of bounced checks or bad checks (*chèque en bois*— wooden checks). It can be difficult to stop payment on a check (*faire opposition à un chèque*) and French law is unrelenting concerning writers of bad checks.

## Savings Accounts

*Un compte d'epargne sur livret* (savings account) can also be opened. Most banks will pay modest interest on funds left in savings accounts for extended periods. Your current balance will be noted in *le livret* (passbook) after each deposit or withdrawal. In France, many people also have a P.E.L. (*Plan d'Epargne Logement*), a government-subsidized savings account designed to accrue interest and credits toward the purchase of a house or apartment at low interest rates.

## Credit Cards

In France the *Carte Bleue* (CB) offered by each bank has truly become an institution in daily life. The French attraction for computerized systems has been married to this centralized form of payment. The CB (part of both the VISA and Mastercard/Eurocard network) is widely accepted. Although it exists in both direct debit and credit forms, it is not really a credit card; it's a payment card in that even the credit version debits cash withdrawals directly. Purchases and automatic cash withdrawals are debited from your checking account. You do not receive a monthly credit card statement and you cannot run up large bills. You do not have a credit line. Your use of the card is debited automatically. The idea of real credit, that great and abusive invention that permits people painlessly to live beyond their means, is still rather foreign in Europe. The main advantage of the *Carte Bleue* is its surprisingly wide acceptance. You can pay your tolls on the *autoroute* with your CB; you can pay all your supermarket purchases with your CB; you can even stick your CB into a ticket machine in selected Métro stations to buy your monthly *Carte Orange* or purchase a museum admission ticket in the lobby of the Louvre with your CB. And of course you can get cash (up to 1800 FF per week) at any bank's 24 hour automatic teller with your CB. Careful, though; these automatic tellers will only accept CB issued on French banks, so don't stick your Visa, Master Card, or American Express cards into one of them. It may retain the card and you'll have to return the next day with your passport to retrieve it.

All major credit card companies are represented in France. Here are phone numbers in case of lost or stolen cards:

**American Express**
tel: 47.77.70.00
Lost cards: 47.77.72.00

**Diners Club de France**
tel: 47.62.75.00
(Info and Lost Cards)

**(Master Card) Eurocard**
tel: 45.67.53.53
Lost cards: 45.67.84.84

**(Visa) *Carte Bleue***
tel: 42.25.51.51
Lost cards: 42.77.11.90 (Paris)
54.42.12.12 (provinces)

# Transferring Funds From Abroad

Having money telexed to your Paris bank account can be done quickly if the issuing bank is directly affiliated with the receiving bank so that the money does not have to go through intermediaries. If you plan to receive a regular transfer of funds over a period of time, and if the issuing bank is not directly affiliated with your bank in Paris, count on the transfer to take as long as four weeks. Therefore, it is a good idea to ask your home bank if it is affiliated with a French bank before you open an account.

## Getting Cash Fast

One of the most important questions you may someday have about banking is "How can I get money quickly from home?" Despite assurances made by many issuing banks in other countries, the majority of money orders and interbank checks—and all personal checks—must normally be cleared through the issuing bank before they can be credited to your account. This can take weeks. Other, quicker possibilites include:

**1)Wire**: the sender can wire money directly to a French franc account, specifying the branch name and the address of your bank—this normally takes 48 hours. Always note the *siège* (branch) number and *clé R.I.B.* (bank code).

**2)American Express**: if you have no account in France, wire transfer can be made through American Express.

**3)**Have a **bank check** drawn in French francs at your Paris bank's foreign branch and sent to you through the mail.

**4)Pray**.

# HEALTH

Although France has a highly impressive and widely democratic system of socialized medicine, this might not undo the feelings of loneliness and despair if you fall sick in a foreign country and are not sure where to turn for sympathy or help. This feeling is compounded, of course, if you are unsure about your language skills. For that reason, services in English have been included here. If you feel like braving the language barrier, you will find that almost any pharmacist is eager and willing to give you advice and to recommend remedies. He or she may go so far as to give you the number of a doctor around the corner. Pharmacists play an essential intermediary role between doctor and patient. And pharmacies are not cluttered with all the non-medical goods found in US drug stores. Medication comes with a two-part sticker on the packaging (*vignette*). One part is peeled off and stuck on the orange and white *feuille de soins* used for reimbursement from the *Sécurité Sociale*, the national health administration. Prescribed drugs are reimbursed up to 75%. Don't be surprised, however, that treatment varies from one country to another. You may find yourself using methods you had never even conceived of at home. For instance, the French are keen on the use of suppositories, for many different problems, including a cough. Pharmacists are even trained to know about the mushrooms you find in the woods and will offer free advice on the delicious and deadly.

A lot of misunderstanding about French medical practices is a matter of aesthetics and style. French doctors' *cabinets* (offices) are surprisingly unclinical in feel, and doctors, particularly specialists, appear more like professors than physicians. Doctors' offices in France are not teeming with paramedical practitioners, nor do doctors' offices maintain extensive medical records. For children medical records are maintained in a *carnet de santé* (health book) which accompanies the child throughout his/her early life. Very little lab work is done in doctors' offices, and the white-coat sterility associated with North American and Scandinavian medical facilities is virtually absent. One does not get the feeling of being dynamically treated; however, there is no denying that French medical procedures are wisely oriented towards prevention instead of intervention. Because the *Sécurité Sociale* reimburses most of the cost of visiting the doctor of the patient's choice, people don't wait until they're seriously ill to see a doctor.

Don't be overly judgmental if the waiting room is drab, there is no air-conditioning and the doctor inspects you in an alcove of his study. The French are not highly obsessed with the aesthetics of hygiene. A normal consultation should run about 100 FF. Many doctors don't require appointments and simply receive walk-ins during fixed hours.

## Hospitals

**The American Hospital** (*Hôpital Américain de Paris*): This is a private hospital which employs British, American, and French doctors on staff and is totally bilingual. It is much more expensive than the French hospitals. You can, however, pay in dollars. Those covered by Blue Cross-

Blue Shield have their hospital-ization covered, provided they fill out the appropriate paperwork first.

**Hôpital Américain de Paris**
63, Bd. Victor Hugo
92200 NEUILLY-SUR-SEINE Cedex
tel: 47.47.53.00
Outpatient Clinic (Emergency Unit)
Recorded information in English
tel. 46.34.59.65

Another hospital which employs English-speaking doctors:

**Herford British Hospital**
3, rue Barbès
92300 LEVALLOIS-PERRET
tel: 47.58.13.12

# Medical Practitioners

Practioners in France are either *conventionné* (abiding by the *Sécurité Sociale* system's schedule of fees) or *non conventionné* (charge higher rates). The following English-speaking doctors are recommended in The American University of Paris' medical bro-chure:

**General Practitioners**
Dr. Hubert Gamon
20, rue Cler
75007 PARIS
tel: 45.55.79.91

Dr. Stephan Wilson
44, av de Ségur
75015 PARIS
tel: 45.67.26.53

Dr. Donald Stangler
American Hospital
63, Bd Victor Hugo
92200 NEUILLY-SUR-SEINE
tel: 47.47.53.00

**Chiropractor**
Marc Tourneur, D.C.
44, rue Laborde
75008 PARIS
tel: 43.87.81.62

**Dentists**
Dr. Celine Bismuth
7, rue Bernard de Clairvaux
75003 PARIS
tel: 48.87.61.61

Dr. Gauthier
47, av Hoche
75008 PARIS
tel: 47.66.33.25

Dr. Chagari
22, rue Cler
75007 PARIS
tel: 47.03.40.10

**Dermatologists**
Dr. Marchal
40, av Bosquet
75007 PARIS
tel: 45.51.04.40

Dr. Metter
29, av Franklin Roosevelt
75008 PARIS
tel: 43.59.88.17

**Gynecologists**
Dr. Richet
109, rue de l'Université
75007 PARIS
tel: 45.51.82.32

Dr. Tatiane Oppenheim
17, Bd. du Temple
75003 PARIS
tel: 48.87.22.63

Dr. Sarrot
6, av Sully-Prudhomme
75007 PARIS
tel: 45.56.03.30

**Laboratories**
Laboratoire Trivin-Vercambre
14, rue Dupont des Loges
75007 PARIS
tel: 47.05.84.37

Laboratoire Lobar-Philippe (x-rays only)
199, rue de Grenelle
75007 PARIS
tel: 47.05.51.87

**Ophthalmologist**
Dr. Fitterer
9, av Bosquet
75007 PARIS
tel: 47.05.52.43

**Optician**
Walter's Paris
107, rue St. Dominique
75007 PARIS
tel: 45.51.70.08
(15% discount on frames, lens
& contacts for students)

**Psychiatrists/Psychologists**
Emmanual Ansart, M.D.
43, rue La Bruyère
75009 PARIS
tel: 48.78.04.60

Barbara Cox
115, rue du Théâtre
75015 PARIS
tel: 45.75.74.61

Mary Larounis
65, quai d'Orsay
75007 PARIS
tel: 45.50.26.49

Nancy Sadowsky
12, rue Marie Stuart
75002 PARIS
tel: 42.33.10.07

Joseph Shesko
4, rue Michel Chasles
74012 PARIS
tel: 43.47.19.72

**Sports Medicine**
Dr. François Manier
64, rue de Rennes
75006 PARIS
tel: 45.44.03.21

**Free A.I.D.S. Testing Clinics**
*Centre Anonyme et Gratuit
des Médecins du Monde*
1, rue du Jura
75013 PARIS
tel: 43.36.43.24

**Dispensaire**
35, rue de Ridder
75014 PARIS
tel: 45.43.83.78

**Hôpital La Pitié Salpétrière**
47, Bd de l'Hôpital
75013 PARIS
tel: 45.70.21.73

# Reproductive Health

A prescription is necessary for contraceptive devices and drugs. There is no age limit. Male contraceptive condoms *(préservatifs)* and female contraceptive sponges *(ovules, tampons)* are available without prescription only in pharmacies. Family planning centers provide information on contraception. Among others, *Le Planning Familial* has centers at 10, rue Vivienne 75002, Métro Bourse, 42.60.93.20, and at 94, Bd. Massena 75013, Métro Porte-de-Choisy, 45.84.28.25. Do-it-yourself pregnancy tests are available in pharmacies at a cost of about 60 FF. Ask for *G-Test*, *Elle-Test*, or *Predictor*. When positive, these tests can be believed absolutely. When negative, they should be repeated five to seven days later. Abortions are legal in France.

Free, anonymous courses of treatment for venereal diseases are offered by the *Ligue de Préservation Sociale*, 29, rue Falguière 75015, 43.20.63.74, Métro Falguière, from 14h00-16h30 and 17h00-19h00 Monday through Saturday; by the *Institut Prophylactique*, 36, rue d'Assas 75006, 42.22.32.06,

8h00-15h00 Monday through Friday and Saturday 8h30-12h00, Métro Saint-Placide; and by the *Institut Alfred Fournier*, 25, Bd. Saint-Jacques, 75014, 45.81.46.41, Métro Saint-Jacques.

# Other Health-Related Services

## Support Groups

**WICE** (Women's Institute for Continuing Education)
20, Bd. Montparnasse
75015 PARIS
tel: 45.66.75.50
Offers courses (in English) in Career & Personal Development, Arts & Humanities, Living in France, Women's Support Group. Open House each Tues.(11h00-16h00) & Friday (11h00-15h00) Métro Duroc or Falguière.

**Alcoholics Anonymous**
3, rue Fréderic Sauton
75005 PARIS
tel: 46.34.59.65

**Alcoholics Anonymous**
American Church
65, quai d'Orsay
75007 PARIS
tel. 47.20.17.92

**Alcoholics Anonymous**
American Cathedral
23, av George V
75008 PARIS
tel. 47.20.17.92

**American Aid Society of Paris**
Talleyrand Building
2, rue Saint-Florentin
75382 PARIS Cedex 08
tel: 42.96.12.02 ext. 2717
President: Mde. Dorothy LOBL
(helps U.S. citizens who encounter problems in France)

**American Women's Group in Paris**
49, rue Pierre Charron
75008 PARIS
tel: 43.59.17.61

**British & Commonwealth Women's Association**
7, rue Auguste Vacquerie
75016 PARIS
tel: 47.20.01.36

**Canada Welcome**
24, Bd. Port Royal
75005 PARIS
tel: 43.37.43.96

**Europ Assistance**
23-25, rue Chaptal
75445 PARIS Cedex
tel: 42.85.85.85

**International Counseling Service**
65, quai d'Orsay
75007 PARIS
tel: 45.50.26.49
Mon.-Sat: 9:30-1:00pm

**Parenting Plus**
(seminars in communication)
745, av du Général Leclerc
92100 BOULOGNE
tel: 46 21 64 29
Contact: Julie DAVIS

**Paris Therapy and Women's Center**
27, rue Daubenton
75005 PARIS
Mon.-Sat.: 9:30-6:30pm
tel: 47.07.74.14

**Weight Watchers France**
18, av. Parmentier
75011 PARIS
tel: 43.57.65.24
Director: F. MANTELIER

**AIDS Support Group**
American Church
tel. 45. 50.26.49.

For more information regarding English-speaking medical personnel, a good resource is *Health Care Resources in Paris,* a comprehensive guide in English. Contact WICE (Women's Institute for Continuing Education), tel. 45.66.75.50 to order a copy.

# Pharmacies

To match a prescription in France be sure to have the following information, since finding the equivalent may be difficult: an up-to-date prescription with the medication's trade name, manufacturer, chemical name, and dosage. If you don't speak French, you may have an easier time if you go to the English and American Pharmacy, since they are used to having to match prescriptions. The pharmacists are very helpful and speak English. In most pharmacies, for many prescription drugs, you will be asked to give your address.

**Anglo-American Pharmacy**
**Pharmacie Swann**
6, rue de Castiglione
75001 PARIS
tel: 42.60.72.96

**British and American Pharmacy**
1, rue Auber
75009 PARIS
tel: 47.42.49.40
**Pharmacie des Champs**
(24-hour pharmacy)
84, av des Champs-Elysées
(passage des Champs)
75008 PARIS
tel. 45.62.02.41

At night and on Sundays you can call the local *commissariat de police* for the address of the nearest open pharmacy and that of a doctor on duty. You can also check the door of a closed pharmacy for the address of the nearest open one.

---

## Useful Words at the Pharmacy

| | |
|---|---|
| *indications* | ailments treated by the product |
| *voie orale* | by mouth |
| *gelules* | capsules |
| *mode d'emploi* | directions for use |
| *posologie* | dosage |
| *gouttes* | drops |
| *effets secondaires* | eventual side effects |
| *sirop* | liquid or syrup |
| *poudre* | powder |
| *ampoules* | small glass containers |
| *sachets* | small packets of soluble powder |
| *cuillère à soupe* | tablespoon |
| *comprimés* or *pillules* | tablets or pills |
| *cuillère à café* | teaspoon |
| *suppositoires* | suppositories |
| *contre-indications* | warnings (when medicine should not be used) |
| | |
| *Ne pas dépasser la dose préscrite* | Do not exceed prescribed dosage. |
| *mal des transports* | motion sickness |
| *le rhume* | cold |
| *la toux* | cough |
| *la diarrhée* | diarrhea |
| *les maux d'oreilles* | earache |
| *mal de tête, migraine* | headache |
| *l'indigestion* | indigestion |

# Natural Medicine

The French are great believers in traditional medicines. *Homéopathie* (homeopathic medicine) uses only herbs and other natural products in very carefully compounded mixtures whose composition is fixed by law. In many *cafés*, *infusions* (herbal teas) are served, largely for complaints such as nervousness, weakness, etc. Two of the calming herb teas available in most *cafés* are *tilleul* and *fleur d'oranger*. There are also a number of fortifiants (tonics, mild stimulants) available in pharmacies, as well as preparations for just about any common ailment. Pharmacies specializing in homeopathic medicine will be clearly marked and can be found throughout the city.

# Medical Emergencies

**Ambulances Municipales**: tel: 47.05.44.87 Rapid transport to the closest hospital emergency room.
**SAMU** ambulances: tel: 45.67.50.50 Life-threatening situations; detailed information will be required by phone.
**Ambulances de l'Assistance Publique**: tel: 43.78.26.26 Handles transportation from one hospital to another.
**Burns** (severe): tel: 42.34.12.12 Hôpital Cochin, 27, rue St. Jacques, 75005.
**SOS Médecins**: tel: 47.07.77.77 24-hour emergency medical housecalls—150 FF before 19h00, 275 FF after 19h00.
**SOS Dentistes**: tel.43.37.51.00 24-hour emergency dental help. Similar prices.
*Association des Urgences Médicales de Paris*: tel: 48.28.40.09 Sends a doctor in an emergency.
**Police Secours**: tel: 17.
*Pompiers* **(Fire)**: tel: 18.
**Anti-Poison Center**: tel: 40.37.04.04 24-hour service.
**Poison Control**: tel: 42.05.63.29.
**SOS Rape**: tel: 42.34.82.34.
**SOS Help**: In English, tel: 47.23.80.80. Crisis hotline every night from 15h-23h.
**SOS Help**: In French, tel: 46.08.52.77.

**SOS Drug Center**: tel. 45.81.11.20
**SOS Vétérinaire**: tel: 48.32.93.30.

# Health Insurance

Before coming to France, you should find out whether or not you are insured overseas and in what instances. Certain firms will expect you to pay your bills in France and then reimburse you after you send them the receipt (*feuille de soins*). It may take several weeks for the reimbursement to come through.

French law requires that students have complete medical coverage during their stay in France. Copies of official documents attesting to this fact are required when you request a student visa from the French Consulate in your home country and by the *Préfecture de Police* when you apply for your *carte de séjour*. The law requires that the medical plan provide for the following coverage: hospitalization in Europe, short and long-term, outpatient treatment, visits to the doctor, dentist and laboratory expenses, pharmaceuticals, medical repatriation, (transportation back to country of residence), medical recommendation. Most national health plans in Europe meet these requirements. Many private plans in the United States and Canada do not. However, if you have substantial coverage by your health plan in North America (inquire for the UK and the rest of Europe) and can get a clause to include a provision for medical repatriation, you may meet the necessary coverage requirements. Several American university programs do provide a special student health insurance plan for students who require it. Students and non-students who are not covered by an employer but who legally reside in France can also take advantage of the French *Sécurité Sociale* (referred to in conversation as the *Sécu*) by paying the annual fee. Inquire at the office of the *Sécurité Sociale* in your *arrondissement* for information.

**Insurance Exemptions for Students**: Those who are covered by European National Health plans (e.g. French Social Security or British National Health), International Organizations, or a particularly extensive private plan in North America, may apply for an exemption. You must send a copy of your insurance policy to the Administration or Bursar or your program when paying the tuition fee to determine if your coverage meets exemption requirements. Please note that you will need official copies of your insurance policy translated into French to apply for your visa and your *carte de séjour*. In most cases, exemptions must be approved prior to registration or you may be enrolled in your program's plan automatically.

# SAFETY & SECURITY

Safety is always relative to what you're used to. Although Paris is a big city and a degree of prudence and common sense should always be applied, it is fair to say that Paris streets, day or night, are safe. In fact, there's little sense in even comparing the safety of Paris to that of any city in the United States. Visitors often ask "how safe is Paris?" Well, let's put it this way, you could walk down by the Seine in the center of Paris at 2h with 500 FF notes pinned to your shirt and not be accosted. A bigger problem is learning how to leave at home the defensiveness that you were most likely, and for sound reasons, brought up to maintain. For all practical purposes, you should not be frightened to take the Métro anytime during its operating hours—5h45-1h.

It's true that certain *quartiers* can be a bit intimidating or less reassuring but even here, danger is minimal. Women, on occasion and in certain neighborhoods, may feel the harrassment of being followed or catcalled by interested men. As unpleasant as this may be, these encounters are in almost all cases harmless. Just ignore such advances and carry on. Of course, it's never a bad idea, especially when going out at night into areas you're not familiar with, to have a friend or friends along. If you feel harassed or simply bothered by someone in the street or in a *café* or club it's best to ignore them at first. If they persist, a clever retort works better than an insult. Try one of these: "*J'attends mon mari*," "*J'attends ma femme*" or "*Est-ce que je t'ai donné la permission de me parler?*" Make sure you have these mastered before you attempt them, however. Common sense is the key, but don't forget that Paris just isn't like New York. You need not be frightened. *Au contraire*, Paris is a city that has a relatively late social life and needs to be negotiated on foot.

Paris is dense; the space between people is often less than in cities in other countries. The social coding between individuals is different. The rules are not always the same. The Body Language is as distinct as the verbal language. For example, some women have complained that French men in clubs or discotheques become aggressive if they don't get their way after their graciously offered drinks have been accepted. As a rule, you should remember that Americans are more open, verbal, and casual than the French in initial social contacts. This difference can lead to misunderstandings which, although not usually unsafe, can be uncomfortable.

Areas of town that are known to be a bit less comforting to foreign students, especially women, include the area between Place de Clichy and Barbès-Rochechouart which delineates the Pigalle district. This area is filled with a lot of porno shops and single men. Being one of the poorer areas of Paris, there are a lot of immigrants, mostly Algerian, Moroccan and African. Although crime is higher here than in the chic parts of central Paris, immigrants usually get an unfair reputation. There is nothing to be frightened about but it's always good to have an idea about where you're going.

Street people, called *clochards*, are for the most part harmless, despite their frequent drunkenness, desperate look, and sometimes angry-sounding comments. Some of the side streets near the Gare Montparnasse and the desolate backstreets of the 14th *arrondissement* are known to be frequented by drug dealers. The drug situation in Paris is a fraction of what it is in North American cities. Far more dangerous than anywhere in Paris are some of the stark concrete HLM projects in the northern suburbs. There would be little reason for you to head out that way. Also try to avoid the larger Métro stations such as Châtelet/Les Halles late at night, as they can be a refuge for late-night partiers of the slightly dubious type and generally a hang-out for unsavory characters. The same goes for the area around Les Halles/Beaubourg—the Rue St. Denis, a notorious sex shop/prostitution street, not far away. But, in any case, compared to any city in the US, Paris' worst is tame.

## Crime Statistics

In 1985 there were 22,358 homicides in the United States, which translates to 8.3 per 100,000 citizens. France only has 2,413 annual homicides, or 4.0 per 100,000 citizens. In the greater Paris area, 306 homicides were committed in 1985, that is, less than five per 100,000 and almost one fifth the rate of Washington, D.C. There are 100,000 homeless and 19,000 *clochards* (street people) in France.

Crime that does exist is primarily directed to property. House or apartment theft is called *cambriolage*. A great many apartment dwellers and home owners have steel enforced doors called *portes blindées*. You won't see grilled-over windows like you do in New York or nineteen locks per door, but you will see these heavy doors and peek holes. In many apartment buildings, there is a *concierge* who adds to the safety. Most break-ins happen in France during the month of August when a large percentage of Parisians leave for holidays. Be somewhat dubious about individuals who knock on your door offering services and wanting to check the inside of your apartment. This is an old trick for determining which apartments are worth hitting. Thieves have an entire hieroglyphic language of codes which they leave for each other in chalk by the door or outside the apartment building.

## Pickpockets

Like in any big city, incidents occur. There is some pickpocketing in the flea markets, in the Métro, and on buses. If you're careful with your possessions you will have no problems. Muggings are not very common, but do occur. Ironically, they can seem to occur more frequently at night in the quiet, wealthy and residential parts of the 16e or 17e rather than the seedier, densely populated areas near Pigalle!

There are bands of immigrant children, falsely labelled *gitans* or gypsies, that hang out between Place de la Concorde and the Louvre. Their M.O. is to swarm around a confused tourist and pick him clean like the sharks and the great fish in Hemingway's *Old Man and the Sea*. This has not been as acute as in the past, however, be careful with your wallet, passport, camera, and jewelry, especially in crowds in the summer. You could be targeted on the street, Métro or bus. To minimize problems, try to always look as if you know where you're going, even if you don't. Professional thieves can quickly spot foreign tourists who look like fair game. Otherwise, don't worry about this. But keep your passport and money well concealed.

## Police, Law & Authority

Every person in France by law has a legal status and an identity card. Americans often see the question of "papers" as a psychological hurdle. The United States does not have a National Identity Card, like most countries in the world. Any policeman has the right to demand to see your papers at any time. No reason or provocation is required. So, it's advisable to carry your Passport or *Carte de Séjour* with you at all times. If you're *contrôlé* (stopped) and you don't have identification or valid papers, say you're a tourist. Don't speak French; smile and be submissive. Show the *agent* (officer, *le flic* in slang) that you respect his power, and in most cases you'll get a banal warning and be sent on your way with a polite salute.

The relationship that citizens have to authority is different in all countries. In France, the police control the public; in the US one tends to feel that the police work for the public. In France, the police are employees either of the Ministry of the Interior or the Ministry of Defense, thus the federal government. The police represent the State. In the US, aside from the FBI, the police work for the municipality; they attempt to enforce the law but they are not the law itself. A large psychological difference.

If you do get ripped off, go to the nearest Police Station and fill out a report *(déclaration de vol)*. You may want to check the city's lost and found at 36, rue des Morrillons, 75015, tel: 45.31.14.80 in that papers are often turned in. (For lost credit cards or traveler's checks, see Banking).

There are several types of police

in France. Basically, the *agent de police*, the local officer, is an employee of the Ministry of Interior. The *gendarmes*, the ones you see on the highways out of town and in the small towns, are connected to the Ministry of Defense. Thus, all police are functionaries of the State. The police who ride around in grey-green armoured vans and carry plexiglas shields are the CRS *(Compagnies Républicaines de Sécurité),* the National Security Police. They are called in to enforce order and maintain security in situations of demonstrations, strikes, riots, protests, or upheaval. France experiences numerous national strikes and scores of organized *manifestations* (*manifs*) (demonstrations) each year. Be prepared to be inconvenienced. *En masse,* these guys are scary looking. In general, you'll find the police to be polite, formal, and mildly helpful. Not more.

You'll see systematic control points in the streets for drivers. Although you may not be used to this, and may even be repulsed by the idea, don't be alarmed.

Remember, in France you're guilty until proven innocent, in keeping with the Napoleonic Code, and this concept is applicable in numerous sectors of French life. Aside from the obvious cases of legal accusation, everyday inter-actions with individuals and administrators are laced with an initial *méfiance* (mistrust). When dealing, for example, with the French tax authorities, even if you are certain that there has been an error, you're obliged to pay first. Justice will follow in due course.

## A Word on Terrorism

Many visitors have been highly concerned over the past few years with the risks and fears of terrorist activities in Europe. Although there was a short period in Paris when an atmosphere of suspicion and caution permeated the air, the actual risk of being subjected to any danger of this sort is highly remote and should not figure in your thinking about life in Paris. Despite the reality that a shopping complex on the Champs-Elysées and a popular working-class department store, Tati, near Montparnasse had been targeted, the international media keyed-in on these incidents and phobia grew disproportionately in the imaginations of individuals overseas. Even Sylvester Stallone refused to come to the Cannes Film Festival in 1986. The hesitations were real, the dangers were exaggerated. In any case, the climate has certainly stabilized considerably since that time. Leave your fears at home! It's a shame to begin with a psychological block.

# CAFÉS

*Cafés* are places where people go
to be among friends and acquain-
tances. They are meeting places,
solariums (the French are notorious
sun-worshipers) or shelters from bad
weather; places to sit, talk, dream,
make friends, make out, or eat. They
are also handy for their telephones
and *toilettes*. *Café-* and bar-sitting are
an integral part of daily French life.
Knowing a little about how *cafés*

function will save you from a lot of surprises. First of all, the large, well-
situated *cafés* on the Champs-Elysées, on the Boulevard Saint Germain in
Saint Germain-des-Près, at Montparnasse, along all the major boulevards,
and in the Latin Quarter are expensive. But remember, you are not paying
for your cup of coffee or glass of beer as much as for your right to sit in a
pretty spot for as long as you like and talk, read, watch, or daydream. If
you're spending 12 FF for an *express* or 20 FF for a *demi* (half a pint of
draught beer), think of it as rent for the time and space. You should know
that the prices of drinks in *cafés* depend on whether you're standing at
the *zinc* (counter bar) or sitting, and then, of course, where you're sitting.
Drinks are less expensive if you are served at the bar. The outside terrace
is always the most expensive. And then don't forget that the price of
drinks goes up after 20h. Also, you can order some drinks at the bar
which you cannot order sitting down. A glass of draught lemon soda
(*limonade*), the cheapest drink available and very refreshing on warm
days, can only be ordered when you're standing at the bar. Otherwise
you get the more expensive and overly sweetened bottled lemon soda.
No matter where you're sitting or when, the tip is always included.
Although not required or even really expected, it is customary to leave
the copper-colored coins in your change as a little extra tip. At the
counter, you'll be presented with a little plastic dish for payment, which is
then flipped over to signify that the barman has collected from you. At
the tables, the *serveur* leaves a slip of paper from the cash register
indicating what you owe. Usually, you pay at the end of your stay, but
sometimes the *serveur* (not to be called *garçon*, even though old
guidebooks will still indicate so) will come around to collect as he goes
off duty. When you've paid he'll crumple or rip slightly the paper
indicating that you've paid. The verb to pay is *regler*.

*Cafés* are open very early for coffee and *croissants*. One of the more
delightful and simple practices is to ask for a *tartine*—a buttered stick of
*baguette*—to dunk in your coffee. *Très parisien*.

The most common beverage in a *café* is obviously a *café* (coffee), and
the nuances need enumeration and explanation: When you just want to
sit and talk, read, write or pass away the time and you don't want to
spend much, order *un café*.

*café noir, un café* (*express*)—classic strong coffee served in
    a tiny cup
*café noir double*—twice the dose of an *express*
*café au lait*—*express* with steamed milk
*petit crème*—*express* with steamed cream
*grand crème*—larger version of the *petit crème*
*café allongé*—*express* with extra hot water, also called *un
    café long* or un *café américain*
*cafe serré*—extra strong *express* with half the normal amount
    of water
Note: Very weak coffee is humorously labelled *jus de chaussettes* (sock juice).

In the daily cycle of most *cafés*, there are three periods of peak activity: at breakfast time (before 9h30); at lunch (between 12h00 and 14h00); and before dinner at the *heure de l'apéritif* (*apéro*) (aperitif hour) from about 17h30 to 19h30. It is not unusual to see two different sets of regulars at different times of day, one at breakfast and lunch and the other at the *apéritif* hour. Between the peak periods customers come for a rest from their work, to meet other people, or simply to sit alone with their thoughts.

The choice of beverages in a Parisian *café* is superb. The French make popular drinks by mixing syrups with either Vittel water or milk. Thus, you can order a *Vittel menthe* (or *menthe à l'eau*) or *Vittel grenadine*, or a *lait fraise* or *lait grenadine*. As for beer, you can order *un demi* (8 ounces), *un sérieux* (pint), or *un formidable* (liter). Or a *panaché* (a mixture of draught beer and draught lemon soda), a popular drink in the summer and one that foreigners acquire a taste for after four or five tries. Other drinks include:

| | |
|---|---|
| *un thé citron* | tea with lemon |
| *un thé nature* | plain tea |
| *un thé au lait* | tea with milk |
| *un chocolat froid* | chocolate milk |
| *un chocolat chaud* | hot chocolate |
| *un citron pressé* | fresh-squeezed lemon juice (served with water and sugar) |
| *une orange pressée* | fresh orange juice (served with water and sugar) |
| *un jus de fruits* | fruit juice |

Many *cafés* will specialize in a certain brand of beer on tap (*en pression*), usually marked clearly on the *café*'s awning.

| | |
|---|---|
| *un demi* | a quarter liter of draft beer |
| *un demi Munich* | a quarter liter of German beer |
| *une bière* | beer in a bottle |

**Wine**: You should not judge French wine by what is served in most *cafés* other than the *nouveau Beaujolais* when it comes out each fall. Cheap *café* wine is seldom very good. *Cafés* normally serve wines in two sizes of glass, *un ballon* (large) and *un petit* (small). Other popular wine drinks include:

| | |
|---|---|
| *un blanc sec* | dry white wine |
| *un kir* | white wine and cassis |
| *un kir clair* | white wine with a touch of cassis |

There are a variety of *apéritifs* served in *cafés*, usually served over ice with a twist of lemon. These drinks are mixed with water and sometimes *sirop de menthe (un perroquet)*. A martini in France is not the dry thing with the olive; it's a brand of vermouth ordered by itself as an *apéritif*. Ice is provided only with certain cocktails, whisky, Pernod, Pastis, or Ricard, that glorious Mediterranean anise *apéritif* that pours out rich and yellow and goes cloudy when mixed with water. Great on a hot afternoon on a *café* terrace with Lawrence Durrell's *Justine* in hand. If you do prefer bottled water, there's Perrier or Badoit on the sparkling side *(avec les boules)*, and Vittel and Vichy on the flat side *(plat)*. The only mixed drink served correctly in most *cafés* seems to be a *gin-tonique*. Other drinks include:

| | |
|---|---|
| *un grog* | hot rum with lemon, water, sugar |
| *un cognac* | brandy |
| *un calvados* | apple brandy from Normandy |
| *une poire William* | pear brandy |

**A word on *café-restaurants***: if the tables are set with cloths, they are reserved for those wishing to dine and should not be taken if you only plan to have a drink.

## Café Services

Toilets and telephones are always found in *cafés*—usually downstairs in the *sous-sol* or somewhere at the back. If you want to use the restroom of a *café* without consuming anything, you have the law on your side. But getting away with it can sometimes be another matter. Be somewhat discreet. In chic *cafés* there might be a toilet attendant who has a plate out for a franc tip. Some toilets require a franc coin, but most don't. Although it is becoming rarer, the old Turkish toilet (hole in the porcelain floor with spots for your feet) is still common. They are a bit hard to get used to, but a highly Parisian experience. Just get ready to jump out of the way before you pull the flusher if you want to avoid soaking your feet. Toilet paper is usually available, but not always, and very often a stiff, crinkly kind that is not very comfortable nor practical. The telephones in *cafés* usually take one franc coins for local calls, but some *cafés*, mostly the smaller or older ones, still have booths with regular phones and the barman has to activate the line for you. You have to ask for a line out for each call *(Est-ce que je peux avoir une ligne, s'il vous plaît?)*. You pay afterwards at the bar, where there is a counter, usually one franc per unit. Occasionally, you'll still find the old phones that require a *jeton* (token) from the bar. These are becoming rare and are a bit quirky to use.

## Le Café-Tabac

*Le tabac* plays a curious but dynamic role in daily French life. *Le tabac,* clearly marked with a red elongated diamond shaped sign hanging in the street, has a monopoly from the State to sell cigarettes, cigars, and tobacco. You cannot buy cigarettes anywhere else in France. In exchange for this privilege, the *tabac*, which is usually also a *café*, performs certain services at face value, such as selling stamps. If you need some stamps for letters or cards, you can easily buy them from the cashier in a *tabac*. Don't expect total cooperation, however, if you want postal rates for the Ivory Coast. That's not their job. You will always find a mail box outside every *tabac* (always yellow and usually divided into two parts— Paris and its suburban codes 75, 77, 78, 91, 92, 93, 94 and the rest of the world). A *carnet* of stamps is a unit of ten basic letter stamps for France (currently 2.30 FF) (often sold in little booklets). Here are what French letter stamps look like:

Single envelopes and writing paper can also be purchased in a *tabac*. This is handy when you have to mail something off in a hurry. You have envelope, stamp, and mailbox at hand—but you have to know postal rates yourself.

*Le tabac* also handles in many cases off-track betting called PMU.

And *le tabac* sells national Lottery tickets (LOTO).

*Le tabac* sells *timbres fiscaux*. This is important in that if you happen to get a parking ticket, you pay for it by purchasing a *timbre fiscal* (State Stamp Tax) and pasting one portion to the return portion of the ticket and keeping the other half as your proof of payment. Similarly, you often need a *timbre fiscal* when you renew your *Carte de Séjour* and other official documents. *Le tabac* sells these, although they are frequently out of precisely the denomination you need and you will have to walk until you find a better-stocked *tabac*.

If you own a car, you'll soon find out that your annual car registration tax is paid in any *tabac* in the *département* in which you live. You'll receive a *vignette* sticker for your windshield.

## A Selection of *Cafés,* Bars, Bistros, Brasseries

The following establishments have been listed here for their original style and glorious tradition. Be prepared to pay a premium, though, for the reputation. These places should become part of your working knowledge of Paris, but they probably won't become daily hang-outs. Otherwise, you'll end up watching tourists watch other tourists. But it is undeniably pleasant just to sit on the terrace and enjoy the moment. Bring out-of-town visitors or your parents for a look at the grand style they associate with Paris. Some of the best known, celebrated *cafés*, bistros and brasseries in the great Parisian tradition include the following. For a more complete list of *cafés* with illustrious literary lore see Noël Riley Fitch's little book: *Literary Cafés of Paris*.

**La Coupole** 102, Bd. Montparnasse, 75014 PARIS, 43.20.14.20
**Le Sélect** 99, Bd. Montparnasse, 75006 PARIS, 42.22.65.27
**Le Dôme** 108, Bd. Montparnasse, 75014 PARIS, 43.35.25.81
**La Closerie des Lilas** 168, Bd. Montparnasse, 75006 PARIS, 43.21.95.37
**Les Deux Magots** 6, Pl. St. Germain-des-Près, 75006 PARIS, 45.48.55.25
**Café de Flore** 172, Bd. St. Germain, 75006 PARIS, 45.48.55.26
**Le Balzar** 49, rue des Ecoles, 75005 PARIS, 43.54.13.67

# Wine Bars, Late-Night *Cafés*, & Special Places

Here is a list of great little finds that can make daily life in Paris truly delightful, although the act of finding your own place will be a matter of personal discovery:

### Au Petit Fer à Cheval
30, rue Vieille-du-Temple
75004 PARIS
A tiny bar with a horseshoe *(fer à cheval)* shaped bar—there are very few of these remaining.

### La Tartine
24, rue de Rivoli
75004 PARIS
One of the oldest, most reasonably priced, and best wine bars in Paris. Also serves great *Pain Poilâne* sandwiches. The decoration is Deco 20's and seventy years of cigarette smoke have mellowed the interior.

### La Palette
43, rue de Seine
75006 PARIS
The room behind the bar has some delightful tile caricatures of Parisians in the Twenties. A favorite meeting place for artists and gallery people.

### Le Cochon à l'Oreille
15, rue Montmartre
75001 PARIS
The walls of this *café* are covered with painted tiles showing the old "*Les Halles*" market halls. Early in the morning you can share breakfast (or a last drink if you've been out all night) with the butchers from rue Montmartre.

### Le Clown Bar
114, rue Amelot
75011 PARIS
Next to the Cirque d'Hiver, this tiny *café* has its original painted ceiling depicting clowns and circus entertainers.

### Brasserie Lipp
151, Bd. Saint-Germain
75006 PARIS
Reservations must be made in person. Favorite Friday night spot of literary media star Bernard Pivot and a host of well-known entertainers and politicians. There are a few tables inside to the left where you can order a drink without eating (the enclosed terrace is stuffy and boring). *Fin-de-siècle* decorations. The length of the waiters' aprons denotes seniority.

### Brasserie de l'Ile St. Louis
55, quai Bourbon
75004 PARIS
Stand at the bar and try one of the white Alsatian wines whilst listening to the street musicians on the Pont St. Louis. There is a beautiful old coffee machine at the bar.

### Le Petit Gavroche
15, rue Sainte-Croix-de-la-Bretonnerie
75004 PARIS
On the corner of the bar of this café/restaurant is one of the few remaining examples of the water-holders used in the ritual of absinthe drinking (sale was prohibited in 1915). Water was dripped onto a sugar cube and into the absinthe.

### Le Train Bleu
Gare de Lyon
20, Blvd Diderot
75012 PARIS
Sweep up the curved staircase from the inside of the station and through the revolving door into one of the most astonishing *fin-de-siècle* interiors in Paris. To the left is the bar with its soft leather sofas and an atmosphere of luxury and calm. While most of the travelers below sit at orange plastic chairs drinking over-priced *demis,* you can be sipping a Pimms, wearing a linen suit and sporting a panama hat, dreaming of taking the Blue Train to the Mediterranean. The restaurant has maintained its elegance amidst sprawling frescos; but the prices are high and the cuisine has slipped.

### Le Gutenberg
29, rue Coquillière
75001 PARIS
One of the prettiest *cafés* in Paris dating from 1913—original lights and mirrors. Try a *café-calva* (coffee and calvados) .

### Twickingham
70, rue des Saints Pères
75007 PARIS
The young French intellectual *(intello)* watering hole.

### Le Balto
rue Mazarine
75006 PARIS
A local *bar-tabac* near the Académie des Beaux Arts. Once a week the "Fanfare des Beaux-Arts" (brass band of the Beaux Arts) practices here.

### Au General Lafayette
52, rue La Fayette
75009 PARIS
Popular French beer bar trying to look like an English pub. Great selection of beers—greater selection of beer mats, mugs, memorabilia and old Guinness posters.

## Good & Sleazy

### Académie du Billard
84, rue de Clichy
75009 PARIS
A huge 19th century billiard hall with a small bar where you can watch the intensity of Frenchmen at play.

### Polly Maggoo
11, rue St. Jacques
75005 PARIS
Revoltingly sleazy but can you leave Paris without saying you've been there?

### Chez George
rue des Canettes
75006 PARIS
Has to be experienced at least once.

### Café Noir
65, rue Montmartre
75002 PARIS
Like a bad 50's or 60's French movie.

### Le Baragouin
17, rue Tiquetonne
75002 PARIS
An enormous late-night bar packed with French "rockers." If you can push your way to the back you'll find some serious dart-playing going on.

# EATING

Eating in France is a ritual and a religion. No city in the world has a greater density of eating establishments than Paris. Nothing of importance happens in France without food, somehow, being included. Amidst the French adoration of quality-filled form exists another important but unwritten rule: anything you do at the table that enhances your enjoyment of a meal is permissible.

For advice and information on everything food-related in Paris, Patricia Wells' *The Food Lover's Guide to Paris* is an excellent resource. It has information on shopping for food, restaurants and *cafés*, as well as comprehensive restaurant recommendations, including hours of operation, restaurants open on weekends, restaurants open after 23h, restaurants open in August, and restaurants with sidewalk tables or outdoor terraces, as well as cross-listings by price, regional specialties, and location. Her book is a must for frequent restaurant-goers and food lovers.

## Restaurants

There is no reason for not eating well in Paris. However, learning how to eat very well, with good value, maximum *ambiance* (atmosphere) and exciting variety is an art. Restaurants are run by a *patron* or *patronne* who on the whole regards his/her position more as one of host than business person. As in all human interactions in France, a smile and a polite *bonsoir monsieur/madame*, lots of *s'il vous plaît* and *merci bien* during service as well as an *au revoir monsieur/ madame, merci* upon leaving will serve you well in getting friendly service and recognition when you return. The quick meal is not really understood so don't get too impatient if service is too slow for you to catch your 21h30 movie. Next time, eat earlier or see a late film. It's hard to rush service in Parisian restaurants. And waitresses and waiters don't work for tips. 15% is always included. *Service compris* means that 15% is built into the prices. *Service non compris* means the 15% will be automatically added to the bill. Don't tip on top of the tip, other than a few coins you leave in the dish as a token of your pleasure.

First, a word about the strictness of eating hours. As of about 11h30 or noon most restaurants have their tables set for the onrush of lunchers. In Paris, 13h is the start of the lunch rush hour. You must be seated for lunch no later than 14h if you want to eat anything greater than a sandwich or a *salade composée* (mixed salad), 14h30 at the extreme if you're lucky. In the provinces, lunch is served between 12h30-13h. At 14h you could beg and plead and offer your first born child and still be refused a hot meal. Between 15h-18h it's pretty much impossible to have a sit-down meal. An early dinner would be at 19h; a normal time to dine would be between 20h-21h. But later than 21h30 is getting dangerous again. At 23h it's too late, except in pizzerias, *couscousseries,* some brasseries and bistros, and some American style restaurants in Paris. There are exceptions, of course, as noted in Patricia Wells' book.

The typical French meal—from simple to elaborate—is graceful and balanced: an opening course, a main dish, cheese, a dessert, and coffee. And of course, wine. Most people ask for a pitcher of tap water *(une carafe d'eau, s.v.p.)* with their meal. This is highly expected. No real need to order a bottle of mineral water; Paris city water is perfectly fine. Don't expect ice cubes though—very little ice is consumed in France. It's hard, if not impossible, to purchase cubes by the bag. The French are not in the habit of drinking their beverages at extreme temperatures. When something is very cold or very hot, the French will tell you, the flavor is less prominent. And flavor is more important, *n'est-ce pas?* They're right. Flavor and quality come before superficial exterior appearances. French people are often disappointed by American supermarket fruits and vegetables; the huge, colorful, waxed objects are visually pleasing but the intensity of flavor is often *fade* (bland). So, to get back to the point, don't expect ice with your water. Paris' culinary diversity and the keen attention Parisians give to food should contribute to the richness of your experience. There are about 30 guidebooks on Paris in which eating establishments are featured. Here are a few operating principles when selecting a restaurant, followed by a few of *Paris Inside Out's* favorites.

—In general, don't plan on eating in a large *café* on a major boulevard. You'll pay a lot of money for quickly prepared, average food and rapid, not particularly careful service.

—Distinguish yourself from the unknowing tourist. Running shoes, maps, cameras, and loud voices are give-aways. If you're caught between hours and you're famished, use the *café* for a quick *croque-monsieur* or a hardboiled egg with salt (less than four francs at the counter).

—Read the menu posted outside before entering. It's uncool in Paris to be seated and then change your mind.

—Be prepared in advance to be squeezed into tight tables and booths. Paris restaurants can be densely packed, but privacy is respected.

—*Steak tartare* is raw, but delicious. *Carpaccio,* thinly sliced, cured beef, is also raw.

—If the food (or service) is absolutely horrible, don't eat it—and leave.

—Avoid the Champs-Elysées area unless someone else is paying. And even then suggest somewhere else.

## Le Menu

The lunch or dinner composed daily by the owner or chef of a restaurant is called *le menu* (don't get confused between the words *menu* and *carte;* the French *carte* is the English menu, and menu is the English complete and prescribed meal). In simple restaurants there is often just one *menu;* otherwise there may be two or three packages to chose from, each a bit more complex or complete and expensive than the former. You can still find little restaurants with *menus* under 50 FF but these are getting rare. Some couscous restaurants or Chinese or Vietnamese restaurants have *menus* at 35 FF. These are getting rarer and are always in the less chichi neighborhoods, but a number still linger in the Latin Quarter.

The hot dish of the day is called *le plat du jour* and may very well consist of roast veal and a heap of braised brussel sprouts, or a thin steak and some French fries, or salted pork with lentils.

In a restaurant, if you try to order something *à la carte* that breaks the rhythm or balance of the meal, you may find that the agreeableness of the service is reduced. This will be true if you try to order two appetizers (called *entrées,* because they are your entry into the meal)—or want to share a dessert or compose anything else that is original, personal or outside of the way that things are usually done. So beware.

When ordering red meat, remember that the French *cuisson* (cooking degrees)—*saignant* (rare), *à point,* (medium rare) and *bien cuit* (medium well)—tend to run rarer than you're used to. The French medium is the American medium-rare on the rare side. So either compensate accordingly or let the chips fly and you may find that you've been really eating meat overcooked for years. In some restaurants frequented by tourists, waiters exasperated at sent-back steaks automatically compensate for Anglo-Saxon preferences. If there truly is a problem with your food, don't eat it. If you eat some of it, it may be difficult to get the waiter not to charge you. The art of public relations has not really made it yet into the average French eatery. A waiter or maitre'd may end up arguing with you that your *magret de canard* is fine when you contend that it's inedible. Stay cool and polite, but hold your ground and don't eat half before complaining. Many small restaurants do have ketchup, but they're certainly not obliged to. The French use mustard in a rather expansive way. And the French mustard is so flavorful you should try a dab or two if you're not in the habit. Note: the cheaper Dijon mustard that comes in jars that can be used as glasses when the mustard has been finished, tends to be wickedly strong.

## Good Value

### Chartier
7, rue du Faubourg Montmartre
75009 PARIS
tel: 47.70.86.29
This is a late 19th century gem that, despite its lively tourist crowd, has preserved its authenticity. Extremely casual, inexpensive, and lively. You're often seated with strangers, share baskets of bread, and conversation. Large menu of typical, everyday French cuisine. Waiters are lively. The bill is

tallied up on the paper tablecloths. Notice the little wooden drawers in the walls; these were for the linen napkins of the "regular" customers. Get there before 21h. Crowded but worth it. Dinner for two–100 FF with wine.

### Le Drouot
13, rue Richelieu
75002 PARIS
tel: 42.96.68.23.
Owned by same people as Chartier. Same concept although a bit less picturesque—but also fewer tourists. Good idea for lunch.

### Le Commerce
51, rue du Commerce
75015 PARIS
tel: 45.75.03.27.
Another restaurant in the Chartier family. Open every day.

### Le Polidor
41, rue Monsieur le Prince
75006 PARIS
tel: 43.26.95.34.
(very reasonable prices, *cuisine traditionnelle*, *"vieux Paris"* ambiance)

### Le Petit St. Benoît
4, rue St Benoît
75006 PARIS
tel: 42.60.27.93.
Also very *vieux Paris*. *Cuisine traditionnelle* (*hachis parmentier, cassoulet,* etc.) Sartre and Simone de Beauvoir were customers; Marguerite Duras dines here occasionally.

### Julien
16, rue du Faubourg St. Denis
75010 PARIS
tel: 47.70.12.06.
Pleasant, fashionable, an in-spot. Plan on spending a bit more. Reservations essential.

### Roger la Grenouille
26, rue des Grands Augustins
75006 PARIS
tel: 43.26.10.55
Great spot for fun-loving bawdiness with style, excellent French provincial cooking. *Coq au vin* and *canard à*

*l'orange* stand out. So do the not-so-timid waitresses. Good house wine. Order the *dessert spéciale* to be rid of Puritanism for good.

**Le Gamin de Paris**
49, rue Vieille du Temple
75004 PARIS
tel: 42.78.97.24
This Marais restaurant has captured fine food, soulful atmosphere, and an unbelievable chocolate mud pie.

**Chez Marianne**
2, rue des Hospitalières St. Gervais
75004 PARIS
tel: 42.72.18.86
Great pickles, corned beef, cheesecake. Friendly atmosphere in the midst of the Jewish sector on rue des Rosiers in the Marais. Ask for André, the spirit of the street.

# American Food

You obviously didn't come to Paris to eat American food. However, for those nostalgic moments when you're *croque-monsieured* to death, and tripe doesn't fit the bill, you'll be reassured to know that there are over 30 Anglo/American/Tex-Mex/etc. style restaurants now in Paris. Without much difficulty you can find ribs to root beer, chile to cookies, although a few cultural culinary icons such as bagels, real maple syrup and the bottomless cup of coffee are still rare. A few stand-by American joints include: Joe Allen, Cactus Charly, Café Pacifico, Harry's New York Bar, Marshall's, Mother Earth's, Rio Grande, Sam Kearny, Chicago Pizza Pie Factory and The Studio. Although the cuisine here is pretty much authentic, these places tend to fill up with a certain type of trend-seeking French clientele that emulates "the American way of life." They also tend to be on the expensive side and haven't quite captured the spirit of the huge American portion.

For commercial peanut butter, crumpets, corn meal, or brownie mix, try The General Store at 82 rue de Grenelle, 75007, and Marks & Spencer, 6-8 rue des Mathurins, in the 9th, across from the Galeries Lafayette. For complete listings of Anglo-leaning eateries consult *Paris-Anglophone* or *Passion Magazine*. Here are a few useful anglo culinary leads:

**Susan's Place**
51, rue des Ecoles
75005 PARIS
tel: 43.54.23.22
Tex-Mex cuisine, excellent carrot cake.

**Hayne's**
3, rue Clauzel
75009 PARIS
tel: 48.78.40.63
Original soul food since the 50's.

**MilleBreakFirst**
tel: 43.45.76.53
Call night before for breakfast at home.

**Mother Earth's**
66, rue des Lombards
75001 PARIS
tel: 42.36.35.58
Jazz on weekends.

**Slice Pizza**
62, rue Monsieur le Prince
75006 PARIS
tel: 43.54.18.18
New York style pizza by the slice; home delivery.

**Randy and Jay's**
14, rue Thouin
75005 PARIS
43.26.37.09
Barbequed ribs.

**Spizza 30'**
43.44.91.11 (call for other locations)
Free delivery of American style pizza.

**Natural's**
15, rue Grenier-Saint-Lazare
75003 PARIS
tel: 48.87.09.49
Macrobiotic take-away.

# International Cuisine

Paris is an international cross-roads for cuisines from all corners of the world, Kurdistan to Korea. One could almost trace the colonial history of France in the restaurants of its capital, from North Africa to Vietnam to the Caribbean *(Antilles)* to black Africa to the Middle East.

## Lebanese

Currently, one of the best international cuisines in Paris comes from Lebanon. With the political upheaval and economic instability in Lebanon, there has been a veritable exodus of Lebanese wealth from Beirut and subsequent investment in Paris. Lebanese business people have preferred to invest substantially in Paris knowing that at least their capital is protected against run-away inflation and the risk of violence and terror. Lebanese restaurants in Paris tend to be both elegant and casual at the same time, and the quality, quantity, and prices are all rather favorable.

**Al Dar**
8, rue Frédéric Sauton
75005 PARIS
tel: 46.34.64.46

**Marrouche**
32, bd St. Michel
75006 PARIS
tel: 46.33.22.11

## Chinese

Paris has hundreds of Chinese restaurants, a number of which can be a good deal for days when your wallet is thin. Many, especially in the Latin Quarter, can be extremely reasonable if you order the menu. On the whole, the best and most authentic Chinese food in Paris is concentrated in Paris' two China-towns: the 13e *arrondissement* between the Place d'Italie and Porte de Choisy, and Belleville, in the northeast part of the city, formerly dominated by North Africans, or Maghrebins. Many Chinese restaurants in the city, ironically, are run by Vietnamese. The result is a mixed bag of Vietnamese, Chinese, and Thai influences, overpowered by the tastes and demands of the French palate. Go to the 13e or Belleville for the real thing. There are too many to list.

## Japanese

The Japanese have recently been investing heavily in France, from 18th century *châteaux* to Paris real estate, especially in the area around l'Opéra, which has become a kind of "Japanese quarter" with many Japanese restaurants and luxury boutiques. Lots of new restaurants around the Opéra as well as in the St. Germain area. Avoid Shogun, the boat-restaurant on the Seine—an amazing rip-off.

## Spanish

If you're looking for Spanish food here are a few suggestions:
**L'Auberge Espagnole**
1, rue Mouffetard
75005 PARIS
tel: 43.25.31.96
Closed Monday noon. Service until 12:00 PM.

**Burro Blanco**
79, rue Cardinal Lemoine
75005 PARIS
tel: 43.25.72.53.
Dinner only, served until 1:00 AM.

**Casa Pepe**
5, rue Mouffetard
75005 PARIS
tel: 43.54.97.33. Dinner only.

**Don Quixote**
10, rue Rochambeau
75009 PARIS
tel: 48.78.01.90. Closed Sunday. Service
until 11:30 PM.

**Roberto**
8, rue des Tournelles
75004 PARIS
tel: 42.77.48.37. Closed Sunday noon.

## Mexican
**The Studio**
41, rue du Temple
75004 PARIS
tel: 43.29.78.73

## Greek

The Latin Quarter is now noted
for its Greek restaurants complete
with extravagant window displays
of brochettes of seafood, stuffed
eggplant, and suckling pig. Also
complete with aggressively affable
male hosts beckoning the tourists.
Most of these places serve reasonably priced, good food.

## North African

There are hundreds of North
African restaurants specializing in
couscous. The Bebert chain is
good but a bit more expensive
than others. Here's one unusual
find:
**Le Méditerranée/Couscous Flash**
14, rue Robert Giraudineau
94300 VINCENNES
tel: 43.74.80.56
Although located on the edge of Paris
in Vincennes, this is one of the only
couscous restaurants that also offers
home delivery service. Copious, stylish,
and not too expensive, owned and
managed by Asdin, a charismatic
marathon runner from Djerba, Tunisia.

## Vegetarian

The choice for vegetarians in
Paris is slim, but new restaurants
seem to appear every week as
health consciousness becomes
more *à la mode*.
**Banani**
148, rue de la Croix Nivert
75015 PARIS
tel: 40.28.73.92
Closed Sunday. Service until 11:00 PM.
Indian food, wide variety of curries.

**Bol en Bois**
35, rue Pascal
75013 PARIS
tel: 40.07.27.24
Closed Sunday. Service until 10:00 PM.
Natural and macrobiotic specialties,
with adjacent bookstore and *épicerie*.

**Rayons de Santé**
8, place Charles-Dulin
75018 PARIS
tel. 42.59.64.81
Closed Friday evening and Saturday.

**Country Life**
6, rue Daunou
75002 PARIS
tel: 42.97.48.51

# Resto U

Students can also take advantage
of the French university-run stu-
dent restaurants called Resto-U,
managed by the CROUS *(Centre
Régional Oeuvres Universitaires
Scolaires de Paris)* tel: 40.51.37.13.
**Assas**, 92, rue d'Assas, 75006, Métro
Notre-Dame-des-Champs
**C.H.U. Bichat**, 16, rue Henri Huchard,
75018, Métro Porte de Saint Ouen
**Bullier**, 39, av. Georges Bernanos,
75005, Métro Port-Royal
**Censier**, 31, rue Geoffroy Saint Hilaire,
75005 Métro Censier-Daubenton
**Châtelet**, 10, rue Jean Calvin, 75005 ,
Métro Censier-Daubenton
**Citeaux**, 45, Bd. Diderot, 75012, Métro
Gare de Lyon
**Clignancourt**, rue Francis de Croisset,
75018, Métro Porte de Clignancourt

**Cuvier-Jussieu**, 8bis, rue Cuvier, 75005, Métro Jussieu
**Dareau**, 13-17, rue Dareau, 75014, Métro Saint Jacques
**Dauphine**, av. de Pologne, 75016, Métro Porte Dauphine
**Grand Palais**, cours la Reine, 75008 Métro Champs-Elysées
**I.U.T.**, 143, av. de Versailles, 75016 Métro Chardon Lagache
**Mabillon**, 3 rue Mabillon, 75006, Métro Mabillon
**Mazet**, 5 rue Mazet, 75006, Métro Odéon
**C.H.U. Necker**, 156, rue de Vaugirard, 75015, Métro Pasteur
**C.H.U. Pitié**, 105, Bd. de l'Hôpital, 75013 Métro St. Marcel

These are crowded and noisy but the food is plentiful and really cheap. You'll need to purchase tickets, available at a *guichet* (counter) in the lobby of each of these establishments.

## Fast Food

Fast food, which is anything but truly fast, has unfortunately over-run the Paris cityscape in the last five years. McDonalds and Burger King, along with their French competition, Quick, which has recently bought-out Free Time and has 27 locations in Paris, have impressive franchises along the high-rent Champs-Elysées. French business people, office workers, students, and kids flock to these meccas of American hamburger prestige, and at lunchtime it's often nearly impossible to get into one of these places, especially on Wednesdays, when there is no school, and school children line up for their "Happy Meal." The McDonalds in the Latin Quarter is a fine example of well-studied kitsch. The walls are lined with façades of fake bookshelves of fake leather editions of the classics of French literature—this being the traditional student quarter of the city, a hundred meters or so from the front door of the Sorbonne. McDonalds has flourished wildly in Paris and even has cornered a share of real prestige, after a rocky period in the Seventies when the king of American burgers pulled out of France due to the shoddy standards of local franchises.

## Les sandwiches

Sandwiches are commonplace in Paris as more and more Parisians give up the Latin tradition of long meals in favor of the pursuit of more healthful and individual pleasures or simply to save time. Sandwiches usually consist of a third of a *baguette* with either butter and ham, *pâté*, gruyère (really French emmenthal; the real gruyère, which has fewer holes, comes from Switzerland and is twice the price), camembert, or *rillettes,* a flavorful but fatty pork paste—delicious with those crispy and vinegary *cornichons* (pickles). In a *café*, a sandwich will cost you between 10 FF and 17 FF, depending on where you are. Again, careful about asking for variations. One student once asked for a piece of lettuce on a ham sandwich and was charged double. "But *Monsieur,* you ordered a sandwich *fantaisie*," he was told. When you see signs for *Poilâne* bread, take advantage of the occasion. This coarse whole rye bread is both a tradition and delicacy in French culinary life.

When the weather is fine, or at least not too gray and sad (*triste*) as Paris can often be, you can always buy some bread, cheese, *charcuterie* (deli goods), etc. and sit in one of the parks (see Parks)—but not on the grass, as the *"pelouse est interdite"*—the grass is off-limits. Or you may want to sit down by the Seine. In the fifth *arrondissement,* it's very pleasant to duck into the *Arènes de Lutèce,* an uncovered Roman amphitheatre that is hidden behind a row of apartment houses on the Rue Monge just below the Place Monge. In the seventh *arrondissement,* the Champs de Mars, the open space below the Eiffel Tower, is lovely. Other options—the Luxembourg Gardens, the Bois de Vincennes, the Bois de Boulogne, the elegant Parc Monceau, or wherever there is a likely-looking bench.

You will see people in restaurants, *cafés,* and even McDonalds paying for their food with coupons called *les tickets restaurants.* These are like money—35 FF each—that employers offer their personnel at half price as an additional benefit. They're cumulative. Establishments that accept them have stickers on their windows.

## Weight

At first you may think you've come to a country where being overweight is against the law; where fatness is a mortal sin. You may wonder how it is that in a country with such a passion for food, everyone seems underfed. You may find yourself perplexed to see so many vices being committed with impunity. You may ask yourself how, with so much sugar being consumed, the population can be so uniformly *mince* (thin). It is true that much of what one associates with classical French food is the rich sauce, the buttery and sweet bakery delights. But these do not constitute the average

diet—they are special treats. Quality is important, and as in every aspect of French life, so is moderation.

A second reason for the relatively *petite* waistlines of the French comes from the fact that Parisians are obliged to be rather active in their daily routines. There is less reliance on cars, more steps to climb, more stops on the shopping circuit, and fewer hours spent mindlessly glued to televisions. The emphasis on form also contributes—meal times are adhered to rather strictly, compared to the haphazard snack times, missed meals, and dinners in front of the TV or over work. One must remember also that in France, personal style and the public self is taken seriously. The French don't like going out if they don't look great. The importance of one's physical appearance is thus primordial.

## Typical Dishes & Specialty Foods

The following is a sampling of specialties commonly found in France:

**Bouillabaisse:** a Mediterranean-style fish stew with tomatoes, saffron, mussels, shellfish, and the catch of the day. Each version is different from the last one, depending on the whim of the creator. Good ones are becoming hard to find.

**Cassoulet:** A casserole of white navy beans, shallots, and a variety of meats such as pork, lamb, sausage, and goose or duck, originating in the southwest region of France. Beans and meat are alternated in a casserole and topped with bread crumbs, then baked until crusty. Perfect for the winter.

**Couscous:** Specialty of North Africa originally brought to France by colonialists. A hearty blend of mutton, chicken, and a spicy beef sausage *(merguez)* in a light stock with boiled zucchini, carrots, onions, turnips, and chick peas. It is spooned over a fine semolina-like meal, called *couscous,* from which the dish gets its name. A very hot red paste called *harissa* can be stirred into the broth.

*Fondue:* A Swiss Alps specialty popular in France, especially in the ski regions. There are two types: *bourguignonne* —small chunks of beef cooked on long forks in pots of hot oil and accompanied by a variety of sauces; and *Savoyard* cheese—melted and flavored with kirsch or white wine, lapped up with chunks of stale French bread on long forks.

*Farce:* Spiced ground meat, usually pork, used for stuffing cabbage *(chou farci),* green pepper *(poivron vert farci),* or tomatoes *(tomates farcies).*

*Hachis parmentier:* Mashed potatoes and ground meat topped with a bechamel, or white sauce, served in a casserole.

*Moussaka:* A heavy Greek casserole dish combining slices of eggplant, tomatoes, and ground lamb, baked with a bechamel topping.

*Paella:* A Portuguese and Spanish dish with a rice base, saffron, pimiento, chicken, pork and shellfish; cooked in a special two handled metal pan.

*Choucroute:* Of Alsatian origin, this dish is often served in brasseries as it is a good accompaniment to a strong draft beer. It consists of sauerkraut topped with a variety of sausages, cuts of pork, ham and boiled potatoes.

# SHOPPING

Upon arrival, one may be struck by the charming inconveniences of the Parisian shopping system. First and foremost, remember to bring along your own shopping bags, basket or backpack. Only thin and tiny baggies are given away for free. One must also consider the flow of time, as most businesses close between noon and 14h or between 13h-15h and most small shops and grocery stores are closed on Mondays. The lack of many large supermarkets *(grandes surfaces)* in convenient locations often means having to frequent the many small neighborhood shops and having to stand, waiting to be served in line after line. Though these circumstances may discourage one at first, taking part in the markets and different shops is a valuable way of enjoying a very basic and material aspect of the culture. The subtle varieties one finds in these shops prove to be intriguing as you'll discover that the merchant *(commerçant)* is an expert in his field and can give you all sorts of interesting tips. Going frequently to the same baker or butcher can also be helpful as they are very quick to remember a face. This is one direct way of participating fully in daily Parisian life.

The larger supermarkets tend to feel like open air markets that have been roofed in. The largest chains are Codec, Monoprix, Carrefour, Auchan, Prisunic, Ed, Inno, and Felix Potin. Often the food section is in the basement of a department store. Don't expect much service. There are no baggers and your tender goods can get smashed as you scramble to bag them yourself as they pile up at the end of the check-out counter.

There is, obviously, a wide range of shops, and the differences are sometimes very subtle, especially when food is concerned. This explains the chain of names one often sees on the awnings of shops. For example, a *Boulangerie-Pâtisserie-Confiserie* will have bread, pastries, and candies.

## Boulangeries

Most *boulangeries* sell prepared sandwiches, mini-pizzas, *quiches,* onion tarts, and *croque-monsieur* (the classic French common food available at all hours in all *cafés,* consisting of two slices of buttered toast, a slice of ham with grilled cheese on top—the *croque-madame* is the same thing topped with a sunny-side-up egg) on the streets for about 12 to 20 FF. They'll microwave food for you upon request.

It'll take some time before you become agile with all the nuances in the French *boulangerie.* The bread alone will stun you in its variety. The following are a few main items:

**Baguette:** (flour, water, yeast and salt), weight (250 grams) and price (3,20 FF) are all government regulated and nationally uniform in weight and price.

**Demi-baguette:** half baguette, 1,70 FF.

**Bâtard:** Same weight as a *baguette,* but shorter and less elegant, made from the squatty end of the rolled out dough.

**Boule:** round loaf, small or large.

**Chapeau:** small round loaf topped with a chapeau (hat).

**Couronne:** ring-shaped *baguette.*

**Le fer à cheval:** horseshoe-shaped baguette.

**Ficelle:** thin, crusty *baguette.*

**Fougasse:** a flat, rectangular-shaped bread made of *baguette* dough filled with onions, herbs, spices, or anchovies.

**Miche:** large round country-style loaf.

**Pain de campagne:** can be a white bread dusted with flour, giving it a rustic look (and a higher price) or a hearty loaf that may be a blend of white, whole wheat, and rye flour with added bran. Also called *baguette à l'ancienne* or *baguette paysanne.* It comes in every shape, from a small round individual roll to a large family loaf.

**Pain au Levain:** sourdough bread. Usually found in health food or specialty stores and relatively expensive. Sold by weight. Delicious with butter.

**Pain complet:** bread made partially or entirely from whole wheat flour.

**Pain fantaisie:** "fantasy bread"—any imaginatively shaped bread.

**Pain de mie:** a rectangular white and crusty sandwich loaf used for toast.

**Pain aux noix** and **pain aux noisettes:** rye or wheat bread filled with walnuts or hazelnuts.

**Pain aux raisins:** rye or wheat bread filled with raisins.

**Pain de seigle:** closest thing to pumpernickle bread in a *boulangerie.* Two-thirds rye and one third wheat flour.

**Pain au son:** a dietetic bread that is "quality-controlled," containing bran flour.

**Pain Viennois:** milk and sugar are added to the baguette dough.

**Pain Brioché:** a rich dough made with milk, eggs, and sugar. *Brioche* comes in all sizes and a variety of shapes. Proportionately expensive, but a real delight for those lazy mornings. Great to dunk in *café au lait.*

**Note**: you will often hear customers asking for their bread *"Bien cuit"* (well done and crusty), *"Pas trop cuit"* or *"Bien tendre"* (less baked and doughier). You can also ask for *"une baguette coupée en deux"* (a baguette cut in half). This facilitates transportation and prevents the bread from breaking *en route.* All of your requests, whether they be at the bakery, the cheese shop, or the hardware store, should of course be accompanied by a smile and followed by *"s'il vous plaît,"* two things that will go a long way towards making any transaction simpler and easier. Also, get accustomed to carrying your bread in your hand, bag, or under your arm. Bread is never wrapped or bagged. Sometimes, in the more bourgeois *boulangeries,* your *baguette* will come with a square of tissue paper wrapped around the center where you are to grasp the bread. If you ask for a second square of paper you'll probably get a strange look if not an outright *non.* Don't worry, though, in four centuries there are no documented cases of anyone getting sick from unprotected bread.

**Note:** It's annoying, but that's the way it is—if you ask for your bread sliced on the slicing machine, expect to pay an additional franc. Don't even bother complaining.

After bread, the most common items in the *boulangerie* include the following:

*Croissant ordinaire:* these are the crescent shaped puff pastry rolls now found all over the world. When the points are curled towards the center, this is the legal indication that the *croissant* has been made with margarine and has not been glazed with butter before baking. Price is always about 50 centimes less than the *croissant au beurre.*

*Croissant au beurre:* these croissants have their tips pointing straight out, signifying their pure butter content. Richer and definitely worth the extra half a franc.

*Pain au chocolat:* a rectangular flaky pastry filled with a strip of chocolate. If you are lucky enough to catch a batch coming out of the oven, the chocolate will still be warm and soft.

*Pain aux raisins:* a spiral-shaped *croissant* cooked with raisins and a light, egg cream.

*Croissant aux amandes:* topped with slivered almonds and filled with a rich almond butter paste.

As for individual *gâteaux,* most *boulangeries* that are also *pâtisseries* offer:

*Millefeuilles (Napoleon):* puffed pastry with pastry cream.

*Eclairs: chou* pastry filled with chocolate or coffee cream.

*Religieux:* same as *éclair* but shaped like a hat.

*Tartelette au fruits:* small fruit tarts.

*Croissants* are usually purchased in the morning, cakes in the afternoon or evenings. *Boulangeries* also sell *bonbons* (candy) by the piece to kids, as well as soft drinks and bottled water that are cool but never really cold. It's nearly impossible to get a napkin. Not all *boulangeries* are open on Mondays so expect lines for bread on that day. Also, if you wait too long on Sundays by midday it might get a bit tough to find bread. Most *boulangeries* sell out their bread every day. Some *boulangeries* freeze unsold *baguettes* and rebake them later at a slight compromise of taste and texture. You can detect this by the pattern of cracks on the sides of the *baguette* crust. Don't make a scene, just change *boulangeries.*

## Boucheries

The Parisian butcher shop has a fine array of its own ideosyncracies. First of all, most butcher shops sell pork, beef, mutton, lamb, veal, liver and some sausages, pâtés, poultry, rabbit, and game. Specialized poultry like turkeys, pheasant, pigeons, cornish hen should be bought in a *marchand de volaille,* your neighborhood poultry shop. If you see a butcher's shop with nice photos of thoroughbreds on its walls, get the message. Here is where horse meat is sold. Horse is reputed to be the finest meat on the market. Try some. You can buy steaks, roasts, hamburger meat, etc. at your local *Chevaline* shop. They're usually decked out with a gold horse's head over the shop door.

The cuts of meat are particular to France. Steaks are not pre-cut nor is chopped meat previously packaged. If you're used to thick steaks you have to ask for one *très épais*. French meat is very tasty but on the whole not as tender as US beef. Less hormones though! The superior cuts of beef—*côte de boeuf, entrecôte, filet mignon*—are expensive. Pork, though, is excellent and relatively cheap. As are certain cuts of lamb and mutton. Don't be alarmed by scrawny slabs of lean red meat hanging above bellowed cutting boards on nasty aluminum hooks. The blood-stained butchers cut steaks out of these hanging slabs as they go. Fresher. Here's some helpful vocabulary:

| *boeuf* | beef |
|---|---|
| bavette | tender steak |
| bifteck | ordinary thin steak |
| bourguignon | cubed beef stew |
| châteaubriand | porterhouse steak |
| faux-filet | sirloin |
| entrecôte | rib steak |
| steak haché | ground beef |
| rosbif | roast beef |
| tartare | ground beef with zero percent fat |
| tournedos | filet wrapped in fat |

| *mouton/agneau* | mutton/lamb |
|---|---|
| brochette | skewer |
| carré | roast rack |
| côte | chops |
| épaule | shoulder |
| gigot | leg of lamb |
| noisette | choice loin |
| selle | saddle |

| *porc* | pork |
|---|---|
| andouillettes | pork belly sausage |
| boudin | blood sausage |
| jambon | ham |
| épaule | less-expensive ham, comes from shoulder |
| jarret | pork knuckle |
| pied | foot |
| rôti | roast |
| travers | spare ribs |

| *veau* | veal |
|---|---|
| blanquette | stewing meat |
| escalope | cutlet |
| paupiette | rolled and stuffed |
| riz de veau | sweetbreads |

| *triperie* | tripe |
|---|---|
| cervelle | brain |
| coeur | heart |
| foie de génisse | calf liver |
| gesier | gizzard |
| langue | tongue |
| rognons | kidneys (not to be confused with *reins,* human kidneys) |
| gibier | wild game |
| chevreuil | young goat |
| lapin | rabbit |
| lièvre | wild hare |
| marcassin | baby boar |
| sanglier | adult boar |

| *volailles* | poultry |
|---|---|
| coq | cock |
| cuisse | thigh |
| suprême | breast |
| dinde | turkey |
| dindonneau | young turkey |
| caille | quail |
| canard | duck |
| magret de canard | breast of duck |
| oie | goose |
| pintade | guinea hen |
| pigeon | pigeon |

## Charcuteries

These are France's delis. The assortment of sliced meats, fish, sea-food in aspic, *saumon fumé*, avocados with crabmeat, *pâtés*, salads, fancy vegetables and prepared dishes like *brandade de morue, hachis parmentier, choucroute* are always a savory delight. These stores tend to be expensive but highly pleasurable. They offer a whole gamut of dishes guaranteeing instant culinary success when entertaining or when you want to treat yourself to something tasty and beautiful. When buying cold cuts, order by the number of slices, indicating if you want them *fines* (thin). When buying *pâtés* and *terrines,* you indicate the quantity by where the clerk places the knife. To avoid buying more than you want, state *"un peu moins que ça, s'il vous plaît."*

## Epiceries

Literally "spice shops," these are simply grocery stores that sell a little bit of everything. In most *quartiers* there are independent grocers as well as one or several chains, the old standby being Felix Potin, an institution in Parisian grocery shopping. In recent years, Codec, which has numerous large supermarkets, has taken over many *épiceries.* The ones owned and operated by North Africans usually stay open late—often until midnight in some of the outlying neighborhoods. This is convenient for finding munchies and beverages late at night.

## Poissonneries

The variety of fish available in Paris is remarkable. The French eat a lot more fish per capita than North Americans or Brits. After a number of visits to your local *poissonnerie* you'll learn the names of the fish and decide which ones you like best and which are the best buys. Whole fish are cleaned and scaled by the fishmonger at your request for no extra charge. Sprigs of fresh parsley are given away too if the customer requests such. Especially in the cool months, a particularly French and extremely reasonable meal consists of fresh mussels. Purchase one liter per person. You can clean off the shells quickly by hand and dump the shiny black mussels into a big pot of chopped shallots and garlic; dump in a half a bottle of cheap white wine and steam them until they open. Dump in some chopped parsley and serve. Don't eat the ones that don't open. Drink white wine with the dish and mop up the briny wine and shallot broth with hunks of *baguette*. Two people can have a great time for about 30 FF.

| *fruits de mer* | **seafood** |
|---|---|
| coquilles St. Jacques | scallops |
| crabe | crab |
| tourteau | rock crab |

| *crustacées* | **shellfish** |
|---|---|
| crevette | shrimp |
| langoustine | sea crayfish |
| homard | lobster |
| huîtres | oysters |
| langouste | spiny lobster |
| moules | mussels |
| praires | small clams |
| oursin | sea urchin |

| *poissons* | **fish** |
|---|---|
| anchois | anchovies |
| bar | bass |
| barbue | brill |
| cabillaud | cod |
| morue | dried salt cod |
| congre | eel |
| calamar | squid |

| | |
|---|---|
| *haddock* | smoked haddock |
| *éperlan* | smelt |
| *hareng* | herring |
| *lotte* | monkfish |
| *merlan* | whiting |
| *raie* | skate/ray |
| *rouget* | mullet |
| *sole* | sole |
| *saumon* | salmon |
| *thon* | tuna |
| *truite* | trout |

## Crémeries/Fromageries

Charles de Gaulle is reported to have once said: "How can anyone govern a country with so many different cheeses?" Some people put the current cheese count at more than 400. The pungent cheese shops offer a wonderful sampling that you should take advantage of. A few things you should learn to appreciate during your *séjour* in France include *chèvre* (goat cheese), especially the *frais* (fresh) ones that are covered in *cendres* (ash). *Fromageries* also sell fresh butter, cut off of huge mountains in chunks, *fromage blanc* (white cheese that falls between sour cream and smooth cottage cheese), *crème fraîche* (a wonderfully rich, slightly sour cream that is used generously in sauces and on desserts), and fresh milk. In France, you'll find whole and skim milk also in vacuum packed cartons that need not be refrigerated and can last for many months unopened. This milk is called *longue conservation* and permits you to stock up all at once. Eggs too are bought in the *crémerie* in packages of six or by the unit. When cutting *brie*, never cut off the nose *(nez)*, or point.

| Fromage | Cheese |
|---|---|
| *Vieux Cantal* | cheddar |
| *chèvre* | goat cheese |
| *fromage carré frais* | cream cheese |
| *rapé* | grated |
| *gruyère, emmenthal* | Swiss cheese |

| Lait | Milk |
|---|---|
| *lait fermenté léger* | buttermilk |
| *lait frais* | fresh milk |
| *homogenéisé* | homogenized |
| *demi-écrémé* | low-fat milk |
| *lait écrémé* | skim milk |
| *lait stérilisé longue conservation* | sterilized milk |
| *lait entier* | whole milk |

| Yaourt | Yogurt |
|---|---|
| *maigre* | no fat |
| *nature* | plain |
| *nature sucré* | plain but sugared |
| *avec des fruits* | with fruit |

## A Note on Quality

An American friend related a story which says a lot about the differing concepts of quality in his country and in France. He set out to make a simple chocolate sauce for a dessert after returning home from a period of time spent in France. It was then that he discovered that Hershey Bars don't melt, they bubble and crack like melted plastic. The cocoa content was less than three percent. The cheapest Monoprix (the French equivalent to K-Mart) brand chocolate in France has at least 20% cocoa. The more cocoa, the higher quality the chocolate. So, quality is on the whole higher and with it, importantly, are expectations. After a year or so in Europe it's doubtful, for example, that you'll be able to chomp on American chocolate, down American beer, or munch industrial white bread.

For the *crème de la crème* of fine sweets and specialty items, a tour of the famous Fauchon at Place de la Madeleine is a must. Better to look than to buy.

## A Brief Comment on French Wines

A few shopping tips: remember, square-shouldered bottles are from Bordeaux and round-shouldered bottles are from Burgundy (there are both square and round-shouldered bottles from smaller, lesser important wine regions in France). When buying inexpensive wines try to select ones with green-colored lead tops rather than the blue or black-colored ones. These are not blended wines; they come from one vineyard and tend to be better quality, although the price is not necessarily higher. The nation-wide chain, Nicolas, can be found in most neighborhoods and offers a wide selection of wines and spirits from every region at a full range of prices.

The French drink more wine per capita than any other people (an average of 1/4 litre per day). Wine is almost always drunk at dinner and quite often at lunch. If wine is forgone, water is the only replacement, never soft drinks with a meal. If you don't drink wine already, Paris is a good place to start. Wine appreciation is, like music and art, part of being a discerning individual. Imported French wines are limited to wines that are able to travel and that are produced in large quantities. In Paris you'll have the chance to try (*déguster*) lots of *petits vins* at *petits prix*.

## Food Markets

Paris offers three kinds of food markets: the permanent street markets, the moving open air markets and the indoor markets. In all of these markets, unless you are encouraged to do so, you should not touch the produce which is carefully displayed for everyone's enjoyment. You should, however, feel free to specify exactly what you want.

The **street markets** are open Tuesday through Saturday from 9h00 to 12h30 or 13h00 and from 16h00-19h00. On Sundays they are open from 9h00-13h00.

**Rue des Belles Feuilles:** Begins av Victor Hugo, 16e. Métro: Victor Hugo.
**Rue Cler:** Begins av de la Motte-Picquet, 7e. Métro: Ecole Militaire.
**Rue Lévis:** Begins Bd. des Batignoles, 17e. Métro: Villiers.
**Rue Montorgueil:** Begins rue Rambuteau, 1e. Métro: Les Halles. Les Halles was formally Paris' central marketplace.
**Rue Mouffetard:** Begins rue de l'Epée-de-Bois, 5e. Métro: Monge. One of the oldest and most animated markets in Paris.
**Rue Poncelet:** Begins av des Ternes, 17e. Métro: Ternes. Exceptional fruit.
**Rue du Poteau:** Begins pl. Jules Joffrin, 18e. Métro: Jules-Joffrin.
**Rue de Seine/rue de Buci:** Begins Bd St. Germain, 6e. Métro: Odéon.

The **moving markets** move from neighborhood to neighborhood, making their appearance on fixed days. They often include clothing and other articles as well as food. These are open from 7h00 to 13h30.

**Alésia:** Rue d'Alésia, 14e. Métro: Alésia. Wednesday and Saturday.

**Alibert:** Rue Alibert and rue Claude-Vellefaux, 10e. Métro: Goncourt. Thursday and Sunday.

**Amiral-Bruix:** Bd. Bruix, between rue Weber and rue Marbeau, 16e. Métro: Porte Maillot. Wednesday and Saturday.

**Auteuil:** Between rue d'Auteuil, rue Donizetti, and rue La Fontaine, 16e. Métro: Michel-Ange-Auteuil. Wednesday and Saturday.

**Avenue de Versailles:** Rue Gros and rue La Fontaine, 16e. Métro: Jasmin. Tuesday and Friday.

**Av. du Président Wilson:** Between rue Debrousse and pl. d'Iéna, 16e. Métro: Alma-Marceau. Wednesday and Saturday.

**Belgrand:** Rue Belgrand, rue de la Chine and pl. de la Puy, 20e. Métro: Gambetta. Wednesday and Saturday.

**Belleville:** On the island of bd. de Belleville, 11e. Métro: Belleville. Tuesday and Friday.

**Bercy:** Bd. de Reuilly, between rue de Charenton and pl. Félix-Eboué, 12e. Métro: Daumesnil. Tuesday and Friday.

**Berthier:** Angle of av de la Porte d'Asnières and bd. Berthier, 17e. Métro: Porte de Clichy. Wednesday and Saturday.

**Bobillot:** Rue Bobillot, between pl. Rungis and rue de la Colonie, 13e. Métro: Maison Blanche. Tuesday and Friday.

**Breteuil:** Av. de Saxe and av. de Ségur, toward pl. Bréteuil, 7e. Métro: Ségur. Thursday and Saturday.

**Boulevard Brune:** Between passage des Suisses and N°. 49, bd. Brune, 14e. Métro: Porte de Vanves. Thursday and Sunday.

**Bd. de Charonne:** Between rue de Charonne and rue Alexandre-Dumas, 11e. Métro: Alexandre-Dumas. Wednesday and Saturday.

**Carmes:** Pl. Maubert, 5e. Métro: Maubert-Mutualité. Tuesday, Thursday, and Saturday.

**Cervantes:** Rue Bargue, 15e. Métro: Volontaires. Wednesday and Saturday.

**Cité Berryer:** Begins rue Royale in the passage of the Cité Berryer, 8e. Métro: Madeleine. Tuesday and Friday.

**Clignancourt:** Bd. d'Ornano, between rue du Mont-Cenis and rue Ordener, 18e. Métro: Ordener. Tuesday, Friday, and Sunday.

**Convention:** rue de la Convention, between rue Alain-Chartier and rue de l'Abbé-Groult, 15e. Métro: Convention. Tuesday, Thursday, Saturday.

**Cours de Vincennes:** Between Bd. de Picpus and av. du Dr. Arnorld Netter, 12e. Métro: Porte de Vincennes. Wednesday and Saturday.

**Crimée:** 430, bd. Ney, 18e. Métro: Porte de Clignancourt. Wednesday and Saturday.

**Davout:** Bd. Davout, between av de la Porte de Montreuil and 94, Bd. Dabout, 20e. Métro: Porte de Montreuil. Tuesday and Friday.

**Dupleix:** Bd. de Grenelle, between rue Lourmel and rue du Commerce, 15e. Métro: Dupleix. Wednesday and Sunday.

**Edgar-Quinet:** On the island of bd. Edgar-Quinet, 14th. Métro: Raspail. Wednesday and Saturday.

**Exelmans:** Along pl. de la Porte-Molitor, beginning av. du Général-Sarrail toward bd. Exelmans, 16e. Métro: Michel-Ange-Auteuil. Tuesday and Friday.

**Gobelins:** Bd. August-Blanqui, between pl. d'Italie and rue Barrault, 13e. Métro: Corvisart. Tuesday, Friday, and Sunday.

**Javel:** Rue St. Charles, between rue Javel and Rond-Point-St.-Charles, 15e. Métro: Charles-Michel. Tuesday and Friday.

**Jean-Jaurès:** 145-185, av. Jean-Jaurès, 19e. Métro: Pantin. Tuesday, Thursday, and Sunday.

**Joinville:** At the angle of rue de Joinville and rue Jomard, 19e. Métro: Crimée. Tuesday, Thursday, and Sunday.

**Lariboisière:** Bd. de la Chapelle, across from Lariboisière hospital, 18e. Métro: Barbès-Rochechouart. Wednesday and Saturday.

**Lecourbe:** Rue Lecourbe, between rue Vasco-de-Gama and rue Leblanc, 15e. Métro: Place Balard. Wednesday and Saturday.

**Ledru-Rollin:** Av. Ledru-Rollin, between rue de Lyon and rue de Bercy, 12e. Métro: Gare de Lyon. Thursday and Saturday.

**Lefèbvre:** Bd. Lefèbvre, between rue Olivier-de-Serres and rue de Dantzig, 15e. Métro: Porte de Versailles. Wednesday and Saturday.

**Maison Blanche:** Av. d'Italie and rue Bourgon, 13e. Métro: Porte d'Italie. Thursday and Sunday.

**Monge:** Pl. Monge, 5e. Métro: Monge. Wednesday, Friday, and Sunday.

**Montrouge:** Along rue Brézin, rue Saillard, rue Mouton-Duvernet, and rue Boulard, 14e. Métro: Mouton-Duvernet. Tuesday and Friday.

**Mortier:** Bd. Mortier, at av. de la Porte de Ménilmontant, 20e. Métro: St.-Fargeau. Wednesday and Saturday.

**Navier:** Among rue Navier, rue Lantier, and rue des Epinettes, 17e. Métro: Guy-Moquet. Tuesday and Friday.

**Ney:** Bd. Ney, between rue Jean-Varenne and rue Camille-Flammarion, 18e. Métro: Porte de Clignancourt. Thursday and Sunday.

**Ordener:** Between rue Montcalm and rue Championnet, 18e. Métro: Guy-Moquet. Wednesday and Sunday.

**Père-Lachaise:** Bd. de Ménilmontant, between rue des Panoyaux and rue de Tlemcen, 11e. Métro: Père-Lachaise. Tuesday and Friday.

**Place des Fêtes:** Pl. des Fêtes, alongside rue Pré-St.-Gervais, rue Petitot, and rue des Fêtes, 19e. Métro: Place des Fêtes. Tuesday, Friday, and Sunday.

**Popincourt:** Bd. Richard-Lenoir, between rue Oberkampf and rue de Crussol, 11e. Métro: Oberkampf. Tuesday and Friday.

**Poniatowski:** Bd. Poniatowski, between av. Daumesnil and rue de Picpus, 12e. Métro: Porte Dorée. Thursday and Sunday.

**Point du Jour:** Av. de Versailles, between rue Le Marois and rue Gudin, 16e. Métro: Porte-de-St.-Cloud. Tuesday, Thursday, and Sunday.

**Porte Brunet:** Av. de la porte Brunet, between bd. Sérurier and bd. d'Algérie, 19e. Métro: Danube. Wednesday and Saturday.

**Port-Royal:** Bd. Port-Royal, alongside Hôpital du Val-de-Grâce, 5e. Métro: Port-Royal. Tuesday, Thursday, and Saturday.

**Pyrénées:** Rue des Pyrénées, between rue de l'Ermitage and rue de Ménilmontant, 20e. Métro: Ménilmontant. Thursday and Sunday.

**Raspail:** Bd. Raspail, between rue du Cherche-Midi and rue de Rennes, 6e. Métro: St.-Placide. Tuesday and Friday.

**Réunion:** Pl. de la Réunion, between the place and rue Vitruve, 20e. Métro: Alexandre-Dumas. Thursday and Sunday.

**Richard-Lenoir:** Bd. Richard-Lenoir and rue Amelot, 11e. Métro: Bastille. Thursday and Sunday.

**Saint-Eloi:** 36-38, rue de Reuilly, 12e. Métro: Reuilly-Diderot. Thursday and Sunday.

**Salpétrière:** Pl. de la Salpétrière, alongside bd. de l'hôpital, 13e. Métro: St.-Marcel. Tuesday and Friday.

**Télégraphe:** Rue du Télégraphe, to the right of Belleville cemetery, 20e. Métro: Télégraphe. Wednesday and Saturday.

**Tolbiac:** Pl. Jeanne-d'Arc, 13e. Métro: Nationale. Thursday and Sunday.

**Villemain:** Av. Villemain, on the island between av. Villemain and rue d'Alésia, 15e. Métro: Plaisance. Wednesday and Sunday.
**Villette:** 27-41, bd. de la Villette, 19e. Métro: Belleville. Wednesday and Saturday.

---

The **covered markets** are generally open Tuesday through Saturday, from 8h00-13h00 and 16h00-18h30, and on Sunday from 9h00-13h00. Little has changed since the turn of the century in many of these markets.

**Batignolles:** 96, rue Lemercier, 17e. Métro: Brochant.
**Beauvau-Saint-Antoine:** Between rue d'Aligre and rue Cotte, 12e. Métro: Ledru-Rollin.
**Chapelle:** rue de l'Olive, 18e. Métro: Max-Dormoy. Open until midnight on Friday and Saturday.
**Enfants Rouges:** 39, rue de Bretagne, 3e. Métro: Filles-du-Calvaire.
**Europe:** Rue Corvetto, between rue Maleville and rue Treihard, 8e. Métro: Villiers.
**Passy:** Angle of rue Boi-le-vent and rue Duban, 16e. Métro: La Muette.
**Porte Saint-Martin:** 31 and 33, rue du Château-d'Eau, 10e. Métro: St.-Martin.
**Riquet:** 36-46, rue Riquet, 18e. Métro: Riquet. Open until 8:00 pm on Friday and Saturday.
**Saint-Didier:** Angle of rue Mesnil and rue St.-Didier, 16e. Métro: Victor-Hugo.
**Saint Germain:** By rue Lobineau, rue Clément and rue Mabillon, 6e. Métro: Mabillon.
**Saint-Honoré:** Pl. du Marché-St.-Honoré, 1e. Métro: Tuileries.
**Saint-Quentin:** 85 bis, Bd. de Magenta, 10e. Métro: Gare-de-l'Est.
**Secrétan:** 46, rue Bouret, and 33, av. Secrétan, 19e. Métro: Bolivar.
**Ternes:** rue Lebon, rue Faraday, and rue Torricelli, 17e. Métro: Ternes.

---

## *Les Marchés Biologiques* (Organic Markets)

These are the equivalent of old-fashioned country farmers' markets. From thirty to fifty independent organic farmers set up stalls on the weekends in Boulogne and Joinville (Parisian suburbs easily reachable by Métro). They sell organically grown fruits and vegetables; homemade breads; dried fruits and nuts; *charcuterie,* farm-raised chicken, ducks, and geese, and natural wine. There are stands selling things like freshly-made pizzas, whole-wheat breads, apple or pear cider, a huge variety of artisanal goat cheeses, sausages, and beer, and dried flowers. Go early in the day for a good selection.

**Le Marché Boulogne:** 140, Route de la Reine, 92 Boulogne-sur-Seine. Métro: Boulogne-Pont de Saint-Cloud, or via the No. 72 bus. Open 8h00-16h00 the first and third Saturdays of each month.
**Le Marché Joinville-le-Pont:** Place Mozart, 94 Joinville. Métro: RER Line B to Joinville, then via the suburban No. 106 and 108N buses. Open 8h30-13h00 the second and fourth Saturdays of each month.
**Le Marché Sceaux-Robinson:** rue des Mouille-Boeuf. Métro: RER Line B to Robinson. Every Sunday, 8h30-13h00.

For additional information on these markets, call *Nature et Progrès,* 47.00.60.36.

# Flea Markets & Special Markets

**Marché de Montreuil:** av. de la Porte de Montreuil, 20e. Métro: Porte de Montreuil. Saturday, Sunday, & Monday. This is probably the least touristy of the flea markets. Located on the eastern edge of Paris, Porte de Montreuil is noted for its huge, cluttered tables of used clothes. Here, if you're not overly bothered by the idea of rummaging through old clothes and are filled with patience you may find high quality and other wrinkled sweaters, skirts, dress shirts, ties, etc. of fine materials for tiny prices. Ten francs for a shirt, for instance. Otherwise, there are loads of old junk, some fine antiques, and piles of useless bric-à-brac. You may not be able to bargain quite as much as you imagined, but you usually can get things for 20-30% less than the asking price. It's not incorrect to try in any case.

**Marché de la Place d'Aligre:** Pl. d'Aligre, 12e. Métro: Ledru-Rollin. Daily from 9:00 am to noon.

**Marché de la Porte de Clignancourt (St. Ouen):** Rue des Entrepots, 18e. Métro: Porte de Clignancourt. This is the largest and most overwhelming of all Paris flea markets. Careful of pickpockets.

**Marché de la Porte des Lilas:** 19e. Métro: Porte des Lilas. Sunday and holidays.

**Marché de la Porte de Vanves:** Av. Georges-Lafenestre, 14e. Métro: Porte de Vanves. Saturday and Sunday.

**Marché aux Timbres:** Rond des Champs-Elysées, 8e. Métro: Franklin Roosevelt. Sunday mornings. Stamp collectors unite to trade and sell.

**Marché aux Fleurs:** Ile de la Cité, 1e. Métro: Cité. Daily assortment of fresh flowers and exotic plants.

**Marché aux Oiseaux:** Same location as the Marché aux Fleurs. Sunday mornings. Bird amateurs from all over bring their birds to sell, trade, and exhibit.

# Department & Chain Stores

**FNAC**—leading up-beat cooperative for books, records, photo and video and audio and electronics equipment. Also concert tickets and *après vente* service.

**Darty**—large appliance chain, wide variety of brands at reasonably good prices. Noted for service, delivery, and repair services. Salespeople wear blinding red jackets.

**Galeries Lafayette**—major department store with principal location at Auber/Opéra. All major fashion houses are represented here.

**Samaritaine**—largest and oldest department store in Paris. It has everything. Roof-top terrace on Building 2.

**Au Printemps**—major department store with principal location at Auber/Opèra. All major fashion houses are represented here.

**Au Bon Marché**—large department store chain, noted for its Left Bank location. A bit less visible than Galerie Lafayette and Printemps.

**Bazaar de l'Hôtel de Ville (BHV)**—a stand-by for all your needs. The chaotic basement is particularly well-equipped for hardware and houseware.

**Tati**—working-class department store for inexpensive clothes.

# Duty-free/Détaxe

Value-added tax (TVA) in France is steep—18.6% for most consumer goods and 28% for luxury items including certain food specialties. The exorbitant price of gasoline is a result of a hidden tax of 74%! Books, on the other hand, are taxed at only 5.5%. For purchases that are being taken out of the country, a part of the TVA can be recovered *(récupérée).* Anyone over 15 years old who is a foreign resident when purchasing goods and spending less than six months in France can benefit from duty-free shopping. If you have a *carte de séjour* you don't comply with the law. Items which cannot be detaxed are the following: tobacco, medicines, firearms, unset gems, works of art, collectors items and antiques, private means of transport (cars, boats, planes and their equipment), and large commercial purchases. To benefit from the duty-free allowance, ask the vendor at the point of purchase to give you a three-slip form called a *bordereau* (export sales invoice) and an addressed, stamped envelope. Non-EEC Nationals must present the detaxed purchases, the three slips (two pink, one green) and the stamped envelope provided by the shop to the French Customs agents at the airport, border crossings, or train crossings.

At the airport there is a window marked DETAXE. Make sure you don't send your duty free items in your checked baggage before presenting them to Customs in that you risk being denied the tax refund. If you leave the country by train, have your three slips validated by the Cus-toms agent on board. French Customs will keep the pink copies and send them in the envelope directly to the point of purchase, who will then reimburse you the amount indicated on space B3 of the form via check or credit card credit; keep the green copy for your files. Sometimes you will be reimbursed at the time of puchase, however, you still must undergo the above process. If you are an EEC resident, you will get a yellow invoice consisting of three copies, two yellow and one green. Upon reaching customs in your country, have all three slips validated by the Customs agent. Send the two yellow slips to the *Bureau des Douanes de Paris-La-Chapelle,* 61, rue de la Chapelle, 75018 Paris. Keep the green slip for your files. Your purchases, including tax, and from any single store, must amount to at least 1200 FF for foreign nationals or 2800 FF for EEC citizens.

# ENTERTAINMENT

You don't have to be in Paris very long to notice that the French pay much more attention to the sensual side of life than to the practical side. This is not only good news for the late night *bon vivant* who likes to wander home through the empty streets at dawn after a night of major-league clubbing. The daylight hours, too, are often packed with possibilities for tasting a bit of what the Parisians call *la qualité de la vie*. It would take a very dull mind and a seriously withered heart to be bored in this city.

The great battle in Paris over the last two centuries, in art and in life, has been between the avant-garde and classical: the Impressionists, for example, shocking the academics in the 1800s, the Dada and Surrealist movements shocking the *bourgeoisie* in the 1920s and 30s, the writers of the *nouveau roman* shocking the reader in the 1950s and 60s. The avant-garde and the classical act like tides that ebb and flow, one temporarily conquering the other. The waves caused by their inevitable clashes tend to keep things bubbling, and interesting for the casual observer and leisurely partaker of all kinds of entertainment, French or foreign. Though much has changed over the decades, Paris remains a place where the new and strange are not only tolerated, but welcomed and even proudly displayed. When it comes to the performing arts, this is still in evidence, just as it is in fashion—which in Paris has become a performing art of its own.

## Music

Choices run from the upper-crust, tuxedo and *escargot* atmosphere of the new Opéra de la Bastille to the merely crusty, like the head-bashing rock club Le Gibus near République. There's a lot in between—like jazz, for instance. Paris is one of the world's most jazz-appreciative cities, and France actually has a state-funded National Jazz Orchestra. Even in the years before World War II, black American musicians found the Parisians a better audience than anything in the US, and the trend continues today. The city sponsors a *Festival de Jazz* each fall (usually in October) but year round you can watch and listen to some of the best American and international acts at intimate cellar clubs like New Morning, the two Petit Journal clubs at Saint Michel and Mont-parnasse, the Petit Opportun at Châtelet and a number of others scattered across the city.

Parisians are serious jazz afficionados. Most clubs are small, crowded, smoky and fairly expensive. There is usually a cover charge, and the price of drinks can seriously unbalance the average checking account. But people don't come to these places to drink, they come for the music, which begins at about 22h, lasts long and loud through multiple sets and ends about 4h on weekends. Lots of people stay for the duration. When the band breaks, it's time for a Gaulois and loud conversation, in the honorable Paris tradition. And unlike most American establishments, no obnoxious waiter will force drinks on you and give you the bum's rush if you don't consume enough.

## Rock

For Paris rock, the choice is between the *salle* where you pay to sit and the club where you pay to dance. There's live music in either spot, but the livelier nights tend to be in the clubs. The big venues for live bands start at the new, massive Palais Omnisport de Bercy, one of the city's few buildings that has to have its walls mowed, to the *belle-epoquish,* more human-scale Zénith, La Cigale, Olympia or Elysée-Mont-martre. In general, Paris is not one of the essential stops on every band's concert tour, mostly because of the lack of big-profit-generating stadiums, so the selection for live bands is less than you'd see in some smaller American cities. But the big acts make it through town at one point or another.

**Palais Omnisports de Paris Bercy**
8, Bd. Bercy
75012 PARIS
tel: 43.42.01.23
**La Cigale**
120, Bd. Rochechouart
75018 PARIS
tel: 42.23.15.15
**Théâtre de l'Olympia**
2ter, rue Caumartin
75009 PARIS
42.66.18.25
**Elysée-Montmartre**
72, Bd. Rochechouart
75018 PARIS
tel: 42.52.25.15

## Clubs

The club scene is much livelier and more varied, with different beats for fashion zombies, celebs and apprentice celebs, and people who just like to get out and move it around. There are the "classic" joints that have been on the scene for years, like Le Palace (almost a Paris institution) and Les Bains Douches, where people-watching is at least as important as dancing. And then there are the African clubs, like Le Tango, Mambo Club and Keur Samba, for some serious shaking and a taste of the exotic.

And, of course, there are the high-tech discos like La Scala, lots of glass, aluminum, lasers and decibels in the auditory-damage range. The bouncers in these places tend to be numerous and over-trained in rapid intervention, which is fine if your primary concern is protecting your designer clothes from some drunken *zon-ard,* but bad news if you're not on best behavior. As a rule, American clubs and discos tend to be a lot rowdier than the Paris version. Public drunkeness or other overt signs of altered behavior are in *très mauvais goût* (very bad taste) here.

Not to be missed on the music and dance scene is the tiny Rue de Lappe near the Bastille, home of Le Balajo, one of this area's several ex-tango ballrooms that date from the nineteenth century. The atmosphere on certain nights is surreal in its mix: fortyish prostitutes dancing with African immigrants, French sailors on leave and on the prowl, the young and hip *branché* (connected or plugged -in—the French word for "in") crowd moving to live and recorded music, sometimes retro, sometimes rock. It's an experience. Note: The very *branché* use the invented language *verl'en* (the syllabic reversal of *l'envers,* meaning "backwards," thus *chébran* for *branché).*

As a general rule, the club scene in Paris gets started late, rarely before 23h, and doesn't get rolling until the tiny hours, sometimes, depending on the club, around 3h or 4h. The hard core spill out at dawn.

**Le Palace**
3, Cité Bergère
75009 PARIS
tel: 42.46.12.43

**Les Bains Douches**
7, rue Bourg l'Abbé
75003 PARIS
tel: 48.87.01.80

**Le Tango**
6, rue St. Severin
75005 PARIS
tel: 43.54.69.69

**Keur Samba**
79, rue de la Boétie
75008 PARIS
tel: 43.59.03.10

## Opera & Classical

Paris now has two operas, the ornate Opéra-Palais Garnier which could easily pass for a wedding cake if it were not so large, and the new state-of-the-art Opéra de la Bastille, which looks more like a postmodern ocean liner, only bigger. The Bastille opera now specializes in mega-productions of the repertory classics, while the old Opera features ballet and other forms of dance. Each is well worth the visit, although not always the steep ticket prices. The Palais Garnier, finished in the late 1800s, is a marvel of extreme architectural romanticism—lots of gold paint, red velvet and swarming cherubim. Guided tours are offered. Inexpensive tickets are available; you'll be too far away from the stage to get really involved but close enough to admire the Chagall fresco ceilings.

Other spots for an inspiring dose of Bach or Beethoven are the Salle Pleyel and Salle Gaveau in the 8e, the Théâtre des Champs-Elysées and the Théâtre Musical de Paris/Châtelet. Over in the 16e, Radio France, the national radio network, offers concerts at very reasonable prices in their spacious and comfortable auditorium. Certain churches around the city make good use of their excellent acoustics and sponsor concerts throughout the year, especially in the summer during the annual *Festival Estival*. And for the very latest in contemporary compositions, there is the famous *Ensemble Intercontemporain* led by Pierre Boulez, based in its underground studios next to the Centre Pompidou at IRCOM.

## Theater

If you like theater, you're in the right city. There are about a hundred and fifty theaters in and around Paris within Métro distance, and some two hundred shows a night in the high part of the season. France's rich theatrical tradition, like England's and Italy's, goes back to the late Middle Ages. Today the quantity is not always matched by the quality, but there's a lot to savor no matter what your taste.

At the top of the list is the *Comédie Française,* the famous *Maison de Molière,* founded more than three centuries ago by Louis XIV. Here some of the best actors in Europe perform the ancient and contemporary classics. Productions and costumes are lavish, and the audiences are extremely knowledgeable, especially when one of the French national treasures from Racine or Molière is on stage. Little old ladies in the front rows have been known to shout out the words in the rare event of an actor forgetting his line. The theater itself, called the Salle Richelieu after the Cardinal who was Louis' top cop for culture, is worth the price of entry, if only to witness firsthand its luxurious architecture. The *Comédie Française* offers one of the best ticket deals in town: fifteen minutes before curtain, you can get upper balcony seats for next to nothing.

There are other large and luxurious, state-funded theaters in Paris. The Odéon is also administered by the *Comédie Française* but features more contemporary work, expecially in its smaller theater, Le Petit Odéon. At Trocadéro is the Théâtre National de Chaillot housed within the massive marble interiors of the Palais du Trocadéro, and across town in the 20e is the new Théâtre National de la Colline, while the city-run Théâtre de la Ville is situated next to the Seine at Châtelet. All three program high quality work (at least technically). There are dozens of good middle-size theaters that offer a wide variety of styles and periods, like the Athenée-Louis Jouvet near Opéra, and the Théâtre de la Bastille that presents avant-garde work by younger writers and directors. To these are added the good theaters in the close suburbs that ring the city, like Saint Denis, Aubervilliers, Gennevilliers and Bobigny.

There are also many small theaters where the quality varies widely. The genre of *café-théâter,* usually very small cellar performance spaces that are a lot like jazz clubs, can be fun, but the quality is sometimes as low as their subterranean setting.

The price of theater tickets also varies greatly. The genre of boulevard theater, similar to Broadway in New York or the West End in London is very expensive and snobbish, for the over-forty crowd. The good state-run theaters have subsidized ticket prices, and good seats are available for 80 to 110 FF, sometimes less. Two-for-one tickets are sold on the day of per-formance at the KIOSK at Pl. de la Madeleine.

## Major Theaters in Paris

Amandiers de Paris (Nanterre)
tel: 43.66.42.17
Athénée Louis Jouvet
tel: 47.42.67.27
La Bastille
tel: 43.57.42.14
Comédie Française
tel: 40.15.00.15
Comédie de Paris
tel: 47.81.00.11
Huchette
tel: 43.26.38.99
Espace Cardin
tel: 42.66.33.30
Le Gymnase
tel: 42.46.79.79
Lucernaire Forum
tel: 45.44.57.34
Madeleine
tel: 42.65.07.09
Marigny
tel: 42.56.04.41
Mathurins
tel: 42.65.90.00
Montparnasse
tel: 43.22.77.74
Palais des Glaces
tel: 42.07.49.93
Palais Royal
tel: 42.97.59.81
Paris Villette
tel: 42.02.02.68
Petit Odéon
tel: 43.25.70.32
St. Georges
tel: 48.78.63.47
Théâtre des Champs-Elysées
tel: 47.20.36.37
Théâtre Grévin
tel: 42.46.84.47
Théâtre de l'Est Parisien
tel: 43.64.80.80
Théâtre de la Main d'Or

tel: 48.05.67.89
Théâtre National de Chaillot
tel: 47.27.81.15
Théâtre National de la Colline
tel: 43.66.43.60
Théâtre de Paris
tel: 43.59.39.39
Théâtre de la Ville à la Bastille
tel: 42.74.22.77

## Theaters for English-speakers

**Théâtre Marie Stuart**
4, rue Marie Stuart
75003 PARIS
tel: 45.08.17.80
Director: Robert CORDIER
**ACT (English Theatre Company)**
20, rue du Ct. René Mouchotte
75014 PARIS
Contact: Mme Anne WILSON
**La Galerie 55**
English Theatre of Paris
55, rue de Seine
75006 PARIS
tel: 43.26.63.51
**Theater Workshops**
6, rue Pierre au Lard
75004 PARIS
tel: 42.78.46.42
**Voices** (English & American Actors)
13, rue Chambéry
75015 PARIS
tel: 45.31.65.48

## Dance

The French dance scene is a very healthy one these days, and there's lots of activity in Paris and the close suburbs. The Théâtre de la Ville programs the big, internationally-known dance companies throughout the year. The Opéra features the work of the Ballet de l'Opéra de Paris, as well as another in-house group, *Groupe de Recherche Choréographique*, formerly headed by Rudolph Nureyev, that is more experimental in nature. Both do very high-quality work. Elsewhere, on a less-exalted level, there is some very interesting

dance work shown at the Théâtre de la Bastille, usually during the beginning of the year, as well as at the Ménagerie de Verre and the Café de la Danse, both in the Bastille neighborhood. The Centre Georges Pompidou (commonly referred to as Beaubourg) programs some interesting avant-garde companies from France and abroad. The numerous smaller dance companies based in and around Paris perform at various locations, sometimes in theaters, often in dance studios scattered across the city.

Of a far more rustic nature is the city's annual summer program called *Paris Villages*. In some neighborhoods, mostly the ones on the eastern side of the city, a bandstand is set up in one of the squares, party lights are strung up, and a retro band complete with accordion and female vocalist plays the old French favorites while everybody from the baker to your *concierge* comes out for a drink and a dance. It's lots of fun, very *vieux Paris*. Not to be missed under any circumstances are the local Bastille Day dances held at every fire station (called *Sapeurs-Pompiers)* the night of July 13th. Here you can dance the night away to live music that is usually so bad, it's an experience in itself. Everyone in the neighborhood comes out for these, from infants to the elderly. The wine flows, there are games and prizes, neighbors who steadfastly refuse to speak to each other during the rest of the year are suddenly great friends, while the firemen gallantly dance with every available woman or young girl. You will probably learn more about the French character in one evening like this than in a year's worth of observation and study. And you can work off your *gueule de bois* (hang-over) the next day by watching the Bastille Day parade on the Champs-Elysées.

## Cinema

Paris is a movie lovers' city with its several hundred cinemas, endless film festivals and retrospectives, and numerous film publications, libraries, and the celebrated Cinematéque (Trocadéro and Centre Pompidou). For complete weekly listings purchase each Wednesday *l'Officiel des Spectacles* or *Pariscope* for 2 and 3 FF respectively. The Cannes Film Festival takes place each year in May. And the Festival du Film Américain happens in Deauville each September.

## People Watching

Finally, in the general category of entertainment, it would be unfair not to say a word or two about that time-honored Parisian tradition, people watching. The warm weather months are the best for this, as it is most effectively done from a *café* table on the sidewalk. This city's obsession with fashion makes people watching especially fun in the right *quartier* (tourist areas are the worst; go for the more purely Parisian spots). What might seem like ill-mannered ogling in some societies is simply part of the daily or nightly routine in Paris, all part of what it means to live in and be entertained by this city and the people who make it the exhilarating, exasperating and extraordinary place it is.

## Special Events

**Fête de l'Humanité:** Sponsored by the *Parti Communiste* each September in the northern suburb of La Courneuve, this massive festival features stands from Communist parties around the world. Great music, food, and crafts.

**Fête de la Musique:** One night every June, Paris generously celebrates music of all kinds with neighborhood concerts, balls, and free street bands. Not to be missed.

**Foire du Trône:** Mammoth amusement park in early summer at the Porte Dorée. Try it for kicks.

## Sites & Monuments

Within an hour of Paris and easily accessible by train there are wonderful side trips to take: Versailles, Fontainebleau, Giverny, Chartes, Chantilly. The *Michelin Green Guide for Paris* is your best bet for full explanations. In Paris, the sights and monuments that eventually must be visited include: the Eiffel Tower, *l'Arc de Triomphe*, *Sacré-Coeur*, *Notre Dame*, the *Cimetières Montparnasse* and *Père Lachaise*, *La Bastille*, *La Pyramide du Louvre*, *Les Invalides*, *La Grande Arche de la Défense*, *La Villette*, the Tuileries Gardens, the Latin Quarter, *l'Institut du Monde Arabe*, *Les Halles*, etc. For these, consult a tourist guide (see Bibliography). There are organized bus tours but better, cheaper, and more fun are the public bus circuits recommended in *Pauper's Paris*. Also, take the public boat on the Seine which makes four stops in Central Paris. The *Bateaux-Mouches* can be a lovely way to spend a sunny afternoon or enchanting evening.

**Bateaux-Mouches**
Pont de l'Alma (Rive Droite)
75008 PARIS
tel: 42.25.96.10
**Batobus**
Seine Commuter Boat
Quai de l'Hôtel de Ville
75004 PARIS
tel: 48.87.09.44

# Parks

Paris has fabulous parks for strolling, sunning and recreation. The following are the some of the major parks in Paris:

**Bois de Boulogne:** 16e, Métro: Porte de Neuilly, Porte Dauphine or Les Sablons.

This park has existed as a green wooded space for centuries, and once stood just inside the fortified boundary of Paris. Now it has been transformed into 2000 acres of varied terrain which includes a rose garden, a museum, two world-famous race courses, a small zoo, a polo ground, a "Shakespeare Garden" where all the plants mentioned in the bard's plays can be found and the plays are staged in the summer, two lakes, broad avenues for riding, and paths for biking. You can even stay here in the campground. The *Jardin d'Acclimatation* has a little zoo, a playground, and a restaurant where you can share your table with the goats and chickens on Wednesdays. Nearby is the *Musée des Arts et Traditions Populaires.* There are boats for hire in the *Lac Inférieur,* and the *Parc de Bagatelle* is nearby with its castle and flower garden. At night the park changes character though. Crime and vandalism are not unheard of, and a most interesting variety of outdoor prostitutes and a hybrid of Brazilian transvestites flourish.

**Bois de Vincennes:** 12e, Métro: Porte de Charenton or Château de Vincennes.

Noted for its Parc des Flores, zoo, *hippodrome,* and stables, this park has two lakes with canoes for hire, biking and jogging paths, a medieval castle and dungeon, playing fields, and three fine restaurants.

**Jardin des Plantes:** 5e, Métro: Jussieu or Gare d'Austerlitz.

Houses a formal garden, a botanical greenhouse, the Natural History Museum, a hidden gazebo and a *ménagerie* (zoo).

**Jardin du Luxembourg:** 5e, Métro Luxembourg.

Located at the edge of the Latin Quarter along the Bd. St. Michel, this garden/park captures the contrasts of modern Paris, with its joggers, wooden toy sailboats, wrought iron park chairs, *Guignol* (matinee puppet shows), pony rides, tennis courts, and *pelouse* (lawn) designated for infants. The gardens are formal in the classical French style, with long open vistas and a popular central fountain. On the north side, the Château du Luxembourg, built by Marie de Medicis in 1615 (and which served as German headquarters during the Occupation) now houses the French Senate and a museum of art.

**Palais Royal:** 1er, Métro: Palais-Royale.

In the classic but now out-of-print and difficult to find *Nairn's Paris,* Ian Nairn describes the "luminous melancholy" of the elegant home and gardens of the Duc d'Orléans as "surely among the greyest joys in the world."

**Parc des Buttes-Chaumont:** 19e, Métro: Buttes Chaumont.

Lesser known to tourists and visitors, but absolutely charming, with two restaurants, exotic trees, and deep ravines.

**Parc Monceau:** Bd. de Cour-celle, 8e, Métro Monceau.

One of the loveliest spots in Paris, set in amidst exemplary bourgeois apartments. You'll find artificial waterfalls and ponds, glades and romantic statuary in this park. Nearby (63, rue de Monceau) is the *Musée Nissim de Camondo,* a completely preserved 18th-century mansion.

**Parc Montsouris:** 14e, Métro: Cité Universitaire.

Elegant formal park with unusual temple-like structure, located near the Cité Universitaire, the residential campus for international students in Paris. This Cité is the closest one will find in Paris to the American style university campus, organized according to national "houses", such as the Fondation des Etats-Unis, Casa de Cuba, Sweden House, etc.

**Jardin des Tuileries:** 1er, Métro: Tuileries.

Contains over 20 original Rodin sculptures.

## CULTURAL AWARENESS

Figuring out how French society works and how its people interact will undoubtedly take a fair amount of time. Think about your understanding of the society you live in—all those cumulative years spent learning to participate in a system with its multitude of layers of unspoken rules, codes, and underlying assumptions. With an open mind you will broaden your knowledge of both French society and your own; you'll get sharper in knowing what people are saying when they're not talking.

### Going Out

The French almost always organize their social lives around a meal. This is true also for a lot of professional and commercial activities. So count on a long and langorous dinner if you get asked out by a French person. If you're doing the asking, you should probably count on a meal too, although your guest might be interested in or impressed by a meal indigenous to your culture. It's very common to meet someone at a *café* at 20h or 20h30, have an *apéritif* (a kir or a glass of wine) and then proceed to dinner somewhere. Learn by heart the names of a few *cafés* that you like and that are convenient, so you'll be able to suggest a meeting point. Remember that usually, even among young people, the person who does the inviting also pays for the dinner. For the French this is highly normal. Going "Dutch" is foreign. Often the guest will offer to pay the next time. *Je t'invite la prochaine fois.* You will almost never see French people dividing up a bill at the table. Sometimes they'll fight over who will pay, each wanting to pay, but the idea of determining who ordered what and "did you have wine?" kind of thing is alien, and even distasteful. So be forewarned. Money still has a vulgar connotation.

The French also go to the cinema a lot (see Cinema). Count on about 35 FF per person, with a reduced price on Monday nights. Most cinemas give reductions to students with valid cards (except on the week-ends). The films start usually 20 to 30 minutes after the time of the announced *séance,* the trailers and advertisements. This pre-film stuff can be very enjoyable and aesthetically rich. French cinema commercials are stylish and sensual. After paying 35 FF to get in don't be disturbed by the one or two franc tip per person you'll be intimidated into coughing-up by the usher as you enter the *salle* (projection hall). This is a long Parisian tradition. There is no popcorn in French cinemas, but after the coming attractions a woman will come around selling ice cream and candy *(bonbons)*. As an English-speaking person, you'll want to make sure that if the film you're seeing is originally in English, that you attend a cinema that is showing the film in V.O. *(version originale),* as opposed to V.F. *(version française).* It's a drag seeing Woody Allen dubbed into French.

If you're invited to someone's house in the evening, it's almost always going to be for dinner, unless it has been clearly stated otherwise. It's always appropriate to bring something, usually a good bottle of wine—never a *vin de table* (table wine) or inexpensive, unknown wine. A well-wrapped bouquet of flowers, *pour offrir,* not the plain ones sold in the Métro, is always appreciated. But don't show up empty-handed. Dress slightly better than you think is appropriate. The French, even young people and students, tend to dress well when going out socially. Only in the last five years or so have people dared go out in the streets in sweatpants and sweatshirts, even for shopping.

## Sexuality

It's always very difficult and dangerous to generalize about how people think and act. In the area of sex this is particularly so, but a few comments might be useful. Young French women, although not prudish, can often be highly sentimental. The men, although not extremely macho, tend to embrace a fair amount of Latin attitudes. The French concept of flirting—with the potentiality of "picking up" someone, is called *draguer* (to drag). This is actually closer to "chatting up" than "picking up." It has a million variations and nuances and can be either flattering or annoying. Paris is the northern edge of the Latin spirit. Male attitudes in general aren't as obviously macho as in Spain or Italy, but there are still attitudes here that might seem sexist to you. On the whole, it is fair to say, in any case, that the French are less inhibited or up-tight and have fewer hang-ups about sex, nudity, and human functions than Anglo-Saxons, for instance. Some French men, though, have pre-conceived notions about American women, especially Californians, in terms of accessibility, "openness," "wildness." These can be reenforced unknowingly by the fact that Americans do tend to be publically more expressive and open.

The French don't judge public officials by their private lives, and view sex scandals (like the one which ruined Gary Hart's political career) as silly and typically American in its Puritan values.

The movement for safe sex in France didn't get much further than the sensuous television ads for the use of condoms. The French approach was not to scare the public with AIDS (*SIDA*) but to convey the positive message that sex with condoms is beautiful and exciting.

The gay and lesbian communities in Paris, although more open and public now than ten years ago, are still somewhat discreet. On the rue Vieille du Temple in the Marais a number of busy, gay night spots and bookstores can be found. The gay community has a Paris magazine called *Gai Pied Hebdo,* 45, rue Sedaine, 75011 PARIS, tel: 43.57. 52.05 (which also has an *SOS Ecoute Gai* phone line, tel: 48.06.19.11). Other gay organizations: *Comité Gai Paris/Ile de France,* 56, rue Ordener, 75018 PARIS, tel: 42.64.27.64 and *Autres Cultures/Lieu Associatif Lesbien et Gai,* 46, rue Sauffroy, 75017 PARIS, tel: 42.63.56.89.

On the whole, you will see a general lack of puritanical attitudes. The French are very comfortable with nudity and all that concerns the human body. The same ad in a London Tube station with a clothed woman would show her topless in Paris. Topless advertising is not considered sexist by either women or men. *C'est beau.* Toplessness isn't even really considered nudity. In some boutiques, you may see women try on blouses without stepping into a changing room.

The rue Saint Denis is the main prostitution street in Paris. Women stand out by their doors openly and, for the most part, are un-harrassed day and night. Around 16h it's interesting to observe the undisturbed mixture of prostitutes coming out to work and school kids returning from school. This is indicative of a larger tolerance. Other areas of dense prostitution include the Bois de Boulogne, where prostitutes and transvestites line the dark roadways peddling their wares, as well as all the major boulevards near the *portes de Paris.*

## Drinking

There is essentially no enforce-ment of a drinking age. You'll never get "carded" or turned away in a *café,* bar or liquor store. You can buy whiskey along with your daily groceries. As a positive consequence, public drunkenness by rowdy youths is not very prevalent. It has been estimated that the average French person over 20 years old consumes an average of 53 grams (1.87 ounces) of pure alcohol per day, making him a participant in an impressive percentage: the French remain the world's heaviest consumers of alcohol per capita after the Luxem-bourgeois. Wine is still served with both lunch and dinner in many families, but the meal is no longer considered incomplete without it. Alcoholism in France results in 17,000 deaths a year, caused more by cheap red wine than hard alcohol, and it is a phenomenon which is vastly more common in rural areas.

## Smoking

A very large portion of French society smokes cigarettes. Con-sciousness is changing but very slowly. Restaurants still readily accept smoking at all tables. Only McDonald's and a select few have created Non-Smoking sections. So, if you're intolerant of smokers, be warned. Similarly, those of you who smoke will not experience the ostracism that smokers incur in the US. If you ask others to put out their cigarettes or to re-direct the smoke elsewhere, be prepared for some looks and gestures of displeasure.

Cigarettes can only be purchased in a *tabac.* They are not available in drug stores, gas stations, and department stores. Some *cafés* and restaurants sell cigarettes as a service to their customers. They cost about 10 FF a pack.

If the smoke has a pungent, unfamiliar odor this is because in France hardcore smokers consume the classic, blue packed and filter-less Gauloises or Gitanes, made of untoasted tobacco. Also, a number of people roll their own cigarettes. It's cheaper.

## Drugs

Drug possession is a serious offense in France, and laws are particularly hard on foreigners. Drug use isn't nearly as much of a social problem, though, as it is in the United States. Until recently there was a cinema in Paris where it was understood that marijuana smokers would not be bothered. And late at night in the Métro as well as in certain bars and clubs, a whiff or two of the popular hash and tobacco mixture may come your way. But attention! If you want to remain in France without problems, think twice before breaking the law. Note that the police, who are often undercover, have the right to frisk anyone at any time. Crossing international borders is of course particularly risky, especially traveling from any island of southern latitude or returning from Amsterdam, where charter buses are often searched with the aid of police dogs.

Even at parties, smoking hash—marijuana is nearly impossible to find—can be met with disapproval. Cocaine use is not nearly as widespread as in the US. And in general French youths seem to feel less pressured to spend time, energy, and money on socially rebellious activities and habits.

## Parties

Even among young people parties are rarely given without a specific occasion to celebrate. A party can be called a *fête, une soirée,* or *un boum.* A *fête* is usually a celebration like a birthday or graduation. A *soirée* is a civilized evening party with not necessarily a lot of people. A *boum* tends to be larger and louder, and usually reserved for the high school crowd.

## Holidays

Holidays in France bring out two typically French traits: the respect for ceremony and ritual and the joy of not having to work. The French *jour du pont* (long weekend) is an occasion for most Parisians to exit to the country. The month of May is particularly affected. Beware of heavy traffic on the *autoroutes* and at the main *portes* (gateways to the city). This is good news for those who stay, because the pace of

Paris slows down remarkably, leaving the tourist and others to enjoy the absence of traffic and noise. Being aware of holidays helps you stay in touch with the rhythms of French life (See Annual Events). Plan your activities around these dates since many shops, restaurants, and museums close on public holidays.

## Vacation Time

French law guarantees everyone who works *(salarié)* five weeks of paid vacation. *Les vacances,* a cherished institution among the French, is a right, not a privilege. In general, it's safe to say that the French are willing to trade higher wages for security and benefits, in other words, a higher quality of daily life.

Aside from the five week vacation, which most people divide between summer and winter (three to four weeks in summer, one to two weeks in winter), here is a list of holidays and their respective customs. Note that traditionally Paris empties out in August, with July being the second heaviest vacation month. Avoid traveling on July 1, July 30, August 1 and August 30.

## Annual Events

A new offering from the *Office du Tourisme et des Congrès de Paris* is a comprehensive card called *Carte Paris Sélection.* The cost is 260 FF for an annual membership. Card holders receive monthly mailings of every publication published by the *Office du Tourisme et des Congrès,* including a calendar of the month's *manifestations* (cultural events), spectacles, conventions, information on hotels and restaurants, maps, and a calendar of major annual events. Discounts are also offered at many museums, monuments and *visites conférences* (guided tours of historic sites and art exhibitions and public seminars).

**Office du Tourisme et des Congrès de Paris**
127, av. des Champs-Elysées
75008 PARIS
tel: 47.23.03.02

---

## National Public Holidays

**January 1** *Jour de l'An* (New Year's Day)*
This day is generally devoted to visiting parents and older relatives and exchanging gifts (instead of on Christmas Day). *Concierges* expect to be tipped at this time. Postmen, firemen, street cleaners, etc. solicit their New Year's gifts as early as November, offering tacky calendars in exchange for year-end tokens of appreciation (cash).

**Late March/April** *Pâques* (Easter)
First Sunday following the full moon of the equinox of spring, at the end of March or early April.

**Monday after Easter** *Lundi de Pâques* (Easter Monday)*

**May 1** *Fête du Travail* (Labor Day)*
May 1st was designated an International Labor Day in 1889 and is observed in France as a legal holiday (celebrated everywhere in the world except the US). Labor groups generally parade in different sections of Paris. A custom in France on this day is to present *muguet* (lilies of the valley) to friends and loved ones to bring them happiness and *porte bonheur* (good luck). May 1st is the only day of the year that anyone can sell *muguet* or other flowers without a license. If you find yourself at the Elysées Palace, you might see *Les Forts des les Halles* (porters of the Paris market), dressed in the traditional porters outfits, presenting *muguet* to the President of France.

**May 8** *Victoire 1945* (V.E. Day)*
*Défilés* (parades) take place throughout the city, the largest and most impressive on the Champs-Elysées.

**May 13** *Fête de Jeanne d'Arc* (Joan of Arc Day)

**Sixth Thursday after Easter** *Ascension* (Ascension Day)*

**May (last Sunday)** *Fête des Mères* (Mother's Day)

**June (third Sunday)** *Fête des Pères* (Father's Day)

**July 14** *Jour de la Bastille* (Bastille Day)*
Celebrations begin on the 13th and include fireworks and streetdances. Admission is free to performances in all National Theaters on this day.

**August 15** *Fête de l'Assomption* (Feast of the Assumption)*
Christian holiday commemorating the assumption of the Virgin Mary. Celebrations such as harvest festivals and the blessing of the sea happen on this day.*

**November 1** *Toussaint* (All Saints' Day)* Halloween, the North American celebration related to this Christian holiday, is not acknowledged in France.

**November 2** *Jour des Morts* (All Souls Day)*
It is the custom in France to visit the graves of relatives prior to the *Jour des Morts* or on the day itself. Flowers (usually chrysanthemums) are placed on the graves. Chrysanthemums were the seasonal flowers before greenhouses existed, and are the traditional flowers used on this day. Thus don't even consider offering chrysanthemums when invited for dinner, etc.

**November 11** *Fête de l'Armistice* (Veteran's Day)*

**December 25** *Noël* (Christmas)*
It is the time to eat the holiday foods at the traditional Christmas dinner *(le réveillon): boudin blanc* (white sausage), *fois gras,* pheasants, *saumon fumé, huîtres, and bûches de Noël* (yule log-shaped cake).

*Denotes most schools and businesses are closed.

**January**
Fashion shows (summer collection).
**February**
Bread and Pastry Exposition.
**March**
Palm Sunday, *Prix du Président de la République,* at Auteuil race course, Bois de Boulogne.
**April**
April-May: Paris Fair (commercial exhibition) at Parc des Expositions.
Early April-early October: *Son et Lumière* at les Invalides.
**May**
May-September: Illuminated Fountains at Versailles.
Mid-May: Paris Marathon (foot race around Paris).
Mid-May-late June: Versailles Music and Drama Festival.
Late May-early June: French Open Tennis Championships, Roland Garros Courts.
**June**
Early June: Paris Air Show (odd years only), Le Bourget Airport.
Early June-mid-July: Marais Festival (music, drama, exhibitions).
June: a festival of music, drama, and dance at Saint-Denis.
Mid-June: Grand Steeplechase de Paris at Auteuil race course, Bois de Boulogne.
Mid-June: *Fête du Pont-Neuf* (booths and street performers on the bridge and in the Place Dauphine).
June 21: *Fête de la Musique*—music groups and free open air concerts throughout the city.
June 24: *Feux de la Saint-Jean* (fireworks) at Sacré-Cœur.
End of June: Grand Prix de Paris, Longchamp race course, Bois de Boulogne.
**July**
Early July: Festival St Denis tel: 42.43.77.72 Classical music festival with concerts throughout Paris.
July 14: Jour de la Bastille (celebrations throughout the city and military display in the Champs-Elysées).
Mid-July: finish of the *Tour de France* cycle race in the Champs-Elysées.

Throughout July:
Fashion shows (winter collection).
*Festival International d'Opéra* tel: 42.68.23.32 Numerous eventsheld for two weeks at Versailles.
Mid-July-mid-September: *Festival Estival de Paris* tel: 48.41.98.01 Classical music, concerts, and recitals throughout the city.
**September**
Festival de Montmartre
Late September-early December: *Festival d'Automne* tel: 42.96.12.27 Music, drama, ballet, exhibitions.
**October**
First Sunday: Prix de l'Arc de Triomphe at Longchamp race course, Bois de Boulogne.
Early October: Montmartre wine festival, Paris Motor Show at the Parc des Expositions (even years only).
Beaujolais Festival: when *le nouveau beaujolais est arrivé,* the party starts at midnight as the first bottle of the new harvest is allowed to be opened. People generally stop whatever they are doing and go for a glass at the nearest *café* or bar.
Late October-early November: *Festival de Jazz de Paris* tel: 47.83.84.06 Two-week festival which includes lots of big name jazz artists.
October-November: Festival d'Art Sacré tel: 42.77.92.26. Concerts and exhibitions held in churches throughout the city.
**November**
November 11: Armistice Day ceremony at Arc de Triomphe.
**December**
Christmas Eve: midnight mass at Nôtre-Dame.
For further details call the *Office du Tourisme de Paris,* tel: 47.23.61.72.

## Jim Haynes (Handshake Editions)

Of the Americans in Paris few are as colorful, free-spirited, and community-minded as Jim Haynes, teacher, publisher, spiritual guru of limitless love and spiritual networking. Every Sunday night in his atelier more than 50 friends, visitors, and new guests take part in (for a nominal fee) a wonderful blue-plate dinner with unlimited wine and beer. Proceeds go to buy food shipments for people in oppressed places. Jim's 14 volume address book tells all, as does his autobiography, *Thanks for Coming* (Faber & Faber). Reservations for Sunday are made by phone on Saturday afternoon. Jim Haynes Atelier A2 83, rue de la Tombe Issoire, 75014 PARIS, tel: 43.27.17.67.

# CARS/DRIVING

Coming to Paris as a student you most likely will neither need a car nor want one, but still there are a number of things you might want to know regarding cars, driving, and parking in France. Young people in France are in no way as obsessed with cars as their contemporaries in the US. Driving in France is not seen as a symbol of freedom, status, and virility. Some French students have cars—traditionally the powerless but charming *Deux Chevaux*—but this is certainly not the rule.

The attitudes you may witness among drivers should tip you off to a lot of things. Although the French are fast and aggressive, relatively few acts of real meanness occur in traffic. The largest difference between French and American urban drivers is a question of morality. If you're waiting on a long line to make a left turn, undoubtedly some feisty guy in a Renault 25 will barrel past you in the on-coming lane, zoom to the front of the line and steal the light. In the US, the UK, or Germany this would cause instant anger because it's a violation and it's unfair. In France, drivers might show discontent too but not out of moral outrage; they'd envy him. They'd be angry because he pulled ahead and they were left in the dust. At the risk of over-generalizing, when the French can profit for their own gain and get away with it, they tend to do it. Higher principles are reserved for higher matters than daily traffic. They are filled with facial and hand gestures. They speed up at lights and breeze past slow cars or jay-walkers, but they will never hit you.

The *priorité à droite* (yield right-of-way) is often seen as a peculiarity among North Americans, where the opposite is the rule. Essentially, just remember that anyone coming from your right in almost all situations has the right-of-way. Sometimes a car will pull out onto a busy road from a dinky sidestreet. You must yield unless there is a sign that tells you otherwise. Often drivers take unfair advantage of this rule of the road and swing far to the right and loop around to make left turns or merge into another road. The *priorité à droite* seems well-engrained in the Parisian mind-set in that people tend to follow this even when walking.

In France, the law requires that seat belts be worn by all passengers. Failure to do so can result in a 230 FF fine for the driver and 500 FF for the passenger. Although this law is a good safety measure, it sometimes can be employed as a pretext for the police to stop cars at random. The law also states that you must carry your *permis de conduire* (driver's license), *carte grise,* and *certificat d'assurance* at all times. Failure to present these can mean stiff fines. *Brûler un feux rouge* (running a red light) is a serious offense that will cost you a minimum of 2000 FF and a morning in court. Crossing a solid white line is also seen as a major fault. U-turns are illegal.

## Drivers Licenses

After the first year of residence in France, foreigners are required by law to obtain a French driver's license. You either trade-in your foreign license (subject to certain conditions) and get a French license without a test, or you keep your old license and take the written test *(Code de la*

Route) and the road test. Make an appointment at your *préfecture*. In Paris there can be a six-month wait. In France, almost everyone applies for a license through an *Ecole de Conduite* (Driving School), private companies that practically have a monopoly on the market. Almost no one succeeds in getting a license as a *candidat libre* (independent applicant). Thus with the required 30 hours of road time, getting your license is time-consuming and costly (±2000 FF).

For the first year, though, your national or state driver's license, along with an International Driver's License, will suffice. This license can be obtained at AAA offices throughout the U.S for $10. It's more work getting one in France.

## Purchasing a Car

When purchasing a car, you need to bring the *carte grise,* the French car registration papers of the seller (on which he has written *VENDU,* signed, and dated), to the *préfecture* in your *arrondissement* or *département.* You also need to obtain, at the *préfecture* or *mairie* of the *arrondissement* where the car has been previously registered, a *lettre de non-gage,* which means that there are no liens or outstanding debts on the car. For cars over five years old, the law requires that the owner provide the buyer with a *certificat d'inspection,* which can be obtained for 190 FF from certified service stations and is valid for six months. *Plaques de matriculation* (license plates) must be changed by the new buyer within 48 hours after the new *carte grise* has been issued. New plates are stamped out while you wait at most service stations for about 130 FF.

## Annual Registration Sticker (*Vignette*)

*Vignettes* can be purchased in any *tabac,* upon presentation of the *carte grise,* and are renewed every November. Affix yours on the inside lower right-hand corner of the *parebrise* (windshield) by December 1. You get fined after December 31. However, *tabacs* only stock them until November 30; after that you have to join the line in the tax office. The tax varies depending on the size, age and horsepower of the car.

## Auto Insurance

If you can prove that you've been insured for two years; you can benefit from a French insurer's *bonus* (discount). For the best rates, check the MACIF and MAAF, two large insurance cooperatives. Again, don't expect snappy service.

Here's one American insurance broker who is noted for his service to English-speaking clients.
**Groupe Peulve, S.A.**
Reuben Giles
126 rue Jules Guesde
92300 LEVALLOIS-PERRET
tel: 47.31.40.41

## Car Rentals

To rent a car in France you must be at least 21 years old and hold a valid driver's license (at least one year old). A major credit card facilitates matters.
**Avis Location de Voitures S.A.**
5, rue Bixio
75007 PARIS
tel: 46.09.92.12 (Res. & Info)
**Budget**
4, av. Franklin Roosevelt
75008 PARIS
tel: 42.25.79.89
**Central Rent-a-Car**
3, rue d'Argenteuil
75001 PARIS
tel: 42.60.52.02

**Europcar (National)**
46, rue Pierre Charron
75008 PARIS
tel: 47.20.30.40
tel: 30.43.82.82 (Res. & Info)
**Hertz France S.A.**
tel: 47.88.51.51 (Res. & Info)
Minitel: 3514 HERTZ
**InterRent**
42, av. de Saxe
75007 PARIS
tel: 45.67.82.17 (Res. & Info)
Toll Free: 05.33.22.10
Minitel: 3614 IR

# Parking

Parking in Paris can be a nightmare. There are just too many cars in Paris for the amount of space. Throughout most of central Paris, on-street paid parking is the rule. Instead of parking meters, Paris has adopted a system whereby you purchase a paper ticket from a parking meter machine on the block where you've parked, indicating until what time you have paid. This, you leave on your windshield. The flock of women in blue coats you'll see parading up and down the avenue writing tickets can rarely be charmed. The basic parking ticket is 75 FF, which skyrockets to 220 FF if unpaid after three months. Parking in an illegal spot is an automatic 230 FF, which becomes 500 FF if unpaid.

At the same time, the style of Paris parking is somewhat chaotic, as you'll habitually see cars pulled up on sidewalks, over curbs, and into other seemingly illegal spaces. This is especially true at night in the Latin Quarter and around Montparnasse. If you get towed, call the Police in the neighborhood in which you've parked for the address of the tow yard (*fourrière*). Be prepared to pay in cash or by French check.

Curiously, there is a tradition in France that all parking fines are waived by the winner after each Presidential election, so if elections are coming up within a year, you might want to hold out on paying; otherwise, better pay promptly to avoid the accumulation of penalties. Parking tickets are, of course, paid by purchasing the *timbre fiscal* again in the *tabac,* sticking half on the return portion of the ticket and retaining the other for your records. When you receive a note in the mail and a bill for the penalty on unpaid tickets you can no longer *régler* (pay) with a *timbre fiscal;* you must send a check to or visit the *Trésor Public*. Payment schedules for large fines can be negotiated. With the increase of greater European cooperation, tickets given to other EEC cars are forwarded for collection in those respective countries.

# Motorcycles

Paris hosts a proliferation of motorcycles, scooters, *mobilettes* and other motorized two-wheelers. Most of Paris' internal message and delivery services move this way.

If you see a rambling mass of motorcycles on a Friday night, don't be alarmed. There's a long tradition in Paris of motorcyclists gathering at 23h at the Bastille and making a giant tour *en masse* along the *grands boulevards.* For those considering scooters and mopeds, a special driver's license is not needed for models up to 50cc, although helmets are required. Some of these vehicles run on a special gas/oil mixture called *mélange*.

# SPORTS

It is true that more and more Parisians are becoming fitness conscious, but the fact remains that recreational sports do not yet play a very important role in daily Parisian life. The closest you'll see in Paris to the jogging phenomenon in New York's Central Park or along Boston's Charles River is the Luxembourg Gardens. The air quality in Paris is not ideal for running, although the Bois-de-Vincennes and Bois-de-Boulogne are vast, lush, relatively pollution-free, and well-marked for runners.

In France, you're either *sportif* or *non-sportif.* So make up your mind. *Non-sportifs* outnumber the *sportifs* and most smoke cigarettes. The *sportifs* tend to be very *sportif* and often belong to clubs, where they regularly swim, play tennis or squash. Other *sportifs* only spectate the *le foot* (football/soccer) matches and horse racing and hang around the special *cafés* marked PMU on the awning. Several sports events in France are of great importance. The *Tour de France* international bicycling race; *Paris-Dakar* international car rally; *Roland Garros,* the French Open in tennis; the *Paris Marathon* for runners; and the European Cup soccer matches are a few highlights.

## University Sports

Team sports at French universities are organized by clubs and student organizations. They tend to be only moderately organized and modestly equipped. There are no large scholarships to entice middle linebackers to the Sorbonne. They can be serious, but rarely obsessed, other than insisting that all participants have proper enrollment cards, health certificates, and insurance forms. If you show up at a university sports complex in your gym clothes but have forgotten your active Student ID, a guardian at the door will most likely not let you in. Always carry identification with you.

A few years back, the starting five for the basketball team for the Sorbonne included two short Americans, a scrappy Mexican, a Japanese forward who owned no white socks, and a lanky French student who was more or less flatfooted. So playing organized sports for a French university team can be fun and recreational, but it won't be ruthlessly competitive. American university programs have a variety of facilities available to them. AUP, for example, has an arrangement with the gym and swimming pool at Mabillon-St.-Germain-des-Près. For pickup basketball games go to the courts in the Champ de Mars on Sunday mornings or the American Church on Saturdays. For up-to-date sports information, including upcoming sporting events, call *Allô-Sports* (42.76.54.54)—a recorded phoneline operating from 10h30-17h Monday-Thursday and 10h30-16h30 on Friday. In the last few years the French have become more interested in playing American baseball and football. *Canal Plus* regularly broadcasts Monday Night Football and other sports events. Tennis has become more and more available, although still mostly limited to clubs—and expensive.

Here's a listing of sports contacts in the Paris area:

**Baseball**
**Baseball Club de France**
tel. 43.38.20.00
**Association Club de**
**Baseball & Softball**
3, allée de la Tour d'Auvergne
91150 ETAMPES
tel: 60.80.14.17
President: M. Jérôme LEBRUN

**Basketball**
**Marché St. Germain**
75006 PARIS
**Bir Hakeim**
9, rue Jean Rey
75015 PARIS
**American Church**
65, Quai d'Orsay
75007 PARIS
tel: 47.05.07.99

**Bowling**
**Bowling Club de Paris**
**Jardin d'Acclimatation**
Bois de Boulogne
75116 PARIS
tel: 40.67.94.00
**Paris Université Club (PUC)**
31, av. Georges Bernanos
75005 PARIS
tel: 43.26.97.09
**Bowling Mouffetard**
73, rue Mouffetard
75005 PARIS
tel: 43.31.09.35
(everyday 10h-2h, Fr. and Sat. until 4h)
**Stadium**
66, av d'Ivry
75013 PARIS
tel. 45.86.55.52
(every day 14h-2h)
**Bowling de Montparnasse**
25 rue Commandant-Mouchotte
75014 PARIS
tel. 43.21.61.32
(Mon-Fri, 10h-2h. Sat. & Sun.until 4h)

**Boxing**
**Fédération Française de Boxe**
**de l'Ile de France**
tel: 42.77.42.36

**Cycling**
**Bicyclub de France**
8, place de la Porte de Champerret
75017 PARIS
tel: 47.66.55.92

**Cricket**
**Paris University Club**
tel: 42.77.42.36 or 42.77.38.25

**Fencing**
**Ligue d'Escrime de Paris**
tel: 47.66.93.63

**Football**
**Fédération Française**
**de Football Américain**
37, rue Lafayette
75009 PARIS
tel: 42.41.51.02

**Golf**
**American Golf**
14, rue du Regard
75006 PARIS
tel: 45.49.12.52

**Horseback Riding**
**Bayard UCPA Centre Equestre**
Bois de Vincennes
75012 PARIS
tel: 43.65.46.87
**Centre Hippique du Touring Club**
Rte. Muettte à Neuilly
75016 PARIS
tel: 45.01.20.88

**Ice Skating**
**Patinoire des Buttes-Chaumont**
30, rue Edouard-Pailleron
75019 PARIS
tel: 42.39.86.10
**Féderation Francaise**
**des Sports de Glace**
tel: 40.26.51.38

**Ping Pong**
tel: 42.57.74.13

**Roller Skating**
**La Main Jaune**
rue Caporal Peugeot
75017 PARIS
tel: 47.63.26.47

**Rugby**
**Fédération Française de Rugby**
tel: 48.74.84.75
**American Rugby Company**
171, rue St. Martin
75003 PARIS
tel: 40.27.86.00
**Comité de l'Ile de France de Rugby**
Information on amateur clubs and organizations
tel: 42.46.68.66

**Soccer**
Information
tel: 47.20.65.40
**Stade Suffren**
2, av de Suffren
75015 PARIS

**Squash**
**Squash Puc Pontoise**
19, rue de Pontoise
75005 PARIS
tel: 43.54.82.45
**Squash Rennes Raspail**
149, rue de Rennes
75006 PARIS
tel: 45.44.24.35
**Sporting Club Loisir**
24, rue Richard-Lenoir
75011 PARIS
tel: 43.67.13.98

**Swimming** (selection of best pools)
**Piscine de Pontoise**
19 rue de Pontoise
75005 PARIS
tel: 43.54.82.45
**Piscine Déligny**
Situated on a barge on the Seine
75007 PARIS
**Piscine Buttes-aux-Cailles**
5, pl Paul-Verlaine
75013 PARIS
tel: 45.89.60.05
Art-deco pool built in 1910
**Aqualand**
91 GIF SUR YVETTE
tel: 60.12.25.90
(outdoor pool with waves)

**Volleyball**
**Marché St. Germain**
6, rue Clement
75006 PARIS

# Health Clubs

Over the last several years, there has been a dramatic upsurge of interest in health clubs and fitness centers. Garden Gym is well-adapted for younger people, with seven locations around Paris, while Gymnase Club, with its 15 locations, is the largest and thus a bit more impersonal. A series of discounts are available to students and others. Currently, Gymnase Club offers a 12 month membership to AUP Students at 1400 FF. There are several other alternatives. Most university programs have been offered special discounts for their students. Here are some numbers for inquiries.

**Garden Gym Beaugrenelle**
208, rue de Vaugirard
75015 PARIS
tel: 47.83.99.45
Métro: Volontières
Open Mon-Fri 7h30-9h30, Sat 9h-14h.

**Garden Gym Elysées**
65, av des Champs-Elysées
75008 PARIS
tel: 42.25.87.20
Métro: Franklin D. Roosevelt
Open Mon-Fri 9h-22h, Sat. 10h-17h.

**Gymnase Club Denfert Rochereau**
28, av du Général Leclerc
Les Portiques d'Orléans
75014 PARIS
tel: 45.42.50.57

**Gymnase Club Nation**
16, rue des Colonnes du Trône
75012 PARIS
tel: 43.45.93.12

# Religion

Although France is a deeply Catholic country, religion does not play a highly visible role in Parisian life or values. Church and State formally separated in 1905, and the debate over public *(laïque)* vs. parochial education in France flares up periodically. As does the heated and recurrent issue of racism and anti-semitism.

The Paris area, of course, has some of Europe's most astonishing cathedrals and churches. Attending Mass in Notre Dame or l'Eglise de St.-Germain-des-Prés, for example, can be memorable. Just being in the presence of the stained glass windows at Chartres is a spiritual experience.

As in all big cities, the opportunities for worship are numerous. Here's a list of what Paris offers in English.

**American Church in Paris**
65, Quai d'Orsay
75007 PARIS
tel: 47.05.07.99
Pastor: Dr. Thomas DUGGAN
(non-denominational service)

**American Cathedral**
**Church of the Holy Trinity**
23, av. George V
75008 PARIS
tel: 47.20.17.92
Dean: The Very Reverend James R. LEO
(Episcopalian and Anglican services)

**Christian Science Church**
36, Bd. St. Jacques
75014 PARIS
tel: 47.07.26.60

**Church of Jesus-Christ of Latter-Day Saints**
23, rue du Onze Novembre
78110 LE VESINET
tel: 39.76.55.88
Leader: James JOHNSON

**Church of Scotland**
17, rue Bayard
75008 PARIS
tel: 48.78.47.94
Reverend: Bruce ROBERTSON

**Consistoire Israëlite de Paris**
(synagogue)
44, rue de la Victoire
75009 PARIS
tel: 42.85.71.09

**Emmanuel Baptist Church**
56, rue des Bons-Raisins
92500 RUEIL MALMAISON
tel: 47.49.15.29
Pastor: Dr. B.C. THOMAS

**Great Synagogue**
44, rue de la Victoire
75009 PARIS
tel: 45.26.95.36

**International Baptist Fellowship**
123, av. du Maine
75014 PARIS
tel: 47.51.29.63

**La Mosquée** (Moslem)
Place du Puits de l'Ermite
75005 PARIS
tel: 45.35.97.33

**Liberal Synagogue**
24, rue Copernic
75016 PARIS
tel: 47.04.37.27
Rabbi Michael WILLIAMS

**Quaker Society of Friends**
114, rue de Vaugirard
75006 PARIS
tel: 45.48.74.23
(Sunday silent meditation service)

**St. George's Anglican Church**
7, rue August-Vacquerie
75006 PARIS
tel: 47.20.22.51
Chaplain: Martin DRABER

**St. Joseph's Roman Catholic Church**
50, av. Hoche
75008 Paris
tel: 42.27.28.56
Father Marius DONNELLY

**St. Michael's Church**
5, rue d'Aguesseau
75008 PARIS
tel: 47.42.70.88
Venerable Brian LEA

# ANIMALS

The French are highly indulgent with animals, children, and senior citizens. However, they clearly have a love affair with dogs. Paris alone counts 500,000 dogs, or 4760 dogs per square kilometer, which by far surpasses the number of children. The French equivalent of "pooch" is *toutou,* and *minou* for "kitty." The most popular dog name in France is Rex.

Dogs are allowed in restaurants and most public places, although they must be leashed in parks and "bagged" in the Metro and in trains. For an assortment of dog bags, go to Samaritaine. There is no problem renting apartments if you have pets. No extra fees. There are animal *auberges* for vacation time, and numerous chic dog *salons,* where the poodles recline on mock Louis XIV *fauteuils.* There are several taxi services for pets, as well as pet ambulances.

On the rue Mâitre Albert, in the 5e, there is an animal *dispensaire* for inexpensive veterinary services. Otherwise, call: *SOS Vétérinaires,* tel. 48.32.93.30 This recording gives the telephone numbers for Paris and the suburbs where emergency veterinary care can be obtained. The French S.P.C.A. shelters homeless pets, many of which had been abandoned along the *autoroutes* during vacation times.

It is relatively easy to bring dogs and cats into France. Although a valid health certificate, showing a recent rabies vaccination, is required, chances are you won't even have to show it at the airport. But it's ill-advised to arrive without one. Technically, animals without proper certification can be deported or destroyed! If you're planning on visiting the U.K., be advised that a strict, six-month quarantine is enforced for animals, vaccinated or not! Pets can travel on international airlines, in approved kennel cages, for the price of a piece of extra baggage. The animal travels in the hold of the plane in temperature-controlled and lit storage areas. Be wary of charters.

There are some regulations, though, that should be carefully noted. Animals under the age of three months old are prohibited. You cannot bring more than three animals at one time, only one of which can be a puppy or kitten. Rabies vaccination certificates must state that the vaccine had been administered more than 30 days and less than one year prior to the date of departure. Birds are limited to two *psittacidae* and ten birds of small species with health certificates issued within five days of departure. All other animals require special import permits from the Ministry of Agriculture.

## The Streets

It should be pointed out that the infamous problem of dog *caca,* which had given Paris a bad name for many years, has been somewhat rectified. Although the law stated that you had to curb your dog, directing him to do his *besoins* (needs) in the *caniveau* (gutter) off the curb—and there are even cute graphic reminders painted onto certain sidewalks—you used to have to hop-skip-and-jump to avoid landing in a rude pile. Now, in the nicer neighborhoods at least, the city cleans up with the use of a green-suited technician on a converted motorcycle equpped with a high-powered vacuum cleaner. Much of the eye-sore has been aspirated away. There are no fines for not curbing your dog, just dirty looks.

While on the subject, Paris has other ways of keeping itself clean. You may wonder why water gushes out of sewers and runs through the gutters so often—even when it's not been raining. Paris street cleaners, mostly Africans in green municipal jumpsuits, open valves of clean, but undrinkable water and direct the flow up or down street, by positioning soggy bolts of tied-up cloth. Then they sweeps with their green plastic-branched brooms, loose papers, *mègout* (cigarette butts), trash, and unclaimed *caca* into the moving stream, which drains into the city sewers and eventually into the Seine system for recycling. You can visit the impressive sewers, *Les Egouts de Paris,* daily at Pont l'Alma in the 7e. Every address in Paris has an equivalent one underground. This complex, unlit network was extensively used by Resistance fighters during the Nazi Occupation.

For humans, Paris streets are equipped with automatic, self-disinfecting pay toilets. For two-francs, you gain access to a futuristic compartment whose cleanliness and comfort is guaranteed.

## WEATHER

The word for weather is *le temps,* not to be confused with "time." Otherwise, the weather report is the *Météo.* Autumn in Paris is absolutely lovely, mild and somewhat sunny with a tinge of melancholy in the air. The *feuillage* (foliage) is nice but not always noticeable in the center of the city. Sweaters and light coats are needed.

The winters have tended to be milder and milder over the last few years. There is rarely any snow, other than a few flakes in February and perhaps a strange and short barrage of hail once or twice a year. Nonetheless, winter coats or down jackets can be necessary in that the cold is damp and penetrating and often annoying. Ski jackets aren't usually worn in town, but students can get away with anything.

Spring comes late or winter seems to linger and fuses with summer. The blooming of the nubby, cut-back magnolia and horse chestnut trees along some of the boulevards is a pleasant sight and the leaves give off a sweet but strange fragrance that only seems to be found in Paris.

Summers in Paris can be rather hot and uncomfortable. The pollution gets thick and the air heavy. The tourists start arriving after May 1, but the Parisians don't start leaving until July (see Vacations).

### A Few Weather Expressions

| | | | |
|---|---|---|---|
| *il fait beau* | It's nice out. | *il fait froid* | It's cold. |
| *il ne fait pas beau* | It's not nice out. | *il fait chaud* | It's hot. |
| *il fait mauvais* | The weather is bad. | *il neige* | It's snowing. |
| *ça caille* | It's freezing. (slang) | *il fait moche* | It's ugly out. |
| *il pleut* | It's raining. | | |

Average temperatures range as follows:

| Stations | Altitude (m) | Annual avg. | January Avg. (Temp. in C°) | July Avg. | Precip. (mm) | # days rain |
|---|---|---|---|---|---|---|
| Lille | 44 | 9 | 3.1 | 15.9 | 596 | 185 |
| Lyon | 200 | 11.1 | 4.2 | 19.7 | 973 | 186 |
| Strasbourg | 150 | 9.7 | 0.6 | 17.9 | 585 | 184 |
| Brest | 98 | 10.9 | 7.1 | 15.1 | 1,030 | 204 |
| Paris | 75 | 11.6 | 4.9 | 18.6 | 631 | 193 |
| Bordeaux | 47 | 12.4 | 6.6 | 19.6 | 801 | 184 |
| Marseille | 4 | 14.8 | 8.4 | 23.4 | 498 | 79 |
| Nice | 5 | 15.1 | 9.3 | 22.3 | 576 | 59 |
| Ajaccio | 4 | 14.7 | 10.4 | 20.9 | 433 | 185 |

# Climate

Although the weather in Paris is seldom extremely hot or extremely cold, it is variable since the city lies at the junction of marine and continental climates which have opposite characteristics. During the winter, the average temperature is about 3° Celsius (37° Farenheit) and there are rarely more than 20 very cold days a year. The winters are wet, and warm rain gear and an umbrella are indispensable. In the spring and autumn, temperatures average about 11° Celsius (52° Fahrenheit) with warm days and cool nights. Temperatures in the summer average about 18° Celsius (65° Fahrenheit) with some very warm days, especially in July and August.

# Clubs & Organizations

## Alumni Associations

**Amherst College Alumni Association**
47, av George Mandel
75116 PARIS
tel: 45.53.99.01
Rep: Axel BAUM

**Harvard Business School Club of France**
c/o France-Amérique
9 et 11, av. Franklin D. Roosevelt
75008 PARIS
tel: 42.56.20.98
President: Mme Danielle GOUVE

**Harvard Club of France**
c/o France-Amérique
9 et 11, av. Franklin D. Roosevelt
75008 PARIS
tel: 48.91.15.19
President: M. Philippe KIMBROUGH

**Mount Holyoke College Alumni Association**
41, rue Emile Menier
75016 PARIS
tel: 47.27.14.71
Rep: Mrs. Laura Gott DONDEY

**Princeton Alumni Association of France**
Trade Development Bank
12-14, Rond-Point des Champs-Elysées
75008 PARIS
tel: 42.25.15.16
President: Mr. Tony EDEON

**Tufts Club of France**
19, rue Octave Allaive
78610 SAINT-LEGER-EN-YVELINES
President: Mr. Bill WAINWRIGHT

**Yale Club of Paris**
7, rue de l'Odéon
75006 PARIS
tel: 46.33.37.50
President: Ms Regine LUSSAN

**University Club of Paris**
(a social club for university graduates)
49, rue Pierre-Charron
75008 PARIS
tel: 43.59.24.33
Secretary: Ms Hélène SULLIVAN

## Other English-Speaking Organizations

**AFL-CIO,** European Headquarters
23, rue de Rome
75008 PARIS
tel: 48.87.74.57

**USIS**
2, rue St. Florentin
75001 PARIS
tel: 42.96.12.02 ext. 2382

**The American Center**
29, rue de la Sourdière
75001 PARIS
tel: 40.15.00.88
After years of being situated in a beautiful building on the Bd. Raspail, the American Center, a private institution promoting American arts and culture,directed by Henry Pillsbury and chaired by Judith Pisar, is relocating to the rue de Pommard at Bercy, a former wine producing village of the last century tucked into the 12e. Ground-breaking for the new Frank Gehry building started in July 1990 with the center scheduled to open in October 1992. The American Center provides American cultural programming and language courses.

**American Club of Paris**
49, rue Pierre Charron
75008 PARIS
tel: 43.59.24.33
President: Ms Stéphanie SIMONARD

**American Friends of Blérancourt**
34, av. de New York
75016 PARIS
tel: 47.20.22.28
President: Baron Bernard D'ANGLEJAN

**American Joint Distribution Committee**
33, rue Miromesnil
75008 PARIS
tel: 42.68.05.68

**American Legion**
Paris- Post #1
49, rue Pierre Charron
75008 PARIS
tel: 42.25.41.93
President: Mr. Ray BENNET

**American Tax Institute in Europe SA**
9, av. Matignon
75008 PARIS
tel: 42.56.33.70
Director: Mr. Bernard PFRUNDER

**American Women's Group in Paris**
49, rue Pierre Charron
75008 PARIS
tel: 43.59.17.61

**Amnesty International**
4, rue Pierre Levée
75011 PARIS
tel. 43.38.74.74
Minitel: 36.15 Amnesty

**Anglo-American Business & Culture Center**
20, rue Godot de Mauroy
75009 PARIS
tel: 42.66.14.11

**Association of American Residents Overseas (AARO)**
49, rue Pierre Charron
75008 PARIS
tel: 42.56.10.22
President: Mr. Leo PACKER

**Association of American Wives of Europeans**
49, rue Pierre Charron
75008 PARIS
tel: 42.56.05.24
President: Ms. Irene CHECLER

**Association France-Canada**
5, rue Constantine
75007 PARIS
tel: 45.55.83.63

**Atlantic Institute for International Affairs**
9, av. Hoche
75008 PARIS
tel: 42.25.56.17

**Bonjour Canada**
38, rue Fabert
75007 PARIS
tel: 45.55.64.57

**British European Centre**
5, rue Richepanse
75008 PARIS
tel: 42.60.35.57

**British Community Committee**
9, rue d'Anjou
75008 PARIS
tel: 42.65.13.04
Director: Mr. Mitchell HUGGS

**British Institute**
11, rue de Constantine
75007 PARIS
tel: 45.55.71.99
Director: Mr. Christophe CAMPOS

**Canada Welcome**
24, Bd. Port-Royal
75005 PARIS
tel: 43.37.43.96

**Canadian Women's Group in Paris**
**Canadian Cultural Center**
5, rue de Constantin
75007 PARIS
tel: 45.51.35.73

**Commission Franco-Américaine**
9, rue Chardin
75016 PARIS
tel. 45.20.46.54

**Common Cause**
19, av. Ferdinand-Buisson
75016 PARIS
tel: 46.20.46.42

**Democrats Abroad (France)**
10, av. de Messine
75008 PARIS
tel: 45.63.11.52
Contact: Joseph SMALLHOOVER

**Foundation Mona Bismark**
34, av. de New York
75016 PARIS
tel:47.23.38.88
P.R. Director: Mme DUNHAM

**France-Amérique**
(fosters cultural and
economic relations)
9-11, av. Franklin D. Roosevelt
75008 PARIS
tel: 43.59.51.00
President: Mr. Jean PINEA

**France-Canada**
5, rue de Constantine
75007 PARIS
tel: 45.55. 83. 65
President: Mr. Xavier DE VELLEPIRE

**France-Etats-Unis**
6, Bd. de Grenelle
75015 PARIS
tel: 45.77.48.92
President: Mr. Cyrille MAKINSKY

**France-Ontario**
12, rue des Geais
77200 CROISSY BEAUBOURG
tel: 60.06.44.50
Director: Ms Christine SEARANO

**France-Québec**
24, rue Modigliani
Immeuble Verseau #17
75015 PARIS
tel: 45.54.35.37
President: Mr. Louis THEBAULT

**Franco-American Volunteer Ass.
for the Mentally Retarded (FAVA)**
24, rue Alsace Lorraine
75019  PARIS
tel: 42.45.17.91

**Franco-American
Volunteers Association**
24, rue d'Alsace-Lorraine
75019 PARIS
tel: 42.45.17.91
President: Ms  DE POLIJNAC

**Homestay America**
5, rue Boudreau
75009 PARIS
tel: 42.65.50.40

**John F. Kennedy Memorial Center**
26, rue Eugène Sue
75018 PARIS
tel: 42.62.75.22

**Lions Club International**
295, rue Saint-Jacques
75005 PARIS
tel: 46.34.14.10
Secretary: Mr. Raymond FAGES

**Organization for
Economic Cooperation &
Development (OECD)**
2, rue André-Pascal
75016 PARIS Cedex 16
tel: 45.24.82.00
Secretary: Mr. Jean-Claude PAYE

**OECD British Delegation**
19, rue Franqueville
75016 PARIS
tel:45.24.98.28

**OECD Canadian Delegation**
15bis, rue Franqueville
75016 PARIS
tel: 45.27.62.12

**OECD U.S. Mission**
19, rue Franqueville
75016 PARIS
tel: 45.24.74.77
Head: Ambassador Denis LAMB

**Office of American Services**
2, rue Saint Florentin
75042 PARIS Cedex 1
tel: 42.96.12.02

**Ontario General Delegation
Ontario House**
109, rue du Fbg. St. Honoré
75008 PARIS
tel: 45.63.16.34

**Reader's Digest Foundation**
23, rue Bourgogne
75007 PARIS
tel: 45.51.62.35

**Republicans Abroad France**
6, rue Edouard Fournier
75016 PARIS
tel: 40.72.71.51
Chairman: Ms Phyllis MORGAN

**Rotary Club of Paris**
40, Bd. Emile Augier
75116 PARIS
tel: 45.04.14.44
President: Mr. André NEURRISSE

**Salvation Army**
International Headquarters
76, rue de Rome
PARIS 75008
tel: 43.87.41.19

**Sphinx
(women's literary association)**
175, av. Ledru Rollin
75011 PARIS
tel: 43.67.31.92
Editor: Ms Carol PRATL

**UNESCO**
7, Pl. de Fontenoy
75700 PARIS Cedex 07
tel: 45.68.10.00
Director: Mr. Mayor SARAGOZA

**YWCA**
22, rue de Naples
75008 PARIS
tel: 45.22.23.49
Director: Ms. DE QUATREBARBES

**Youth for Understanding**
69, rue Nicoto
75016 PARIS
tel: 45.03.15.79

**YMCA**
22, rue de Naples
75008 PARIS
tel: 45.22.23.49

**Volunteers of the
American Hospital of Paris**
63, Bd. Victor Hugo
92202 NEUILYY-SUR-SEINE
tel: 47.47.53.00

# Useful Telephone Numbers

Ambulance: 43.78.26.26
Bus Info. (in English): 40.46.42.12
Central Post Office (24 hours): 42.33.71.60
Charles de Gaulle airport: 48.62.22.80
Chronopost: Minitel: 3614 EMS
Customs Information Center: 42.60.35.90
Drug Crisis Center: 45.05.88.88 (free)
Enfance et Partage (Hotline for Kids in Trouble): 05.05.12.34 (free)
Entertainment/Theater Info: (in English) tel: 47.20.88.98
European Insurance Commission: 48.24.02.04
Fire: 18
Fax Office: Service Internationale: 40.28.20.00
Gas & electricity information: 43.87.59.99
Highway Information Center: 48.58.33.33
Information
        Ile de France (Paris region): 12
        provinces: 16.11.12
        international. 19.33 plus country code
Le Bourget Airport: 48.62.12.12
Locksmith (24 hours): 47.07.99.99
Lost American Express Card: 47.08.31.21
Lost and Found/Objets Trouvés: 36 rue des Morrillons, 75015, 45.31.14.80
Lost Animals: 43.80.40.66
Lost Diner's Club Card: 47.62.75.00
Lost Eurocard/Mastercard: 43.23.46.46
Lost Property: 45.31.14.80
Lost Visa Card: 42.77.11.90
Marine Radio Information: 05.19.20.21
Minitel Directory: 11
Movie Info: 46.34.00.00
National Railroad Information: 45.82.50.50
News of the Day: 36.36.11.11
Orly Airport: 48.84.32.10
Paris Culture Listing: 47.20.88.96
Plumber (English): 40.29.99.89
Police: 17
R.A.T.P. (public transport) Info: 43.46.14.14
Rape Crisis Hotline: 05.05.95.95 (free)
Restaurant Information: 43.59.12.12
Search For Hospitalized Persons: 40.27.30.81
SOS HELP English Crisis Hotline: 47.23.80.80
SOS Lawyer: 43.29.33.00
SOS Nurses: 48.87.77.77
SOS Oeil (eye care): 40.92.93.94
SOS Pédiatre: 42.93.19.99
SOS Tailor: 40.15.03.14
Stock Market News: 36.69.10.02
Taxis Bleus: 42.02.42.02
Taxis G7: 47.39.33.33
Taxis Radio Etoile: 42.70.41.41
Telegrams in English: 42.33.21.11
Telephone Complaints, Repairs: 13
Telex Office: 42.33.20.12
Tenant's Information: 48.06.82.75
Theater Information: 47.23.61.72
Tourist Office: 47.23.61.72
Train Info: 45.82.50.50
Wake-up Calls (electronically programmed): * 55 * plus the time in 4 digits (i.e., 7.30 am=0730).
Weather Info: 36.69.00.00 (Paris) tel: 36.69.0101 (provinces) 45.56.71.71 (foreign)
Weather Report: 43.69.01.01

# Selected Bibliography
## Books, Guides, & Sources

*Academic Year Abroad,* Institute of International Education, 1989.
*57 Guide*, Gault Millau, Paris (4500 restaurants)
Ardagh, John, *France Today,* Penguin Books, London (indepth study of French society)
*Bloom Where You're Planted,* The Women of the Church, The American Church in Paris (welcome booklet for new residents)
*Cityscope Paris*, Berlitz (1001 addresses)
Constons, Martine, *Le Guide de Paris*, La Manufacture
Dansel, Michel, *Les Cimetières de Paris*, Denoel
*Dictionnaire de Paris*, Paris, Larousse, 1964
Dinh, Catherine, *Restaurants Etrangers à Paris*, MA Editions (1000 restaurants)
Dournon, Jean-Yves, *La correspondance pratique,* Livres de Poche, Paris
*Economist Business Traveller's Guide to France, The,* Prentice Hall Press, New York
Gramont, Sanche de (also known as Ted Morgan), *The French,* Bantam
*Guide Consommateur Vert*
*Guide des Hôtels de Charme de Paris*, Rivage
*Guide de Paris Mystérieux,* Tchou, Paris
Hillairet, Jacques, *Dictionnaire historique des rues de Paris,* Minuit, *1972*
*Histoire Secrète du Paris Souterrain*, Hachette, (sewers, caves, etc.)
*Insight Cityguide's Paris*, APA Publications, Singapore
Juvin, Hervé, *Paris*, Times Books, London
Kjellberg, Pierre, *Nouveau guide du Marais*, Paris, La Bibliothèque des Arts, 1986
*Le Guide Bleue, Paris,* Hachette, Paris
*Le Guide des Etudes Supérieures 1990*, L'Etudiant, Paris
*Le Guide du Routard Paris,* Hachette, Paris
Lebey, Claude, *Bistrots Parisiens*, Editions Robert Lafont, Paris
Lémoine, Bertrand, *Les Halles de Paris, Histoire d'un lieu*, Paris, L'Equette, 1980
Leprette, Veronique, *Paris Pressé* , Hermé (saves time)
Léri, Jean-Marc, *Montmartre*, Paris, Veyrier, 1983
*Les Villas d'Artistes à Paris*, Les Editions de Paris
Lozareff, *Paris Rendez-Vous*, Guide Hachette (400 addresses for going out)
Martin, Hervé, *Guide de l'Architecture Moderne à Paris*, Syros
Martin, Michèle, *Weekends Plaisir aux Environs de Paris*, Editions de Veccehi
McClure, Bert, *Architectural Walks in Paris*, La Découverte/Le Monde
Mengès, Bernard Stéphane, *Dictionnaire des Noms de Rues* (5000 streets)
*Paris and Environs*, Michelin
*Paris Anglophone*, Frank Books, Paris
*Paris Arts ou Seine*, Autrement (art scene)
*Paris City Guide*, Price Waterhouse, Paris 1989
*Paris en Bouteille*, Flammarion, Paris
*Paris en Marché*, Autrement
*Paris par A + B,* La Documentation Française, Paris
*Paris Pas Cher,* Flammarion, Paris
*Paris sur Seine*, Beaudoin, François, Nathan, 1989
*Paris Trafic*, Editions du May, Paris
*Paris Visa*, Hachette, Paris
*Paris*, Guide Arthaud, Paris
*Paris-Combines,* MA Editions, Paris (3500 inexpensive restaurant addresses)
Simon, François, *Paris Vin*, Editions de Main, Paris
Turner, Miles, *Paupers' Paris*, Pan Books, Ltd., London
Wurman, Richard Saul, *Paris Access,* Access Press
Zeldin, Theodore, *The French*, Collins, 1983.

## EXPRESSIONS /LEXICON OF TERMS

Here is a random list of French colloquial expressions and some *argot* (slang), selected on the the basis of what you might hear in daily conversation or in the street. Although these and others are useful to know, be absolutely sure you understand the context and appropriate usage before throwing them around.

| | |
|---|---|
| *à table* | the meal is served (be seated) |
| *aie!* | ouch! |
| *argot* | slang |
| *berk* | yucky |
| *bêtise* | stupidity, foolishness, nonsense |
| *bof!* | (a noise used to say "I don't know") |
| *bonne chance,* | good luck |
| *bonne continuation* | keep up the good work |
| *bonne courage* | chin up! |
| *branché* | hip/in |
| *c'est absurde* | that's absurd |
| *c'est chouette* | it's really great, fab |
| *c'est comme ça* | that's just the way it is |
| *c'est dingue* | that's crazy |
| *c'est drôle* | that's funny, strange |
| *c'est foutu* | It's over, it doesn't work, it's broken (for events/people/objects) |
| *c'est génial* | that's great, brilliant |
| *c'est impec* | that's impeccable, that's perfect |
| *c'est intéressant* | *(in business)* that's a good deal, oppurtunity, investment |
| *c'est marrant* | that's funny |
| *c'est pas la peine* | it's not worth it |
| *c'est pas mal* | it's not bad, rather good (used as a compliment) |
| *c'est pourri* | that's rotten |
| *c'est ridicule* | it's/that's ridiculous |
| *c'est super* | that's super |
| *ça boum* | it's hopping (as in a party) |
| *ça cocotte* | it smells strongly (perfume) |
| *ça gaze, sa baigne* | everything's going great |
| *ça m'énerve* | that unnerves me, annoys me |
| *ça m'est égal* | I don't mind one way or the other |
| *ça marche* | it works, it's okay |
| *ça me gêne* | that bothers me |
| *ça me gonfle* | that bothers me (literally, that makes my head swell) |
| *ça ne me dit rien* | I'm not in the mood / that doesn't ring any bells |

| | |
|---|---|
| *ça schlange* | that stinks |
| *ça suffit* | enough! |
| *chacun son tour* | each his turn |
| *con, connard* | idiot, clot (male) |
| *connasse* | tart, stupid bitch |
| *connerie* | rank stupidity |
| *coucou* | hi |
| *coup de foudre* | love at first sight |
| *d'acc (d'accord)* | all right, okay |
| *dégage* | get the hell out of here |
| *dégoûtant* | disgusting (polite form) |
| *dégueulasse* | disgusting (slang version) |
| *elle me fait craquer* | she drives me crazy (as in love) |
| *engagé* | committed |
| *ferme ta gueule* | shut your face/trap |
| *flipper* | to flip out, to freak out |
| *fous le camp, barre-toi, casse-toi* | |
| | piss off, beat it, get lost (very vulgar) |
| *fous moi la paix* | leave me alone, leave me in peace |
| *franchement* | frankly |
| *grosses bises* | hug and kisses |
| *il a perdu les pédales* | he's lost control, nuts |
| *il a un grain* | he has a screw loose |
| *il est culotté* | he's nervy, cheeky |
| *il est gonflé, il exagère* | he's got a hell of a nerve |
| *il faut profiter* | to take advantage of something |
| *j'ai d'autres chats à fouetter* | |
| | I've other fish to fry |
| *j'en ai assez* | I've had enough! |
| *j'en ai marre* | I'm fed up with |
| | (this, it, him/her, everything) |
| *j'en peux plus* | I can't go on like this |
| *je craque* | I'm giving in to temptation, I can't resist any longer |
| *je m'en fiche, je m'en fous* | |
| | I don't care a hoot |
| *je n'ai pas envie* | I don't want to, I don't feel like it |
| *je suis crevé, KO* | I'm dead tired, beat |
| *je suis saoûl(e), je suis bourré(e)* | |
| | I'm drunk |
| *je t'embrasse* | I kiss/hug you (for ending friendly phone conversations or letters) |
| *la bagnole, la caisse* | the car |
| *la nana, la gonzesse* | the chick, girl |
| *le boulot* | job, work |
| *le fric, le pognon,* | bread, money |
| *le gars, le mec, le type* | guy |
| *les fringues, les sapes, nippes* | |
| | duds, clothing |

*ma frangine, mon frangin*
my sis, sister; my bro, brother

| | |
|---|---|
| *merde* | shit |
| *mince* (replacement for *merde)* | darn |
| *mon pote* | my buddy, pal |
| *ne quittez pas* | hang on, don't hang up |
| *ne t'inquiète pas* | don't worry |
| *on laisse tomber* | let's forget it |
| *on s'appelle/se téléphone* | we'll call each other (call me/I'll call you) |
| *plouc* | country hick |
| *quel bordel* | what a mess! |
| *salaud, salope* | dirty bastard; son of a bitch; slut, bitch |
| *saloperie* | filthiness |
| *si tu veux* | it's okay with me |
| *sois pas vache* | don't be nasty |
| *ta gueule* | shut up (literally, your snout/face vulgar) |
| *tais-toi, taisez-vous* | shut up |
| *tant mieux* | so much the better |
| *tant pis* | too bad, that's the way it is |
| *truc/machin* | thingamajig, whatchamacallit |
| *tu parles !* | no kidding (sarcastic) |
| *un clope* | a butt, cigarette |
| *un flic, les flics* | a cop, the cops |
| *une toile* | a film |
| *va te faire cuire un oeuf* | go jump in a lake! |
| *vachement* | tremendously, very, extremely |

# GENERAL INDEX

# Les MONUMENTS de PARIS

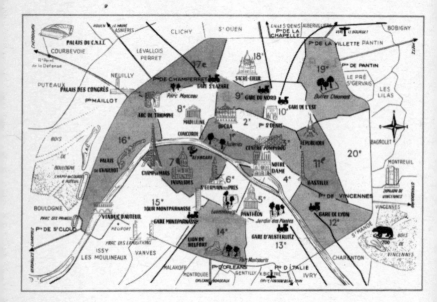

# Noctambus

Toutes les nuits,
à partir de 1 h 30 du matin,
toutes les heures jusqu'à 5 h 30,
10 lignes de bus vous conduisent
du Châtelet à la périphérie
et à Rungis.

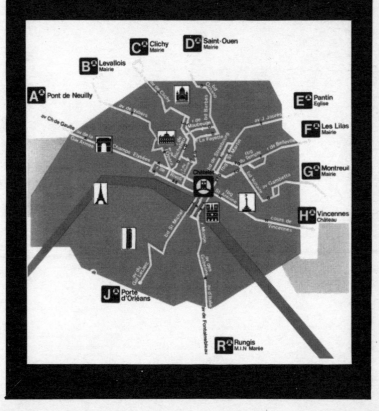

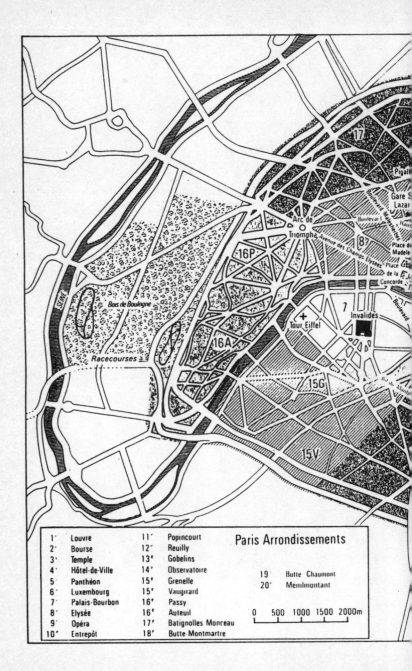

| | | | | |
|---|---|---|---|---|
| 1ᵉ | Louvre | 11ᵉ | Popincourt | **Paris Arrondissements** |
| 2ᵉ | Bourse | 12ᵉ | Reuilly | |
| 3ᵉ | Temple | 13ᵉ | Gobelins | |
| 4ᵉ | Hôtel-de-Ville | 14ᵉ | Observatoire | 19ᵉ  Butte Chaumont |
| 5ᵉ | Panthéon | 15ᵉ | Grenelle | 20ᵉ  Menilmontant |
| 6ᵉ | Luxembourg | 15ᵉ | Vaugirard | |
| 7ᵉ | Palais-Bourbon | 16ᵉ | Passy | 0  500  1000  1500  2000m |
| 8ᵉ | Elysée | 16ᵉ | Auteuil | |
| 9ᵉ | Opéra | 17ᵉ | Batignolles Monceau | |
| 10ᵉ | Entrepôt | 18ᵉ | Butte-Montmartre | |

Sacré Cœur

18

19

Buttes Chaumont

Rue Lafayette

10

CANAL

Place de la
République

1

3

20

Père la Chaise

de

Rivoli

Hôtel de Ville

11

Place des Vosges

ouvre

4

Place de la
Bastille

Notre Dame

rmain

5

Jardin
des Plantes

12

SEINE

13

Bois de Vincennes

# FRENCH COMPANY HANDBOOK 1990

Now, in the 1990 completely revised and updated edition, 200 pages of indispensable information in English on a selection of 82 of the most important French companies, as well as basic facts on other major firms. Includes information on the French economy and major sectors of activity, an introduction to the Paris Bourse, and a bilingual dictionary of French financial terms.

Each profile includes detailed information on: head office, management, major activities, number of employees, sales breakdown, company background, shareholders, principal French subsidiaries and holdings, foreign holdings and activities, exports, research and innovation, 1984-1988 financial performance, 1989 financial highlights and 1989/1990 important developments, strategies and trends.

Indispensable for corporate, government and banking executives, institutional investors, industrial purchasers and other decision-makers who should be more fully informed on major French companies. French Company Handbook 1990 is being sent to 8,000 selected business and financial leaders in the United States, Japan, Southeast Asia, China, the Middle East and Western Europe.

Other interested parties may purchase the Handbook at $59.50 per copy, including postage in Europe. Three or more copies, 20% reduction. Outside Europe, please add postal charges for each copy: Middle East, $4; Asia, Africa, North and South America, $7.

ACCOR
AÉROPORTS DE PARIS
AEROSPATIALE
AIR FRANCE
ATOCHEM
BANQUE INDOSUEZ
BANQUE NATIONALE DE PARIS-BNP
BANQUES POPULAIRES
BÉGHIN-SAY GROUP
BSN
GROUPE BULL
CAISSE DES DÉPÔTS ET CONSIGNATIONS
CAISSE NATIONALE DES TÉLÉCOMMUNICATIONS (CNT)
CANAL +
CAP GEMINI SOGETI
CEA-INDUSTRIE
CEGELEC (ex CGEE ALSTHOM)
C.E.P. COMMUNICATION
CGIP (COMPAGNIE GÉNÉRALE D'INDUSTRIE ET DE PARTICIPATIONS)
CGM GROUP
CHARGEURS S.A.
CLUB MÉDITERRANÉE
CMB PACKAGING (ex CARNAUD)
COGEMA
COMPAGNIE BANCAIRE
COMPAGNIE FINANCIÈRE DE CRÉDIT INDUSTRIEL ET COMMERCIAL-CIC GROUP
COMPAGNIE FINANCIÈRE DE SUEZ
COMPAGNIE GÉNÉRALE D'ÉLECTRICITÉ (CGE)
COMPAGNIE GÉNÉRALE DES EAUX
CPR-COMPAGNIE PARISIENNE DE RÉESCOMPTE
CRÉDIT AGRICOLE
CRÉDIT D'ÉQUIPEMENT DES PME-CEPME GROUP
CRÉDIT LOCAL DE FRANCE
CRÉDIT LYONNAIS
CRÉDIT NATIONAL
DASSAULT
DOCKS DE FRANCE
ÉLECTRONIQUE SERGE DASSAULT
ELF AQUITAINE
EMC-ENTREPRISE MINIÈRE ET CHIMIQUE

EPÉDA-BERTRAND FAURE
ESSILOR
FIMAGEST
FRAMATOME
GMF GROUP (GARANTIE MUTUELLE DES FONCTIONNAIRES)
GROUPE DES ASSURANCES NATIONALES (GAN)
HAVAS
IMETAL
LAFARGE COPPÉE
LEGRAND
L'ORÉAL
LVMH MOËT HENNESSY LOUIS VUITTON
LYONNAISE DES EAUX
MICHELIN
MOULINEX
PECHINEY
PERNOD RICARD
PEUGEOT S.A.
POLIET
PRINTEMPS GROUP
LA REDOUTE
RHÔNE-POULENC
SAINT-GOBAIN
SALOMON
SANOFI
SCOR S.A.
SEB GROUP
SEITA
SEMA GROUP
SGE GROUP-SOCIÉTÉ GÉNÉRALE D'ENTREPRISES
SKIS ROSSIGNOL
SLIGOS
SOCIÉTÉ GÉNÉRALE
SODEXHO
SOMMER ALLIBERT
THOMSON
TOTAL
UNION DES ASSURANCES DE PARIS (UAP)
USINOR SACILOR
VALEO
VALLOUREC
VICTOIRE GROUP

## Herald Tribune
INTERNATIONAL
Published With The New York Times and The Washington Post

### FRENCH COMPANY HANDBOOK 1990

**Published by**
**International Business Development**
**with the**
**International Herald Tribune**

*FRENCH COMPANY HANDBOOK 1990*

International Herald Tribune, Book Division
181 Avenue Charles-de-Gaulle, 92521 Neuilly Cedex, France.

Please send me _____ copies of French Company Handbook 1990.

☐ Enclosed is my payment. Payment may be made in any convertible European currency at current exchange rates

☐ Please charge to my credit card:   ☐ Visa   ☐ Diners   ☐ Amex
                                      ☐ Eurocard   ☐ Access   ☐ MasterCard

CARD NUMBER _____ EXP. DATE _____

SIGNATURE _____
(necessary for credit card orders)

NAME (in block letters) _____

POSITION _____

COMPANY _____

ADDRESS _____

CITY/COUNTRY/CODE _____

# Your
# Key
# To
# The
# Capital

# Only One Name
# Brings You Complete
# Daily Coverage
# Of World Events
# All Rolled-Up In One
# Outstanding News Source.

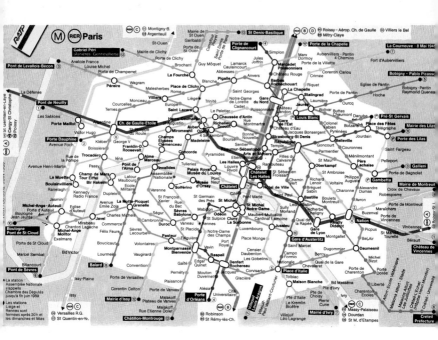

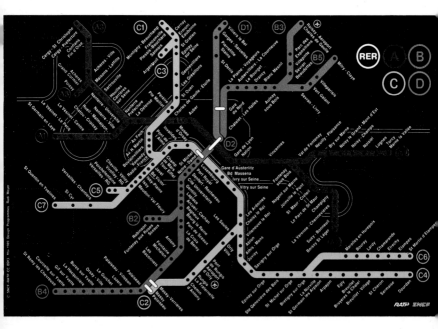